CAGE AND AVIARY SERIES

BRITISH BIRDS IN AVICULTURE

OTHER BOOKS AVAILABLE

BRITISH BIRDS IN AVICULTURE

Edited by Peter Lander
With specialist contributors

Foreword by
Jack Hargreaves

Issued By
THE BRITISH BIRD COUNCIL

SAIGA PUBLISHING CO. LTD.,
1 Royal Parade, Hindhead, Surrey GU26 6TD

DEDICATION

Produced as a permanent memorial to the late Ray Allen,
a good aviculturist and friend: a Member of the British Bird
Council who gave a great deal of his time and energy to the
Council's work and the furtherance of the British Bird Fancy.

Typeset by Ebony Typesetting, West Tremabe,
Nr. Liskeard, Cornwall, PL14 4LT

Printed and bound in Great Britain by
Robert Hartnoll Ltd., Bodmin, Cornwall.

Published by
SAIGA PUBLISHING CO. LTD.,
1 Royal Parade, Hindhead, Surrey.
GU26 6TD.

CONTENTS

Sections not written by Peter Lander are acknowledged with
contributors' names.

MONOCHROME ILLUSTRATIONS

COLOURED PLATES

Between pages xiii and 1

ACKNOWLEDGEMENTS

The British Bird Council would like to acknowledge the following for their contributions to this book:

For the loan of photographs — Dennis Avon and Tony Tilford; also Colin Clark and Judith Domin.

For writing articles and making valuable contributions to textual material — V.A.V. Carr, Malcolm Taylor, Bob Partridge, Cyril H. Rogers, A.C. Wyatt, V.C. Beckett, Colin Clark, A.T. Worrall, Ron McCluskey, Rob Taylor, Ray Allen, Eric Peake, Judith Domin, Walter Lewis and P.W. Beauchamp.

The Council also wish to express their grateful thanks to Jack Hargreaves for writing the Foreword.

FOREWORD

When I was very young there were still men called fowlers – by then on the wrong side of the law – who worked with springes and bird lime and decoy cage traps to catch wild singing birds for sale. I still have a lark-twirler: a piece of hardwood embedded with pieces of broken mirror and made to spin by pulling a string. For some unknown reason this apparatus irresistibly attracted the skylark. It was made by an old man who, in his early youth, had occasionally supplied larks' tongues for the banquets of the very rich. All such doings fell into disrepute and for a long time the whole idea of keeping native wild birds in captivity was frowned upon by most people — though we did not extend this objection to finches, parakeets and the crow family; birds that were native to other countries.

In the meanwhile, those who were concerned about the dwindling butterfly life of Britain had discovered that by breeding them in captivity they could provide reserve stocks of threatened species with which to re-colonise the countryside. At the same time creeping urbanisation threatened our bird stocks and, when I wanted to make a catalogue film of the British finch species, I discovered I could best do it with the help of the specialist fanciers. I remember the day they brought their birds to a group of garden aviaries: we knew by the end of the filming that these people knew exactly what they were doing. We could see how fit the birds were and how attuned to human company.

This book is compiled from the knowledge and experience acquired by the British Bird Fanciers. They know a great deal because amongst them are many specialists who have devoted their time to particular birds. Who, for instance, could know the nuthatch better than the man who has persuaded them to breed in his aviary, the sides of which are covered by tree bark?

Within these pages you will find the details of the stiff and responsible system of licensing which protects the fanciers' standards of practice.

I recommend this book. It has been created by people whose work may one day provide the solution for perpetuating some of our bird species. Why not? Quite a few animals have gained redemption by similar care and study.

JACK HARGREAVES

INTRODUCTION

A book of this nature must, of necessity, have the beginner in mind though it is hoped that the experienced aviculturist will also find something of interest.

The intention in compiling this book has been to give good coverage of those species which are commonly bred by aviculturists and there has been no attempt to cover every British Bird which has or is being bred in aviaries and cages as this would be quite beyond the scope of a volume of this size.

There are many books available on British birds which give descriptions and illustrations of the species and their eggs so that they can be recognised. Few give details of how the birds live and fewer still give details of the birds' natural foods — especially the foods which are fed to the young in the nest. This is partly because it is impossible to see what the birds are bringing to the nest — only examination of the young birds' stomachs can reveal this. Unfortunately this means killing the young birds, something which should only be done for exceptional reasons.

Every aviculturist should, therefore, spend as much time as possible watching the species in which he or she is interested, in the wild. By also quietly watching the birds in the aviary some of the wild birds' actions can be better understood. In this way information is gradually built up and it is hoped that such information will be passed on to the British Bird Council for publication at a later date. Whenever possible an aviary should have growing plants so that it has the appearance of the wild birds' habitat. This is not essential but it goes a long way to assist in the study of the species and helps to ensure successful breeding.

Added to this is the joy of seeing a collection of birds in miniature natural environments. With this in mind, an attempt has been made to give a general guide to the birds' life in the wild though it cannot in any way be said to be complete. Perhaps in a future volume this might be further extended especially if individuals would undertake to collect information on particular species.

In recent years the trend for the individual to specialise in only a few species has become far more popular, with obvious benefits to aviculture. The present-day greenfinch is a good example of what a few years' specialisation can achieve. The information given in this book on keeping and breeding each species is based on articles supplied by aviculturists together with personal experience. It is significant that experiences by different breeders vary and in some cases are even contradictory. This only goes to show that there is no magic formula for breeding these birds. This information can be used as a good guide and the aviculturist has to learn to watch his or her birds and interpret their needs from their behaviour. Nevertheless, given the right conditions and proper management, all birds will breed in confinement. Unfortunately most of us are limited to being able to provide the right conditions for only a small number of species and must choose to keep these species only, rather than others which we might admire even more.

To save constant repetition a brief guide only is given on feeding under each species, therefore readers should also study the chapter on feeding. The same remarks apply to the chapter on cages and aviaries.

It is recommended that all birds bred should be ringed either with the closed ring or the split ring issued by the British Bird Council. Apart from timid species and birds such as the wren where it is difficult to remove the young without damaging the nest, the younger aviculturist with nimble fingers and good eyesight should not have difficulty in using the closed rings provided that the instructions are carefully followed. Do not try to put them on too soon or the rings will either fall off the bird's leg or the parents may throw out the ring — with the youngster — when cleaning the nest. The young should be nicely developed so that their legs are hidden in the nest. Do not expect the rings to fall on; it does require a little time and patience but with practice it is not difficult. Canaries and budgerigars are good birds on which to gain a little experience of ringing. Older aviculturists, whose fingers are not as supple as they used to be and whose eyesight is not as good as it was, will have more difficulty and may be content to use the split rings but must understand that the birds cannot then be legally sold. Again, ringing has been covered in a separate chapter and details have not been repeated under each species.

Included is an appendix on the law where the main provisions, as they affect aviculture, are explained by a layman for the layman. It must be made clear, however, that this is not a legal explanation and is intended only as a help and a guide. Also, from time to time, various alterations are made by 'Orders' (as opposed to Acts of Parliament) to the Schedules and other details. In general these do not really affect the average aviculturist, but one must always be on the look-out for the announcement of various changes. Finally it is very important, if we are to continue to be allowed to keep and breed British Birds, that all aviculturists keep within the law and it is strongly recommended that they do so.

There are also chapters dealing with hybridisation and exhibiting as well as other interesting subjects.

Those who have contributed to this book may not always agree with that which has been written on the various species because, as already explained, experiences vary considerably. It is hoped, however, that these controversial points will spur others to submit their experiences for incorporation in future publications.

On behalf of the Council I would like to thank all those who have contributed; Colin Clark and Judith Domin for the loan of photographs, and the many others who have helped me in so many ways. Without all this help this book could not have been completed.

PETER LANDER

Coloured Illustrations
British Birds

The coloured plates which follow illustrate most of the popular British birds described in this book.
In addition there are black and white illustrations in the text.

Bullfinch (Male)
Chaffinch (Male)

Bullfinch (Female)
Bramblefinch

Plate 1

Crossbills
Greenfinch (Female)

Chaffinch (Female)
Goldfinch

Plate 2

Linnet
Redpoll

Hawfinch
Mealy Redpoll

Plate 3

Twite
Reed Bunting

Siskin
Corn Bunting

Plate 4

Meadow Pipit
Redstart

Snow Buntings
Rock Pipit

Plate 5

Starling
Song Thrush

Black Redstart
Blackbird

Plate 6

Waxwing
Yellow Wagtail

Mistle Thrush
Grey Wagtail

Plate 7

Nightingale
Wren

Tree Creeper
Whitethroat

Plate 8

Wheatear
Magpie

Whinchat
Jay

Plate 9

Fieldfare
Jackdaw

Ring Ouzel
Choughs

Plate 10

Dunnock
Stonechat

Nuthatch
Redwing

Plate 11

Pied Flycatcher
Yellow Hammer

Spotted Flycatcher
Skylark

Plate 12

CHAPTER 1

Conservation of Bird Life

1. THE ETHICS OF AVICULTURE

Issued by the British Bird Council in conjunction with the National Council of Aviculture.

The meaning of the word 'ethic' in this context is to denote what is morally right and "acceptable" and what is morally wrong and "unacceptable" and it is essential that all who keep, breed and exhibit birds live up to this code.

1. **Ethical:** The welfare of the birds is paramount and they must at all times be well looked after, properly fed, housed and protected from their enemies.
   Unethical: Birds must *never* be allowed to be badly housed or not looked after properly.

2.(a) **Ethical:** Those who keep birds must act in an honourable manner and adhere to the Protection of Birds Acts.
   Unethical: It is wrong to take birds from the wild — except under licence, or birds caught legally as pests — and it is wrong to encourage or condone any other person in breaking the Protection of Birds Acts.

2.(b) **Ethical:** It is in the best interest of the species to obtain a licence to take for avicultural purposes some of the seasonal surplus of species, which are abundant in the wild, or birds which would otherwise be destroyed as pests.
   Unethical: It would be morally wrong to obtain licences to take birds which are rare in the wild — except where a properly equipped and run station is set up for the stated purpose of building up stocks and repopulating the wild.

3. **Ethical:** Those who keep birds should be encouraged to join and to conform to the rules and regulations of the Specialist Societies — guided by the British Bird Council.

4. **Ethical:** Those who keep birds should always foster the best possible ways of keeping and breeding birds and preach the Ethics of Aviculture on all possible occasions.

5. **Ethical:** It is right and proper to encourage all species to reproduce in cages and aviaries, and to establish a free breeding, healthy strain.

6. **Ethical:** It is ethical to exhibit all aviary bred birds, as this encourages the production of better specimens.
   Unethical: The exhibition of birds which are likely to bring discredit to the Fancy must be stamped out.

1

7.   **Ethical:** The Fancy should develop better strains of aviary bred birds and give awards for establishing strains, and ensure that no one can throw any doubt on the authenticity of birds on the show bench.

8.   **Ethical:** The British Bird Council should be the R.S.P.B.'s best friend; their knowledge and experience should be of inestimable value in the running of sanctuaries for all birds.

9.   **Ethical:** There is nothing unethical in developing free breeding strains of species which are not yet established, provided that this is done within the law and the original stock is correctly obtained. There is nothing unethical in exhibiting such birds.

10.   Any member who is convicted under the Protection of Birds Acts will be automatically suspended, but will have the right of appeal, in person, to the Council. The Council's decision is binding.

Figure 1.1   Bullfinch

2.   CONSERVATION IN THE WILD

The purpose of conservation of bird life is to promote the richest and most varied bird life possible and embraces the protection of existing species and the establishment of fresh species as breeding colonies throughout Britain. There is no doubt that conservation is well worthwhile: birds bring great pleasure to men and women everywhere and are part of our national heritage which we must never allow to be lost. Birds are also of great scientific interest and there is still a great deal to be learned about them: they have an economic value and play a vital part in the balance of nature.

Almost two centuries ago there was a great deal of virgin country in Britain and many species flourished without interference. The development of agriculture and the planting of hedges around fields enabled most of our common species to increase their numbers and their range. About 100 years ago changes began to take place which have had a tremendous effect — sometimes disastrous — on our bird population. These changes include the reclamation of fens and marshes, the industrial revolution which brought with it railways and roads opening up hitherto unspoiled areas and a big increase in human population. Ominously· improved guns and the preservation of game birds proved to be at the expense of other species, particularly birds of prey.

The potential population increase in most species is very great, as would be seen if every egg hatched and the bird lived to breed in the following year. Nature, however, has a way of maintaining a balance. Many species feed on others, their eggs or young. Squirrels and rats take their toll and, in suburban areas, the domestic cat does untold damage. To combat this the species which are most prone to predation lay the most eggs and have the most broods.

The summer migrants who come here to breed suffer losses in migration and from other causes in their winter quarters. For those species which are resident nature has another way of redressing the balance of numbers so that only the fittest survive to breed the following year. The regulating factor which keeps the numbers down to specified limits is the available food supply in the winter months when many birds starve to death. In severe winters some species suffer drastically and take five or six years to recover their numbers even though more survive through following winters since there is a greater supply of food for fewer birds.

Trouble arises when man either wittingly or unwittingly upsets the balance and the pressures become so great that some species are reduced to such an extent that they become 'endangered'. History has shown that when a species is reduced below a certain level it is no longer able to reproduce itself in sufficient numbers to overcome normal losses, and therefore the species becomes extinct.

The main cause of the reduction of bird life in our country is the alteration and loss of habitat. The constant growth of the concrete jungle; the ripping–up of hedges at the rate of 12,000 miles per year to make way for factories, houses, schools, roads and for farming purposes; the chopping down of trees and disturbance from the public who have better transport and more leisure time — all these factors mean a loss of habitat for the birds. The dreadful habits acquired by many local authorities of spraying the hedgerows with weed killer just when the weeds are seeding and the birds are feeding on them so that many die unseen, as well as trimming hedges with mechanical cutters in the middle of the breeding season destroying many nests and young, can and must be stopped by enlightened public opinion.

The quest for rarities is another unwarranted intrusion on bird life. No sooner is a rare bird reported as having been seen than hordes of bird spotters descend on the area, causing untold disturbance to other birds, just so that they can tick a name on a list. Many appear to have little knowledge of birds' lives and even less interest in conservation. Such intrusions nearly always result in the rarity being driven away within a week or two.

The protection societies have done a great deal of good work in education, the provision of nesting boxes and in setting up bird reserves and sanctuaries. In spite of this it is not unreasonable to suggest that if more is not done to reduce the pressures on our bird life there will only be a few species of common birds left in Britain apart from the small pockets of rare birds or birds which are rare in this country where special measures have been taken to protect and improve their habitat. A great deal of our wonderful heritage would be lost to future generations if we were only left with avocets, blackbirds and house-sparrows.

Aviculturists are conservationists, some more active than others and many are members of the protection societies. They study and have an excellent knowledge of the species in which they specialise and, because they are able to watch the birds throughout their whole life, have a great deal of experience to offer. Sooner or later, and we must do all we can to make it sooner, the protectionists and aviculturists must get together to help the birds.

It is not sufficient just to delegate a piece of woodland or countryside as a bird sanctuary. Much more must be done to ensure the right habitat, to encourage as many species as possible, with adequate food supplies (even if these are artificially produced) and protection. Of course this will cost money and the public must have access, not only to enjoy and understand our heritage of bird life but also to provide the cash flow needed to maintain it.

We believe that Sir Peter Scott showed how this could be done at Slimbridge and other places belonging to the Wild Fowl Trust. What has been accomplished for wild fowl can also be accomplished for other species. We have long cherished the dream of similar places being set up to cater for most of our woodland, heath and scrubland birds. It is not as difficult as it may seem. Some of our national parks and National Trust property would be ideal. Landscaping would be necessary to provide the type of habitat and food supplies with a number of permanent hides at strategic places. The public would be confined to well-defined paths, by thick hedges and banks, leading to each of the hides. To add interest each hide would give a good view of a particular habitat where birds are breeding in the wild and also an aviary built in the habitat in which the same species would also be breeding, so giving a close view for those members of the public who are not used to watching birds. Such an arrangement opens up tremendous possibilities for the further study of each species.

Young bred in the aviaries could be released close by in the following spring and would, in many cases, nest in the same area. Even migrating species could be encouraged to come back to the same place by this means. Releasing birds into the wild must be done in the proper way if the birds are not to perish quickly. An aviary designed for the purpose is erected in the exact location where the birds are to be released; the birds are placed in the aviary for at least two weeks so that they can settle down and become familiar with their surroundings; after this the door is opened quietly one evening after the birds have gone to roost.

This enables the birds to find their way out quietly in the morning and ensures that they will know their way back to feed. The birds must not be disturbed in any way at this stage. Food supplies are kept up for as long as the birds come back to take them, thus ensuring that they have time to learn how to find their own food. This is the way to save the birds and preserve our heritage.

Figure 1.2 Redstart

3. SANCTUARY IN OUR GARDENS

All aviculturists are bird lovers and like to watch the birds in the garden as well as on outings in the country. Some are fortunate in having large gardens in rural areas but others are not so lucky, having only small gardens in urban areas. Yet even in a small garden a lot can be done to help and encourage the birds. Those in the rural areas will, of course, be able to attract a greater variety of birds. Even in urban areas many small gardens often run alongside each other and back to back with the next road, producing quite a sizeable area in which birds can live. Not all the neighbours will encourage birds and some will actively discourage them but even so quite a large community of birds can be sustained with a little help.

First let us examine what are the birds' needs. They need food, shelter, suitable nesting sites and water to drink and bathe in. They need protection from their enemies — man and cats being the worst.

The most obvious way to help birds is to erect a bird table and provide food, especially in the winter. It is surprising how quickly birds will find this and pay several visits to it at regular intervals each day. In addition certain flowers and shrubs can be grown on which the birds will feed but more about these later in this chapter.

One thing which attracts more birds than anything else is a garden pool especially if it is planted. This can be as ornamental or as simple as desired but should have at least one part where the water is shallow with a mud bottom. Birds cannot bathe in water which is more than 5 cm (2 in) deep, although they may be able to drink if there is something low for them to stand on. A bath is, however, most important to birds even in the coldest weather and enables them to keep their plumage in good condition. The planted pool will also provide a host of small insects which are particularly needed in rearing young birds.

The erection of nest boxes will encourage birds to nest and a variety are illustrated. These can either be bought or made at home. Boxes should be so fixed that they slope forward in order that rain runs off and will not be driven by the wind into the entrance hole. Generally it is best to fix them as high as possible to make them less accessible to cats. If possible the hole should face east because birds do not like to have the mid–day sun shining in — neither do they like the wet west winds.

By planting suitable shrubs, creepers and climbing roses a great deal can be done especially if these are judiciously pruned. Strong growers like jasmine, japonica and roses are generally pruned close to the wall or fence, but this does not provide good cover for the birds. By not cutting too close leaving forks strong enough to support nests and allowing some of the top shoots to hang over a fine balance is obtained, giving cover for the birds and a nice display of blossom. In some places a few twigs can be tied in a bunch. Provided that these will resist the wind they will make suitable places for flycatchers' and warblers' nests. Finches like the tops of pergolas because they afford solid foundations and good cover. Shrubs can be treated in the same manner. Thorn hedges are very popular with the birds if they are allowed to

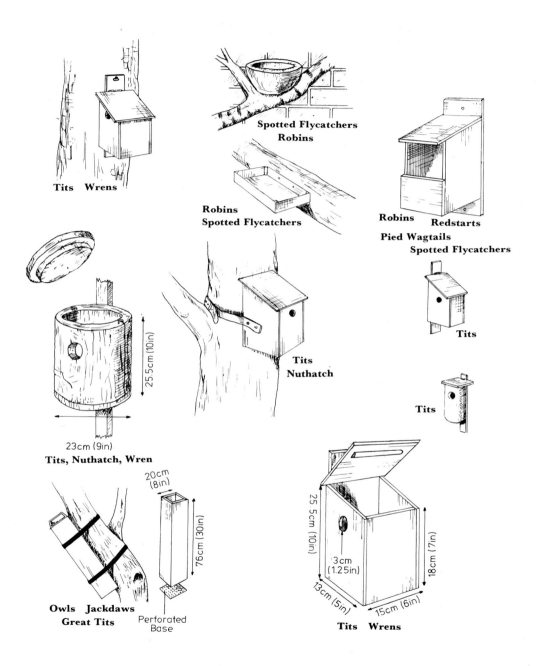

Tits   Wrens

Spotted Flycatchers
Robins

Robins
Spotted Flycatchers

Robins   Redstarts
Pied Wagtails
Spotted Flycatchers

Tits

25.5 cm (10in)

23cm (9in)
Tits, Nuthatch, Wren

Tits
Nuthatch

Tits

20cm
(8in)

76cm (30in)

25.5cm (10in)

3cm
(1.25in)

18cm (7in)

13cm (5in)

15cm (6in)

Owls   Jackdaws
Great Tits   Perforated
Base

Tits   Wrens

Figure 1.3   Various Nest Boxes and Methods of Fixing

grow and are only trimmed to keep them in bounds at the end of the breeding season. Old currant bushes which have been pruned for years so that the old wood has become gnarled with age are very popular. A tangle of wild rose or blackberry in an odd corner or even screens round the rubbish dump can be a veritable heaven for small birds. Old metal teapots and kettles judiciously concealed with the spouts hanging down often appeal to robins. Hawthorn and honeysuckle both provide food and cover. Forget-me-not, antirrhinum and sunflowers are much liked, as are privet berries in the autumn. The berries of cotoneaster attract a lot of birds in the winter. Mountain ash berries attract blackbirds and thrushes. Fieldfares, redwings and other thrushes, like the orange-coloured berries of pyracantha. *Berberis vulgaris* is also sought after. It is amazing what birds can find to eat on a lawn. One cannot find the tiny insects the birds eat even with a powerful magnifying glass — but the birds can spot them. If birds are attracted to the garden they will do a better job of keeping the greenfly down than will spraying with insecticides.

Old walls can be most useful, especially if they have not been too well repaired. Tits are adept at finding weak places. Redstarts and nuthatches will also nest in them. If a brick is removed the shelf left may well be used by a robin. If the wall is not too important holes can be cut into it or old drain pipes cemented in. A dry wall can be built as part of a rockery and will provide a continuous supply of live food for wrens who will work it over several times a day.

Clumps of laurel or rhododendron provide shelter for the winter as well as cypress, yew and lonicera. A list of other useful plants and shrubs is given below:

List of Foods for the Bird Table

Hemp	Crushed and soaked dog biscuits
Millet	Household waste
Wheat	Stale bread
Canary seed	Dried currants
Sunflower	Over-ripe fruit
Peanuts	Mealworms
Coconut	Gentles
Bones	Cheese
Fat	

List of Shrubs and Plants

Arundinaria (bamboo)   Tough evergreen forming clumps for roosting and nesting.
Aster (Michaelmas Daisy)   For insects and seeds.
Athyrium   Small ferns for decoration and ground cover.
Aucuba (laurel)   Evergreen for roosting and nesting.
Berberis   Useful group of shrubs, many varieties to choose from.
Betula (birch)   Attractive to redpolls and siskins.
Buddleia   Flower shrub very attractive to butterflies.
Buxus sempervirens (box)   Evergreen shrub. Good cover for roosting and

nesting.

Centurea Herbaceous plants related to cornflowers – favourite of goldfinches and linnets.

Chamaelyparis (cypress) Evergreen conifers which will provide good cover.

Clematis Evergreen and deciduous climbers. Provide good cover and useful berries.

Cornus (dogwood) Deciduous shrub. Gives good cover if pruned hard.

Cotoneaster Evergreen and deciduous shrubs with useful berries.

Cupressus Evergreen conifers for cover.

Delphinium Herbaceous border plant liked by bullfinches.

Dipsachus (teazle) Liked by finches especially goldfinches.

Dryopteris Ferns for good ground cover and decoration.

Erica (heathers) Tall ones give excellent cover for roosting and nesting. Seeds popular with finches.

Eryngium Similar to Dipsachus (teazle).

Fagus (beech) Useful as a hedge. Host to greenfly.

Hedera (ivy) Good cover and nesting place. Providing insects and spiders.

Helianthus Group includes sunflower. Very popular seeds.

Hydrangea Especially the climbing variety *Hydrangea petiolaris*. Attracts insects.

Ilex (holly) Provides excellent cover and nesting sites.

Jasminum Useful climber often used by flycatchers.

Laurus (bay) Useful evergreen well known for culinary use.

Ligustrum (privet) Well known evergreen. Berries loved by bullfinches and others.

Linum (flax) Annual and herbaceous plants useful for their seeds.

Lonicera (honeysuckle) Useful climbers with popular berries.

Malus Group of trees and shrubs bearing edible fruits liked by softbills.

Onopordum A group of thistle–like plants useful for seeds.

Phalaris arundinacea (gardeners garters) Useful cover for ground nesting birds.

Prunus Includes edible fruiting trees – favourites with softbills.

Pyracantha A group of evergreens, provides dense cover and berries.

Rhododendron Very useful winter cover.

Ribes Group includes black, white and red currants – liked by softbills.

Salix (willow) Form dense thickets.

Sambucus (elder) Host to blackfly, berries, favourite with softbills.

Sorbus (mountain ash) Most useful berries.

Tagetes (marigold) Seeds appreciated by finches especially goldfinch and siskin.

Taxus (yew) Excellent cover and if unclipped good nesting sites.

Viola (pansy) Seeds liked by the finches.

Cupressocyparis leylandii Conifer which can be clipped annually.

Contributions by: Bob Partridge

CHAPTER 2

Our Future With British Birds
by V.A.V. Carr

It is recognised today that most hobbies or sporting clubs have their own rules and regulations governing the general behaviour of those whose interests are served. Such democratically elected bodies have as their main function the correct ethical promotion of the particular interest sponsored. Aviculture over the generations has not been subject to many outside pressures except where Acts of Parliament have been introduced.

The first in 1884 gave certain powers to county councils to legislate on a county basis and several amendments have been made since that time and are likely to be further revised in the future.

I remember as a schoolboy being teased and 'ragged' because I showed an interest in our native birds — almost to the point where I deemed it diplomatic to keep quiet about such interests. It is, perhaps, significant today that anybody with some knowledge or expertise in the study of bird life is listened to and sought after by a large body of public thirsting for knowledge.

Hence we arrive at the situation today where the public, with little knowledge, criticises the activities of many aviculturists whose mode of conduct has not been subjected to scrutiny and whose pattern of behaviour has varied little in the past century.

Perhaps at this point I should emphasise that with knowledge so readily available through books, radio and television, and our nation's general cultural uplift, the public is becoming increasingly aware of nature's place in the industrial and wasteful society we know today. We are all part of a world subject to oil pollution, toxic materials, nuclear fall-out and the rest, which damage whole continents and impose harmful side effects on living creatures. In the light of modern life and its associated hazards we can understand the need for and the creation of environmental lobbyists, ecological and preservation societies, the Countryside Commission, the Society for the Protection of Birds and other bodies.

Protection of Birds Acts

The year 1934 saw the introduction of a Protection of Birds Act which brought under its wing all the previous Protection Acts and stopped the sale of most of our native birds except those bred in captivity, and such aviary-bred birds had to have a close fitting, closed ring placed on one leg when in the nest at about five days old. Before this Act came into force birds could be bought freely from fanciers, bird shops and bird catchers. Indeed, I knew many bird catchers in those days who reared their families on the proceeds of bird catching — there was no social security, no school meals and only an unemployment pay offering subsistence below starvation level.

Putting the bird catcher out of business made the availability of our native species very difficult with the exception of those imported from the continent. On the other hand it stimulated most fanciers to breed their own — with a background of little or no experience — and it was soon found that the fixing of the closed ring caused many problems with the feeding parent birds.

No doubt to encourage the aviculturists and other interests another Parliamentary enactment in the 1950s tightened the security of rarer birds but allowed licences to be issued to responsible people or bodies to take wild birds for avicultural or scientific study. That is the position today. Discussions are taking place with all interested parties to promote another Act of Parliament to control still further those who wish to take birds from the wild. In 1970 the Royal Society for the Protection of Birds was asked by influential people in this country to check on reports that the traffic in wild birds was growing and that these birds were being exhibited in large quantities. A meeting between the protectionists and British bird specialist clubs was called which resulted in the formation of a Council of British Bird Fanciers. These discussions have continued regularly, both sides freely expressing their views and it is likely that another Protection of Birds Act will be presented controlling still further the activities of keepers and exhibitors of our native birds.

The ease with which one may purchase closed rings and advertise birds for sale are both factors which have made it difficult for our hobby to control its destiny because of the abuses of a few. To safeguard our hobby in the future it will be necessary to have closed rings available from one source of manufacture and supply, such rings should be coded and registered. It is to be hoped that new legislation will accept a split ring to be used on birds which have fledged so that there is no interference with the nest and no concern caused to the parent birds, these split rings also to be coded and registered. It should be easy to monitor sales of rings and stock and, if there is any abuse in the use of rings the issuing authority should be empowered to take displinary action.

The stigma of the allegation that exhibition birds are fresh caught has damaged our hobby and it will be difficult to convince our critics until the time comes when all exhibition birds are ringed. For many years breeders have been encouraged to record their breeding achievements and it is understandable that form filling and other clerical work is resented in one's hobby, but proof is required to convince others that progress is being made in a sensitive area of our declining bird population.

After years of discussion within the council members themselves, and with outside organisations such as the RSPB, RSPCA, the British Trust for Ornithology and, latterly, the Department of the Environment, a clear picture is emerging. Some expression of freedom in avicultural circles is the intent — but to what extent Parliament will allow remains to be seen.

CHAPTER 3

Aviaries and Cages

Before obtaining any birds it is essential to have suitable accommodation available. While this need not be either expensive or ornamental, it must be suitable for the birds' needs. To some extent this will depend on the type of bird and species to be kept but the same basic requirements apply to all birds. They must have room to move about freely, they must have shelter from the elements and protection from enemies such as cats, owls, weasels and rats. There must also be sufficient receptacles to provide the necessary food and water.

Undoubtedly birds do look nicer in an aviary, but for those who have neither the space nor the means to provide an aviary, adequate accommodation can be provided in cages. These can be situated in a spare room or in a shed in the garden. Generally there will be enough light in a room in the house, but many sheds need extra windows to allow the birds to feed all day — if the shed is dark they will spend a lot of time roosting. There must be good ventilation allowing continuous free passage of air. Heating is not necessary for any birds which are normally resident in this country throughout the year. On the other hand, as it is essential that the birds can drink at all times during the day and, unless the fancier is at home all day, it is a help to provide sufficient heat to prevent the water from freezing during severe weather. A study of the advertisements in the fancy press will produce information on sheds designed for bird keeping in a variety of shapes and sizes.

Cages for Bird Keeping

There is not as much information on cages, these being generally designed for canary and budgerigar breeding. British Birds do need more room if they are to breed — in fact the larger the cage the better. The minimum size recommended is 91 cm (36 in) long by 60 cm (24 in) high by 46 cm (18 in) back to front with not more than one pair per cage. Far better results will be obtained by having a few pairs in large cages than by having more pairs in smaller cages. Natural branches can be fixed in the cages for perches, these look nicer and are much more comfortable for the birds' feet than the round dowelling often used. In one end of the cage fix a bunch of heather and fir with a forked branch in the middle to support a nest. Alternatively a small wicker basket or canary nest pan can be used. The object is to provide privacy and a feeling of security to the sitting hen, but the bunch must not be so thick as to prevent the birds from entering it easily.

Contrary to advice frequently given, the most consistent results are obtained in sheds and aviaries which face east. The reason for this is that birds, particularly when nesting, do not like being subjected to the mid-day sun and always, in the wild, choose a position which is shaded. They also like protection from the prevailing wet west winds and in the wild choose a situation which is also protected in this respect. It is not always possible to provide the ideal and in such cases it is advisable to fix up some means of providing shade and protection.

Disadvantage of Cage Breeding

The only real disadvantage to cage breeding is the difficulty experienced in providing sufficient small insects which most of the species we are concerned with use to feed their young, particularly when they are first hatched. A bed of nettles in an aviary will enable the birds to find nearly all they require. This means that large quantities of greenfly, blackfly and similar have to be collected. To some extent this can be overcome if the birds can be persuaded to feed the young ones on egg food. More details on feeding are given in Chapter 13. The same remarks apply to small aviaries housing single pairs which is an ideal arrangement if the fancier has plenty of spare time. Most fanciers, however, who are out at work all day, will find it easier with a somewhat larger aviary housing several pairs of birds.

Aviary Construction

An aviary can be any size but the minimum recommended is 180 cm (6 ft) long by 61 cm (2 ft) wide by 180 cm (6 ft) high. This will hold six to ten non-breeding birds, but generally only one pair of breeding birds. In a mixed aviary one should allow at least 2.25 m³/80 cubic feet per pair of birds; much more if possible.

It is not necessary to have an expensively built aviary and the cheapest construction, provided that it meets all the birds' requirements, is perfectly adequate. An example of this is one designed by Mr Hylton Blythe which is easily made as follows. Roofing laths are driven into the ground at 1 m (3 ft) intervals and cut off to the required height, with further laths nailed along the tops and across from side to side — this enables 1 m (3 ft) wire netting to be stapled to the laths. There is a small door at one end for access with a shelf above it for food. A further small door gives access to the shelf so that it is not necessary to enter the aviary to feed the birds. Cover must be provided to keep the seed and shelf dry. The birds also need protection from the wind and rain and shade from the sun. This can be achieved by nailing boards all round along the top to a width of about 30 cm (12 in) and the same along the top of the sides. Roofing felt can be used instead of boards providing there is wire netting underneath to support it. If all the timber is treated with creosote or bitumin it will last a lot longer. Under the boards bunches of heather, gorse or fir are fixed for roosting and nesting sites.

Any simple structure with suitably-sized netting will keep birds in, but it is much more difficult to keep vermin out. Cats can also be a nuisance, especially if they get on the top of the aviary. To overcome this the main frame should be extended about 23 cm (9 in) and this extension covered with 5 cm (2 in) netting, often called chicken wire. Cats cannot walk on 5 cm (2 in) netting, and bunches of gorse hung on the corner posts facing downwards will help to stop them climbing up. Rats, if they gain access, will kill the birds and drag them down their holes, so that they all suddenly disappear. This can be overcome by digging a trench round the aviary 30 cm (12 in) deep and 30 cm (12 in) wide. The wire netting is extended down the side of the trench and along the bottom in the shape of a letter L. The trench is then filled in. Mice are much more difficult to exclude. Although mice do not kill the birds they do cause considerable disturbance which will jeopardise breeding results. Also, where mice can get in weasels will follow and they will kill and eat every bird in sight in no time at all. Mice and weasels can get through ½ in (1.30 cm) netting which is generally used for aviaries: ⅜ in (1.0 cm) netting, which is much more expensive, will keep out all but baby mice. It is therefore very important to keep a sharp look out and take quick action if any signs of mice are seen, by setting traps and putting down poison. Both traps and poison must be suitably protected from pets and children, especially as they cannot be placed inside the aviary.

While a small aviary for each pair of birds is ideal, and with some species necessary, the average fancier who is out at work all day will find it difficult, with this arrangement, to provide all that the birds require to rear their young, particularly when keeping hardbills or seedeaters. This is because all seed eaters rear their young for the first few days on small insects such as greenfly, blackfly, gnats and such and then gradually wean them off onto half ripe seeds, which are easily digested. In the wild the birds do not eat hard seeds until the frosts arrive, by which time they are well through the moult. Large quantities of small flys and seeding weeds are therefore required all through the summer and autumn, and for most people it is necessary to augment them with soaked seeds.

Softbills, those species which live almost exclusively on an insect diet, are highly territorial — both cocks and hens. With these birds it is essential to have separate aviaries for each pair. Indeed, when the cocks come into condition they will often kill the hen when confined together. It is therefore best to have the aviary divided so that the pair can see each other, but are kept separate until the hen shows signs of wanting to nest. The cock can then be allowed through but a careful watch kept. If there are any signs of fighting the cock should be separated off and tried again a little later.

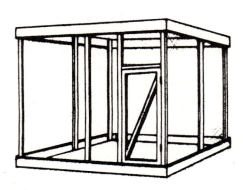

Figure 3.1   Typical Aviary — from an original design by Hylton Blythe

All these points have to be considered before constructing an aviary, and more details are given under the individual species, so study those you intend keeping before making any decisions.

The next point we come to is the floor of the aviary. With softbilled birds small shrubs and climbers can be grown in the aviary, but unfortunately all the finches or hardbills eat the young buds and the shrubs quickly die. The only ones which seem to survive are the elderberry and the blackberry. This is a pity, because birds do look much nicer and there is better chance of success when the aviary is landscaped to resemble the type of habitat in which the particular species lives in the wild. Those who are keen on gardening can do a lot in this respect.

A concrete floor is not really satisfactory for British birds because they need so much that can be obtained from an earth floor. A small plot of well cut grass gives endless pleasure to the birds from which they derive a lot of small insects which we cannot see, as well as minerals. A patch of nettles produces a continuous supply of small gnats and greenfly, but because they spread so quickly they are best grown in a tub or old tank sunk into the ground. A small pool attracts a lot of insects as well. The normal rain will keep the aviary floor nice and fresh, but in prolonged dry spells it should be watered if possible.

Because we cannot have growing shrubs when keeping hardbills we have to provide substitutes. Many fanciers fix up bunches of fir, heather, or gorse in corners, but in an aviary containing more than one pair there is the big disadvantage that pairs take up territories and tend to fight off every other bird. Strange to say, a continuous hedge all down one side seems to overcome this problem and pairs will nest close to each other, without any fighting. This arrangement has been found to be by far the most satisfactory.

The artificial hedge is built in the following way. Vertical spacers about 2 inches (5 cm) thick are fastened onto the side of the aviary. Then laths are nailed horizontally about 10 inches (25 cm) apart, starting from the top. It is not necessary to go below about 30 inches (75 cm) from the floor. If possible choose the west or south–west side. If the outside of this part of the aviary is of wood, or some other solid material, so much the better. If not cover it with hessian or roofing felt to provide protection and privacy. Bare branches containing forks are now placed in the laths to simulate the inside of a hedge. After this fir branches, evergreens, heather and gorse are threaded into the laths producing a finish rather like an uncut hedge. It is important that this should not be too thick and that there are holes in the foliage through which the birds can obtain access to the inside of the hedge where they will build their nests. Do not forget to put a covering 12 inches (30 cm) to 18 inches (46 cm) wide on the outside of the aviary over the top of the hedge to provide shade from the sun and shelter from the rain.

If birds are to be kept in the aviary all the year round, it is best to have some sort of shelter shed attached to the aviary so that the feeding can be done inside, and it may be necessary on occasions to confine the birds inside as well. The shelter shed can be as large or small as may be desired, or it can be the main bird room with the aviary built on the side. A container full of grit and a bath of fresh water are other essentials to the aviary.

Rambler roses and honeysuckle, if grown up the outside of the aviary, look very attractive and help to attract greenfly, so essential to the birds.

It is recommended that all birds be ringed and it is worth bearing this point in mind when deciding on the feeding stations. It is a great help if the feeding stations can be somewhat obscured from the nesting sites. Ringing is best done just before dusk when the parents have finished feeding the young for the day. Put in a fresh bunch of groundsel or some other favourite food and go and wash your hands. By the time you come back the parents will be busily feeding and out of the way. Slip in quietly. Remove the youngsters from the nest and place them in a box of cotton wool. When each one has been ringed, place all the youngsters back in the nest and cup your hand over them for a minute to make them squat down in the nest. Then come away quietly and leave them alone.

As previously mentioned, aviaries can be as large or small, as ornamental or as heavily built as may be desired by the owner, but all will follow the basic pattern of design already described and illustrated in the sketch. All sorts of refinements can be added according to individual taste. One point that should be stressed is that it is better not to have the doors too large unless a safety porch is included: it will be found a considerable help if the bottom of the door is at least 6 inches (15 cm) above the ground so that it does not catch on things on the floor. For safety's sake the door should always open inwards.

Figure 3.2 A Garden Birdroom

CHAPTER 4

Breeding

1. ENCOURAGING BRITISH BIRDS TO MULTIPLY IN AVIARIES
by Malcolm Taylor

Only too frequently we hear of someone who has maintained a pair of birds throughout the winter in good condition only for one of the pair to die or escape, dashing all hopes of a breeding. To obtain replacement birds at this time of the year is virtually impossible as most aviculturists only have their breeding stock left.

Breeding birds in confinement took a big step forward in this country when a group of enthusiasts founded the Avicultural Society in 1894 for the study of British and foreign birds in freedom and captivity. International in character, its membership spans the world. One of its chief objects from the beginning was to bridge the gulf between aviculturist and the scientific ornithologist, in the belief that each had much to learn from the other. This is still true and many aviculturists are good ornithologists. More than ever before the main aim, in my opinion, should be the breeding of pure species of British birds. In attempting to do so we should strive to copy nature as far as possible. The characteristics of those species it is proposed to keep should be studied so that the breeder has some knowledge of the birds under his management.

Most aviary birds whether seedeaters or insectivorous, will breed given the right conditions and understanding. Many species of the finch family breed successfully when housed together in a large aviary with an abundance of cover and adequate nest sites. For example, in an aviary measuring approximately 3.6 × 1.8 × 1.8 m (12 ft × 6ft × 6ft) containing three breeding pairs of finches, such as goldfinch, siskin, linnet or greenfinch or lesser redpoll, breeding success would certainly be possible from two of those pairs. Finches, of course, destroy growing shrubs and trees in an aviary after a time. This does not apply to softbills.

To encourage birds to breed, artificial nest sites of heather, small bundles of pea sticks, privet, gorse, fir branches, evergreen shrubs and small trees should be provided. They must be placed in the aviary at a suitable height, depending on the species. Ensure there are plenty of these sites, making the best use of available space, taking into account the need for adequate light and protection from heavy rain and strong sunlight. Before birds are placed in their breeding quarters all should be ready so that birds need not be disturbed thereafter. The best way of encouraging birds to breed is a controlled aviary, which is one large aviary divided into sections each accommodating a pair of birds. In the case of softbills this is the only way, as they are generally more pugnacious than hardbills. Hawfinches, chaffinches, bullfinches and members of the bunting family are best housed in separate quarters for breeding purposes.

The need for adequate cover cannot be over-emphasised — not only for nesting sites, but to enable the less dominant bird to retreat until a pair bond has been formed. Nesting material should be moistened with water to make it easier for the birds to work. Dried grasses, horsehair, moss, rootlets, fine birch twigs (for bullfinch, hawfinch and crossbill), artificial fibres, a few down feathers and wool should be supplied. Wool should be anchored so that it can be teased out by the birds as in the wild, thus preventing the leg damage which may occur if it is strewn on the aviary ground in a ball. Leaves are necessary for the nightingale and nuthatch. The closer we stick to nature, the better the results. Some species take to nest-boxes of the open-fronted type and others prefer to build a natural nest. Some insectivorous species must be supplied with nest-boxes, hollow logs and the like. These include redstarts, spotted flycatcher and nuthatch. It sometimes helps to place nesting material by a good site as a hint of what is expected of the birds. Nothing is gained, however, by trying to construct a nest, as this can safely be left to the birds who will do a good job if they are given the correct materials.

Once a pair has decided to go to nest they should not be disturbed. They will not tolerate the treatment accepted by budgerigars. A quick glance when tending to them daily is all that is necessary to ensure that all is well. When finches lay and hatch successfully, supply plenty of seeding weeds such as chickweed, sow thistle, dandelion, persicaria, sorrel and plantain together with soaked seed. Live food in the form of maggots, meal worms, greenfly and green caterpillars is necessary for such species as chaffinch, brambling, hawfinch and members of the bunting family which, during the breeding season, are almost exclusively insectivorous. Be extremely careful where seeding weeds are gathered, in view of the poisons used by local authorities on allotments and by gardeners and farmers. Much has been said about mortality in young greenfinches but I have never suffered serious losses when they were fed in this way.

Softbills like to supplement their diet with more varied live food, including ants' eggs, crickets, locusts and as many green caterpillars as possible from oak trees. The food value in these caterpillars is so great that some species in the wild feed their young almost exclusively on them. If only maggots and mealworms are available, dust them in a multi-vitamin powder such as Vionate as a precaution against rickets. It is a nasty shock when what appears to be a nestful of healthy young about to fledge have to be destroyed because of grossly disfigured legs — due entirely to insufficient calcium.

If it is decided to close ring birds this is best done during the evening, using the correct size ring for the species when the birds are seven or eight days old. Provided the nestlings are replaced carefully with rings hidden from the adult birds no mishap is likely to ensue. A parent bird often delves into the bottom of the nest to remove a parasite in the course of nest cleaning and will remove any foreign object. If a ring is visible, out will go the nestling onto the aviary floor. So, after ringing, check the ground around the nest to make sure no chicks have been ejected by the adults. Warm ejected nestlings in the hand and replace them in the nest. Recovery will be promoted by the warmth of others in the brood. At this age nestlings feather fairly rapidly overnight and by morning, hopefully, all should be well.

I do not exhibit birds at shows because this side of the hobby does not interest me, neither does the breeding of mules and hybrids. I feel that in these times greater emphasis should be placed on the breeding of pure species of British birds. It is probably safe to say that most people who keep British birds keep seedeaters as opposed to softbills, because they have been under the misapprehension that the latter are difficult and time-consuming to look after. This may well have been the case more than seventy years ago when there were no proprietary brands of insectile foods available. Of course, softbills do require live food and a great deal of attention, particularly during the breeding season. Softbills are both fascinating and challenging, and well worth the additional time and trouble spent in looking after their welfare. There is aesthetic pleasure in breeding them and keeping them to study.

It is my experience that softbills, unlike hardbills, will never live communally in one large aviary during the breeding season, because they become highly territorially minded and are veritable fiends towards each other. There is only one way in which to breed softbills and that is to house each breeding pair separately. One large aviary could be divided into several breeding compartments or aviaries measuring approximately 1.8 m (6 ft) × 91 cm (3 ft). Height is not of great importance, although it is more pleasing to the eye and the birds are more easily observed if the structure has a minimum height of 1.8 m (6 ft). Quarters such as these would provide ample room for a pair of small insectivorous birds in which to live and breed. At least half the roof area should be covered so that nesting and feeding sites are kept dry. With the remaining part of the roof area left uncovered, the birds can enjoy the gentle rain that is natural for them and which enhances their plumage. They will soon take to the covered area in the event of a downpour.

If certain birds are to remain in such a structure throughout the year, due to their resident nature, more shelter from the south-westerly winds may be required. Each compartment or aviary should be planted with small conifers and shrubs to provide cover which is so essential to the birds, both with regard to concealing the nest site and to enable the less dominant bird of the pair to seek cover during the courtship period. Coniferous trees and shrubs also provide good roosting sites for the more hardy birds during the winter. Prior to the breeding season furnish each aviary additionally to that described, according to the wild breeding habitat of a species. Here, of course, ornithological knowledge is very useful. Most small softbills will breed if housed in separate aviaries, provided that they are steady enough and have confidence in their owners. Depending on the weather, I put my birds into their breeding aviaries during the third week in April, as most of their wild counterparts are arriving into the English countryside by then.

One should consider a bird's wild breeding habitat in attempting to encourage it to breed under controlled conditions. In the case of the stonechat (Saxicola torquata), I spread bracken over the ground of the covered area of the aviary which is collected from a common and I have bred generations of stonechats in this way. The cock will dive into the bracken as soon as it is in position looking for potential nest sites. A tunnel run to the nest is preferred by this species. Lookout perches nearby are essential, as they like to be able to observe the nest from a short distance without disclosing its position, and this is something to bear in mind when planning several choice sites where the nest will ultimately be constructed. The male will select the site and the female will construct a very neat nest from dead grasses, sprigs of heather and rootlets, lined with animal hair.

In the case of the wheatear *(Oenanthe oenanthe)* which in its wild state would nest in a disused rabbit hole or under a rock or large stone, a large earthenware pipe with wide diameter, or similar receptacle, can be used. It must be sited so that in the event of a torrential summer downpour of rain, it does not fill with water and so destroy any chicks. Another way to provide such a nesting receptacle is to pour cement into a corrugated mould approximately 46 cm (18 in) square with one end blocked off. When this has set, repeat the procedure and, with one half placed upon the other, it allows for easy removal for cleaning or inspection of eggs and young, if so desired. Pipits and larks will be at home with a grass area interspersed with several large tufts of grass with earth attached. They will then construct a nest from dead grasses and some moss and line it with horse hair, under a large tuft in a depression on the ground.

The nuthatch *(Sitta europaea)* will make use of an ordinary tit nest-box but will require some clay made quite wet as it likes to plaster the clay around the entrance hole so that it is just large enough for it to enter. Mud is used in parts of the country where clay soils are absent but in my area it has been found that clay is used widely by nuthatches when involved in this task. The only nesting material required is wood, bark strips, chippings, and a few leaves. As the bird spends the majority of its time on the bark of deciduous trees searching for food, it is necessary to construct the back and one side of the aviary, in which a nuthatch pair is to be housed, with planks of timber, preferably oak with the bark left on. The nuthatches will then spend their time on the bark running up and down in their search for hidden grubs. Oak bark has deep crevices and fissures and is best for this job, but almost any bark from a similar species of tree will be very acceptable.

The Redstart (*Phoenicurus phoenicurus*) tends to prefer a hollow log with one end blocked up and placed horizontally off ground level. In all cases provide plenty of natural springy perches and site them so that they are clear of food and water pots and growing shrubs and trees. Softbills will not cause damage, or stunt the growth of any aviary vegetation as will most hardbills. Provide nesting material for the Redstart in the form of dead grasses, moss, animal hair and a few feathers.

Dense ground cover is required for the nightingale (*Luscinia megarhynchos*). Because of its skulking nature, it is more often heard than seen, and is therefore more at home and relaxed in confinement with plenty of cover to withdraw to. If it does not have any cover at all in which to retire when danger is imminent (and this also applies when being wintered in a birdroom) it becomes strung up with nervous tension. The nightingale is a bird which requires great attention in every respect if it is to be kept in good health and be long-lived. Its needs are such that it is one of the more difficult softbills to care for throughout the year. The nest is constructed mainly of dead oak leaves, grasses and lined with some hair and a leaf or two. It is usually better to offer any nesting material moistened with water as then it becomes easier for the birds to work when constructing the nest. If this is not done, the birds will very often do it themselves by dipping it in the drinking water.

The wagtails make delightful subjects for the aviary, the pied wagtail *(Motacilla alba),* grey wagtail *(Motacilla cinerea)* and yellow wagtail *(Motacilla flava)* being the three most popular species among aviculturists. The pied will breed readily and is not particular about a choice of nest site. It will take readily to a tin can, open-fronted nest-box or other receptacle. Fast running water, although necessary for the grey wagtail in the wild, is desirable but not essential for birds in confinement. A miniature pond or large water container, with bogside plants for additional insect life, together with a small loose stone wall constructed from breeze blocks, will enhance the aviary. Similarly, stones can be used to form sufficient crevices and ledges upon which a nest could be constructed, and will be all that is required to encourage a pair of these delightful birds to breed. The potential sites should be partially covered with growing vegetation. Like the pied, the grey is a resident British species, although some do migrate. Both are very hardy when cared for correctly, the pied being almost omnivorous and on a par with the greenfinch *(Carduelis chloris)* when it comes to sheer voracity of appetite. The grey wagtail is more delicate until after the first moult; both species may however be kept in an outside aviary which is well sheltered throughout the year. In the case of the grey, the pair should be separated after the breeding season.

The yellow wagtail *(Motacilla flava)* is a migratory bird which spends the winter in Africa and is a summer visitor to Europe and the British Isles, where it breeds. Although this is mainly a bird of the lush lowland water meadows, it is also found on arable land among growing crops, where it builds its nest in a depression on the ground. For this species a similar arrangement will suffice as for the grey wagtail, with the addition of a few large tufts of grass with clumps of earth attached. Place these around the breeding area and this should be sufficient to encourage a steady pair of these birds to breed. Nesting material should be supplied in the form of grasses, roots and a considerable amount of cow or horse hair which is used to line the nest.

In order to achieve breeding success in most cases one must have true compatibility between a pair of birds. This is very difficult to achieve in softbills. Although it is always good practice when wintering a pair in a birdroom to cage them separately and in view of each other, it does not follow that they will be completely compatible when released into an aviary together, even though the male may have been singing and displaying to the female before spring while still in the bird room. It has been my experience that, although a pair of stonechats will live happily throughout their lives together, very many migratory birds, such as the nightingale and redstart, are not gregarious, and are highly territorial over selection of habitat at all times. Since no pair bond whatsoever exists, it is generally very difficult for them to reach compatibility in confinement. When a male of this species stakes a territory in its habitat, any female that it takes an instant dislike to is driven out of the territory and no harm comes to it. In the aviary, however, compatibility is more difficult to achieve, and perhaps only one pair of a species is available to the breeder. This applies particularly to the redstart and anyone who has a truly compatible pair should think himself very fortunate indeed.

To avoid fatalities, place the male bird in the aviary first. The female should be either in a spare adjoining aviary or in a cage in the aviary containing the male. The male should then begin to sing and display freely. After a week or two has elapsed, it will quite likely accept the female if it is released into the aviary. I hasten to add that this should be heavily planted with sufficient cover to protect both birds from possible savage onslaughts caused in the courtship chases by the more dominant bird of the pair, which is not always the male. A large receptacle for drinking and bathing should be provided. There should be at least two feeding areas out of sight of each other, or the more dominant bird will starve the other one off the feeding pots. This situation is not always apparent to the inexperienced eye as the ailing bird seldom shows any signs of deterioration until it is too late.

It is one thing achieving compatibility among breeding pairs of softbills, but quite another to persuade them to nest, lay fertile eggs and rear their offspring. The foregoing applies to all species of softbills, and a close watch should be made during the first day or two that the birds are together to ensure that no fatalities occur. Young softbills remain blind until the fifth or sixth day, when their eyes begin to open. A constant supply of live food must be supplied as the parents will not touch much static food and the female will fail to brood the young in her effort to search for and provide food. The young will become chilled and fail to respond to the soft call notes uttered by the female on her return to the nest with food. Ultimately, they become so cold that they appear lifeless, subsequently being removed from the nest by the adult birds one by one. Place the feeding pots close to the nest at this stage, then the male can feed the female who in turn will feed the young without leaving the nest. The chicks will keep warm thus ensuring steady, healthy growth. At this stage feed small maggots and mealworms dusted with a multi–vitamin powder to prevent rickets occurring, together with wood ant pupae. As the young thrive so the size of the maggots and mealworms can be increased, and it is very often necessary to chop or pierce them because of their tough skins. Moths can be caught overnight and used to supplement the diet. If any additional culture of live food can be provided this will be to the advantage of the birds.

In the wild the young of pipits, larks and ground nesting species of the thrush family will leave the nest before they can fly and remain in the undergrowth for several days before flying properly. This is purely a survival tactic and by instinct is employed in confinement although the birds are free from predators. Hole–nesting species are safer from predators and therefore remain in the nest very much longer. At the beginning of September the pair, unless a resident species, should be brought into the birdroom and housed separately in roomy cages or flights, according to the species of bird. Pairs of some species will live together amicably while others must be kept apart from each other.

Most species will do quite well in an unheated bird room during the winter but they will be much happier if the room is heated to a temperature of 45 deg F (7 deg C). Those species which are resident in the British Isles can remain in their outdoor enclosures provided that they are sheltered and free from draughts.

2. BREEDING BRITISH BIRDS UNDER LIMITED CONDITIONS
by Bob Partridge

In my experience near natural conditions are far from essential for the breeding of most of the common British hardbills as well as for a few of the softbills. The majority of these common species can be reproduced with the minimum of cover in an aviary or small flight.

Whilst living in the country, I used large amounts of gorse, broom and other evergreens in the aviary, but since moving to the city have had to do without such items, and have found no lack of co-operation from the birds. In fact, results have been good and this could be a pointer to the true domestication of our British birds. Various sized flights or aviaries are used containing from one pair in a small flight to four pairs in the largest aviary which measures approximately 7.62 m × 1.81 m × 1.81 m (25 ft × 6 ft × 6 ft).

For nesting sites use small wicker work baskets with a few twigs tacked around in order to give the birds some degree of privacy; even so, many birds will pick nesting sites completely open to view, despite other more secluded sites being available. Two or three sites should be available to each pair of birds. For any shy specimens of birds, birch brooms (Besom) are very useful. These are fastened securely upside down having previously rammed a sod of earth into the centre. These nesting sites last for years, and the brooms can be purchased from any large garden stores for a few shillings. Other acceptable nesting sites are the square wooden pans with perforated zinc bottoms, as used by many breeders of canaries. Also useful are the straw cones used by wine merchants when packing bottles; these are fixed up in the same way as the brooms.

Plywood strawberry punnets, clay flower pots, and plastic canary pans can be utilised. However, I have had very little success with the plastic pans since they need to have felt linings glued or sewn inside and the birds pull them to pieces leaving the slippery plastic surface on which they cannot shape a nest.

For larger members of the thrush family and waxwings, trays measuring 8 inches (20 cm) square × 3 inches (8 cm) deep are as good as anything. These are secured at various heights. A few twigs can be tacked around, though this is not necessary with this group of birds as even in the wild they will choose completely open sites.

The smaller and more delicate softbills require more natural conditions if a reasonable amount of success is to be obtained in breeding from these species. However, I would not recommend them for the beginner.

3. ESTABLISHING A STRAIN

There are so many species of British birds that the average fancier has neither the time nor the facilities to breed them all or even all the species which are commonly exhibited. In addition it is not possible to consistently breed good exhibition birds without keeping at least six and preferably ten pairs of the particular species chosen. The first step, therefore, is to specialise and most breeders will only have the time and facilities to specialise on one or, at the most, two species. The second step is to decide on which species to specialise. A further point which has to be borne in mind is that most British birds take a long time to mature and are not at their best for exhibition until they are four or five years old. This makes the selection of the young birds much more difficult and generally means that a number of birds bred will have to be kept for a year or two to see how they mature. If they are used for breeding during this period they will not only mature much better, but much more quickly.

Having decided on the first two steps it is necessary to acquire suitable hens which will readily breed. They should be selected with this in mind and home-bred hens are invaluable. The next thing is to obtain the best available cock which, with the hens, will be the foundation of the strain.

The object is to mate this cock with a least four hens but it is unlikely that this will be achieved in one season. It depends on the species, of course, some being most reluctant to mate with more than one hen in a season. Generally it will be necessary to resort to feeders, transferring the eggs to canaries or other suitable species to hatch and rear the young. It is easier to proceed if a good number of young are reared in the first two seasons. With many species the cock can be run with two hens provided that they are given a suitable enclosure on their own. If eggs from the second hen prove to be infertile, the first hen should be removed as soon as young have been obtained. This gives a number of half-brothers and sisters.

In the second season the cock is paired to the other two hens so producing a second line of half-brothers and sisters. At the same time the young from the first season are selected, pairing the best cock from one hen to the best hen from the other original hen. That is, pairing half-brother to half-sister. This will produce a small proportion of young resembling the original cock which should be retained, discarding all the remainder. At this point it is also necessary to pay particular attention to stamina; only retain the most virile stock.

In the third season the original cock can be paired to the best hen obtained from the previous pairings which will be his grand-daughter. The grand-daughter will already have 50% of the cock's characteristics and the purpose of this mating is to produce 75% in the resulting young. The same procedure is followed with the second line, except that this is one year behind the first line. The importance of ruthless culling — so that only the best are retained and the standard of the stock is improved each year — cannot be overemphasised.

In the fourth year cross pairings between the first and second lines can be used. These again will be half-brothers to half-sisters and by now, if you have selected the stock correctly, some birds will be produced which equal or possibly excel the original cock. Most undesirable features will have been bred out of the stock so that they will consistently produce young of this standard.

It may be that a young cock has been produced which is sufficiently good to take the place of the original cock and follow the same procedure all over again. If not, now is the time to obtain a new cock which excels in any points in which the stock are lacking and again follow the same procedure. This time results should be achieved more quickly since the whole stock has already achieved a reasonable standard and you are working with stock which is related and where the full pedigree of each bird is known.

To carry out a breeding programme such as this, it is absolutely essential to keep the most accurate breeding records of every pairing and the results obtained, with every bird and its pedigree recorded. These must be permanent records which are retained for future reference. From these it will soon be seen if any line is showing any sign of infertility. If so the whole line should be discarded no matter how good they may be and not used for further breeding. Failure to do this will result, in a few years time, in a strain which either will not or cannot reproduce itself.

When in-breeding it is important not to go too far and pairing brother to sister should be avoided. In-breeding doubles up on the good points, but can equally double up on the bad points. Useful pairings, apart from the programme set out above, are cousin to cousin, uncle to niece, nephew to aunt and grandfather to grand-daughter, always provided that each pairing has a set purpose in mind — to improve the stock and show this in the youngsters obtained.

4. INHERITANCE OF COLOUR MUTATIONS
by Cyril H. Rogers

In addition to the natural colours of our native birds from time to time abnormally coloured ones appear through mutations. Unless these unusually coloured specimens are preserved and mated correctly they can disappear as quickly as they came. In these notes I will describe how the different coloured mutations can be perpetuated. The same sets of rules are applicable to the same colour mutations whatever the species happens to be. The visual expression of a mutation can be controlled to some extent by the basic ground colours of the species which has mutated. These ground colours are either white or yellow and, in the case of the former, the yellow and red coloured areas are not affected and, with the latter, it is only the red areas.

At the present time specimens of the following mutations are to be found in the aviaries of breeders, some of which are producing quite freely:

Albino (Lutino) — sex-linked reproduction
Cinnamon (Fawn) — sex-linked reproduction
White (Yellow) — dominant or recessive reproduction
Dilute — dominant or recessive reproduction
Pied — dominant or recessive reproduction.

Some of the mutant colour forms, although they look the same, can reproduce in different ways and, if the breeder is not aware of this possibility, time can be wasted and stock lost.

The mutations most frequently encountered are the Albino (Lutino) and Cinnamon (Fawn) kinds and their method of inheritance is sex-linked. When it is said that a mutation is sex-linked it means that the colour characters that cause this mutation are situated on the sex-linked chromosome pair. It is important to the breeder to know if a mutation is sex-linked as the results from pairing a sex-linked cock bird to a normal hen is different to that of pairing a sex-linked hen bird to a normal cock. The rules which govern sex-linked inheritance are simple and straightforward and really quite easy to remember and apply. A sex-linked coloured cock mated to a normal hen will give all normally coloured cocks that are carriers of sex-linked colour and all sex-linked coloured hens. The reverse pairing of sex-linked coloured hen to pure normal cock gives all normally coloured cocks and hens with the young cocks all being carriers of the sex-linked colour. A normal sex-linked colour-carrying cock paired to a normal hen will give pure normal cocks and hens, normal carrying sex-linked colour cocks and sex-linked coloured hens. Unfortunately there is no difference, visually, between the pure normals and the carriers, and this can only be discovered by further test pairing. In the above pairings it will be seen that the sex-linked coloured birds produced are all hens, so the question arises — **how are cock birds produced**?

The answer is quite simple; by pairing either two sex-linked coloured birds together or a normal sex-linked colour-carrying cock to a sex-linked coloured hen. The former mating will, as expected, produce only birds of the sex-linked colour, the latter will give sex-linked colour-carrying cocks, normal hens and sex-linked coloured cocks and hens. When two different sex-linked mutations are paired together the hen bird behaves as though she were a normal; for instance, if a lutino cock is paired to a cinnamon hen all the resulting young cocks are normal in colour, but carrying both lutino and cinnamon, and all the young hens are lutinos. If the pairing is reversed and a cinnamon cock is paired to a lutino hen all the resulting young cocks are normal in colour carrying cinnamon and lutino and the young hens are cinnamons.

If the mutation is a dominant pied then a cock or a hen paired to a normal will give half dominant pieds and half normals as most of the dominant pied birds only have the character in a single quantity. Whenever a pied of the dominant kind is paired to a normal the breeder can expect pied birds from every cross, providing, of course, full nests are reared as single youngsters are invariably of the wrong colour! If the mutation happens to be a recessive pied form then a cock or hen paired to a pure normal will only give normally coloured young all of which will be carriers of the recessive pied colouring. When a pied bird is paired to a pure normal and no pied young are produced from a reasonable number of chicks the breeder can assume that the pied in question is of the recessive kind. When a recessive pied is mated to a normal carrying recessive pied half the young will be recessive pieds and half normal carrying recessive pieds. Two normal carrying recessive pieds give *pure* normal cocks and hens, normal carrying recessive pied cocks and hens and recessive pied cocks and hens. Should a normal carrying recessive pied be paired to a pure normal then half of each kind will be produced with no visual difference. Such matings should only be carried out when the breeder has an odd bird because of the time wasted in testing the progeny.

The dilute mutation, which causes a bird's colour to be expressed in about half its usual depth and sometimes with an altered shade, can be dominant or recessive and very occasionally sex-linked. This being so the dilute mutation will follow the same sets of rules that govern the inheritance of the colour mutations just discussed.

When breeding colour varieties of any species it is important that the breeder keeps strict and accurate breeding records to avoid inbreeding too closely. Close inbreeding can quickly lead to infertility, dead in shell, deformed and weakly chicks. It is my belief that, in the past, colour strains have faded out because breeders have not introduced enough new genes via fresh stock and, therefore, increased infertility rate and general loss of vigour has eventually terminated the line's ability to reproduce worthwhile birds.

RESULTS OF MATINGS

Matings				Expectations in Young	
	Cocks	× Hen	=	Cocks	Hens
1.	Lutino	Lutino		Lutino	Lutino
2.	Lutino	Normal		Lutino carriers	Lutino
3.	Normal	Lutino		Lutino carriers	Normal
4.	Lutino carrier	Lutino		Lutino	Lutino
				Lutino carriers	Normal

If using Cinnamon substitute Cinnamon for Lutino

| 6. | Lutino | Cinnamon | Carriers Lutino/Cinnamon | Lutino |
| 7. | Cinnamon | Lutino | Carriers Cinnamon/Lutino | Cinnamon |

Figure 4.1   Wheatear

CHAPTER 5

British Bird Council Rings

There are two types of rings available: the close ring and the split ring.

The Closed Ring

This is brown and stamped BC across the ring, the size code and an exclusive number are stamped along the ring. A great deal of work has been done over the years to find the best size for each species, although minor alterations may still be found necessary from time to time in the light of future experience.

This ring has to be put on the young bird while it is still in the nest and is acceptable to the authorities as being proof that the bird is aviary bred. A bird wearing the correct size ring can be legally sold, provided that the species is included in the schedule of birds which may be sold, when aviary bred and close ringed. That may sound a bit complicated, but it is important to understand that not every bird can be sold just because it is wearing a ring. Nearly all the birds which are generally kept, however, are included in the Schedule (see chapter explaining the law).

One of the problems with the closed ring is that many birds resent the interference in the nest, therefore, the parent birds should be accustomised to being handled and, if possible, be finger tame before the breeding season. The best time to ring is in the evening just before dusk when the parents have finished feeding the young for the day. Place a large bunch of greenfood in the aviary as far away as possible from the nest, then go and wash your hands. This is important because birds have a sense of smell and handling the young birds will leave alien smells on them so causing the old birds to reject them. By the time you get back the parents will be feeding on the greenfood. This is the time to slip in quietly and remove the young ones from the nest. Place them in a lined canary nest pan or something similar, as this allows much more freedom of movement so the task can be completed more easily and quickly. When all the young are ringed place them back in the nest and cup your hand over the nest for about half a minute. This will cause the young to shuffle down into the nest so keeping them warm and hiding the rings.

The age at which young birds can be ringed does vary and the aviculturist will find that the more experienced he becomes the later he will be able to put the rings on. If the rings are put on too soon they will either fall off or the hen will remove the youngster from the nest when she is cleaning out the faecal sacks. The best time to ring is when the youngsters are just big enough to fill the nest and are beginning to evacuate onto the rim of the nest. This is around the seventh day and the hen stops clearing the nest at this time. **Do not expect to do this the first time you try.** It takes practice and experience.

It is well worth practising on canaries and budgerigars, which are much more tolerant of interference.

The recommended method for ringing is as follows (see illustrations page 31). First, if you look at the rings you will see that the rings are tapered (caused by stamping the number on them). Always place the big end on first. Secondly, it is essential to get the three long toes straight and parallel to each other. If the toes are crossed the ring will not go on. Sometimes it takes several goes to get the ring in this position (fig. 1) because the young bird continually tries to clench its toes. Having got that far a gentle pressure and slight twisting motion will take the ring up over the ball of the foot (figs. 2 & 3). The ring is then slid up the shank of the leg until the hind claw is released (figs. 4 & 5). Do not try to rush the job, it requires care and patience.

The correct sizes are:

A. Tree creeper, Wren, Willow Warbler, Chiffchaff, Goldcrest.
B. Redpoll, Siskin, Linnet, Twite, Spotted Flycatcher, Coal Tit, Longtailed Tit.
C. Blue Tit, Marsh Tit, Whitethroat, Redstart, Blackstart, Meadow Pipit, Tree Pipit, Pied Wagtail, Yellow Wagtail, Grey Wagtail, Goldfinch, Bullfinch.
D. Chaffinch, Bramblefinch, Reed Bunting, Whinchat, Stonechat, Tree Sparrow.
E. Greenfinch, House Sparrow, Dunnock, Woodlark, Nightingale, Cirl Bunting, Yellow Hammer, Blackcap, Bearded Reedling.
G. Wheatear, Snow Bunting, Nuthatch, Great Tit, Skylark.
J. Crossbill, Corn Bunting, Lesser Spotted Woodpecker.
K. Hawfinch, Waxwing.
L. Song Thrush, Redwing, Starling, Greater Spotted Woodpecker.
M. Mistle Thrush, Fieldfare, Blackbird, Ring Ouzel, Shrike.
P. Jay.
R. Jackdaw, Magpie, Lapwing.
S. Chough, Sparrow Hawk, Kestrel, Hobby, Merlin, Little Owl, Scops Owl.
U. Short Eared Owl, Barn Owl, Tawny Owl.
W. Peregrine, Goshawk, Common Buzzard, Marsh Harrier.
X. Red Tailed Buzzard.

Closed rings are issued from 1st February to 30th September each year.

The Split Ring

This ring is used for registration purposes. It can be put on after the young have fledged. The breeder must inform the Ring Registrar on which bird each ring has been used. It is also the breeders' responsibility to inform the Ring Registrar if the bird dies or if it is passed on to another breeder.

The rings are individually numbered and each ring issued is recorded to the breeder concerned. They are made of a special alloy and as the description implies, the rings are open. After being placed on the bird's leg the ring is permanently closed using a special pair of pliers. These pliers have different sized holes to coincide with the different sizes of rings. It is most important to use the correct hole in the pliers otherwise the ring will either not be closed properly or the ends will overlap making it too small for the bird

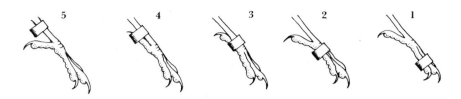

Figure 5.1 Ringing young birds

The ring is first passed over the three forward toes (1) and then drawn up to the metatarsus (2). It is then drawn up the tarsus taking with it the hind toe (3). The ring should be drawn as high up the tarsus as possible (4). In most birds the hind toe will release itself (5). Care should be taken not to dislocate the hind toe or damage the hind claw.

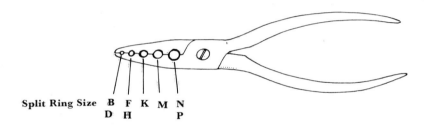

Split Ring Size   **B   F   K   M   N**
                   D   H   P

Figure 5.2 Split Ring Pliers

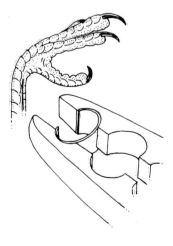

Figure 5.3 Method of using Split Ring Pliers

and causing injury. The pliers are placed over the ring using the correct hole and making sure that the bird's leg is not trapped and will not be damaged when the pliers are squeezed to close the ring. This first action, although closing the ring makes it oval so the pliers should now be turned 90° and squeezed again which makes the ring round, with the two ends butting neatly together so that they are not then a hazard in which the ring might get caught up in wire netting or suchlike. It is a simple operation after a bit of practice, but normal care must always be taken to ensure that the bird is not damaged in any way.

The correct sizes to use are as follows:

B.   Chiffchaff, Goldcrest, Tree Creeper, Willow Warbler, Wren.

D.   Bearded Reedling, Blackstart, Blue Tit, Bramblefinch, Bullfinch, Chaffinch, Coal Tit, Goldfinch, Linnet, Longtailed Tit, Marsh Tit, Meadow Pipit, Pied Wagtail, Redpoll, Redstart, Reed Bunting, Siskin, Spotted Flycatcher, Stonechat, Tree Pipit, Tree Sparrow, Twite, Whinchat, Whitethroat, Yellow Wagtail.

F.   Blackcap, Cirl Bunting, Dunnock, Great Tit, Greenfinch, House Sparrow, Nightingale, Nuthatch, Skylark, Snow Bunting, Wheatear, Woodlark, Yellow Hammer.

H.   Corn Bunting, Crossbill, Hawfinch, Lesser Spotted Woodpecker, Waxwing.

K.   Blackbird, Fieldfare, Greater Spotted Woodpecker, Mistle Thrush, Redwing, Ring Ouzel, Shrike, Song Thrush, Starling.

M.   Jackdaw, Jay, Magpie.

Exhibition

Under the new legislation all birds exhibited must be ringed with a ring of the correct size. The only available rings at the present time to comply with this requirement are the B.B.C. rings. These are obtainable from:

**L.S. Warrilow,
Ring Registrar,
35 Chatham Road,
Kingston–upon–Thames,
Surrey, KT1 3AB.**

CHAPTER 6

Seedeaters

Order: *Passeriformes*
Family: *Fringillidae* (Finches)

GREENFINCH *(Chloris chloris)*

Length — 6 inches (12.25 cm)   **Weight** — approximately 1 oz (28–35 g).
Male: Olive-green with heavy, conical, horn coloured bill. Yellow wing butts, yellow on outer side of the primaries and yellow tail sides. Jonque and mealy forms are easily distinguishable in this species. The jonque, or yellow form, is slightly smaller and much yellower with yellow on the breast. The mealy or buff form is larger and not quite as colourful.
Female: a much browner bird, more like a sparrow but with yellow on the outer sides of the primaries, though not to the same extent as the cocks. The young are similar to the hen but have brown streaks on the breast. An easy bird to sex.

Characteristics

The greenfinch is a common bird, resident and well distributed. A useful bird to gardener and farmer since its food consists mainly of weed seeds and, when rearing young, small insects like greenfly. It frequents almost every part of the countryside which is well supplied with trees, hedges, bushes and evergreens. A sociable bird which often nests in loose colonies in copses, farmland hedgerows, city parks and suburban gardens. Frequent visitors to bird tables where they are particularly attracted by peanuts. The distinctive *Tzee-ee* drawn out call is easily recognised.

In winter some leave the shelter of the gardens to join flocks of other finches and buntings feeding on stubble and waste land. In winter too flocks of greenfinches arrive on the east coast from the continent. These depart again in the spring and do not appear to stay to breed. The continental bird is rather larger and greyer on the wings than our native bird.

The greenfinch is a prolific breeder, commencing nesting in April and will have two or sometimes three broods in the season. The nest is a bulky affair, usually about 6–7 feet (1.83–2.13 m) above the ground, constructed of grass, moss and wool on a foundation of twigs and is lined with fine roots and hair. A normal clutch is four eggs, whitish with a few dark markings. Incubation takes thirteen days and the young fledge in approximately fifteen days. The young are fed on regurgitated food.

The greenfinch's main foods are chickweed, groundsel, dandelion, elm, dogs mercury, charlock, goatsbeard, persicaria, burdock, bramble, yew and hornbeam as well as small flys, gnats and other tiny insects on which they feed their young.

In the wild greenfinches suffer heavy losses said to be mainly from predation which is, of course, why they have so many broods. At the end of the year the proportion of young birds to old birds is said to be 3:1 which means that only 1.5 birds per pair survive through the autumn. The winter will take further tolls of both old and young especially in hard winters when the food supplies run out. It is this which maintains the species at approximately the same level year after year. However, experience in aviaries suggests that there may be other reasons besides predation for the heavy loss in young birds.

Aviary Breeding and Rearing

Greenfinches are ideal subjects for aviaries and a good species with which to commence breeding, British birds being easy to cater for, providing their requirements are fully understood. The basic aviary described in the chapter on Cages and Aviaries is ideal, especially if this is equipped with the artificial hedge also described. The birds are hardy and can be put into the aviary in the autumn. They will winter outside and be all the better for it, provided that they have adequate supplies of food and water. Water is the main problem because it can freeze in hard weather. If the food and water are in a shelter shed to which the birds have access through holes, sufficient heat can generally be provided to maintain the shed just above freezing point which is all that is necessary. If, however, there is any doubt about it they should be kept inside and put into the flight as early in the spring as the weather allows.

Being early nesters it upsets the breeding cycle if the birds cannot commence breeding as soon as spring arrives. A good British finch mixture and sunflower seed forms the basic diet with as many wild seeding plants as can be gathered. Dandelions, which seed in April, can be supplied in unlimited quantities as long as the main crop lasts (about four weeks); chickweed is also excellent and supplies are normally available except in very dry weather. Groundsel, because it dies off so quickly, is best placed in jars of water. If the jars are sunk into the aviary floor they will not tip over. Soaked seed should also be supplied. There are two ways of doing this. The seeds can be soaked in a jar of water for two days but the water should be changed several times, otherwise the seeds go sour and smelly. Only as much as the birds will eat should be given each day because the seeds soon dry out and cease to be useful. The best way, if space permits, is to fork over a small patch away from the main perches and scatter some seed on it. The damp ground and rain is sufficient to start them sprouting. Every few days fork the ground over again and add a few more seeds. If this is not possible use two or three seed boxes full of soil with the seed on top. These should be watered every day and used alternately in the aviary.

If possible, get the breeding birds onto egg food made with hard boiled eggs and described in the chapter on feeding. This will help to supply the large quantities of protein which the young ones require. Young birds grow at a tremendous rate and in approximately two weeks from being hatched — blind, helpless and naked — become full-sized birds with a full set of feathers. To do this they must have animal protein. In the wild this is provided in the form of insects — in this case small flys, gnats and such, with greenfly being particularly useful. Hard boiled egg, cheese and milk are good alternatives but milk is difficult to provide because it soon goes sour and is therefore best avoided.

Supply small birch twigs, moss, roots, dried grass and cow or dog hair for nest building. Also sizal string teased out and cut into 2 inch (5 cm) lengths. Most finches like cotton wool but it must be used carefully, otherwise it may become tangled in their feet. Buy cotton wool in small rolls which should not be unrolled but tied tightly with string or wire and fastened on the branches in the open where the rain can get at it. The birds will then pull off small beakfuls as they require it and no harm will come to them. All nesting materials should be placed on the aviary floor where they will become wet. Dry moss, for example is like a sponge and will keep returning to its original shape so that the birds are unable to mould it into the shape they require. If it is too wet the birds will soon pull it about until it has the right amount of dampness.

A patch of nettles, some rotting fruit — particularly bananas — and horse or cow manure will all help to attract the small flies which are so necessary for the young ones and will keep the parents occupied in collecting them.

Since greenfinches are such sociable birds, several pairs will breed together in the same aviary, and they can also be mixed with other finches. It is best not to have odd cocks because they will quarrel over the hens but good results can be obtained using up to two hens to each cock if desired. It is important though not to overcrowd and the size of the aviary will determine how many birds can be kept.

Young birds are self supporting about two weeks after fledging although the cock may continue to partially feed them longer than this. This is the time when they must have ample and continuous supplies of seeding weeds. Apart from the weed seeds they find many small insects on them. This is also the time when a small patch of lawn is essential. The young greenfinches will eat a lot of grass and spend a great deal of time picking up odd things which we cannot see. Whether these are minerals or small insects or both is not known, but if these young birds are put into cages or otherwise denied the chance of pecking in the soil and not given supplies of wild seeds many of them will not live through the moult. Young birds are best left in the aviary, with or without parents, until they have fully completed the moult into adult plumage which takes place in the autumn. Young greenfinches are particularly prone to going light, that is, they gradually waste away. Nobody actually knows the reason for this, but it appears to be a form of indigestion and although the birds spend all day pecking round the food receptacles they do not actually eat anything. When this becomes obvious the bird is generally beyond saving, except by the use of antibiotics which are not recommended. If it is noticed in the early stages it can be cured by feeding the bird with rather wet egg food. The bird will not take it itself and this has to be done by hand. To avoid this situation is better than trying to cure it and one can do this by carefully following the advice already given above.

A permanent supply of fresh water in a shallow vessel not more than 2 inches (5 cm) deep for drinking and bathing is essential. As with all seedeaters a permanent supply of a suitable mineralised grit and cuttlefish bone must never be neglected.

Many greenfinches have been bred in aviaries for years and have become quite domesticated. Domestication, as with all animals, has brought changes and mutations. Greenfinches reared today are now much larger than the birds in the wild and there are two well established mutations.

Mutations

The green in the greenfinch's plumage is made up of three colours — yellow, brown and black. In the first mutation the black and the brown were inhibited leaving a bird which is clear yellow. This bird has pink eyes and is really a yellow form of Albino which is called Lutino. The mutation is on the sex chromosome and is called sex-linked. This means that it does not breed true unless two Lutinos are mated together. There is a full explanation of the inheritance of abnormal colours in chapter 6.

In the second mutation the black only was inhibited leaving brown markings on the yellow ground. This is a very pretty colour known as cinnamon. As with the Lutino, the cinnamon mutation is on the sex chromosome and again it is sex-linked and has pink eyes. No doubt further colours will arrive in due course and, possibly, pied forms. Other mutations including Silvers, cinnamon winged Lutinos, Slate Blues and Pieds have also appeared but as yet are not established.

There is, therefore, a great deal more to be learned about this species and much experimental work still to be done — a most interesting and worthwhile study.

Exhibition

In an exhibition specimen overall size is important; it should be thick set, having plenty of width and frontal rise in the skull. A well-rounded head set on a thick, well defined neck compatible with body size. Short, compact wings with well defined yellow bars, also well defined yellow edging to feathers in tail, clear and as bright a green as possible, devoid of smokiness. The bird should be sturdy and have an upright stance.

Contributions by: Bob Partridge.

Figure 6.1   Redpoll–Bullfinch Hybrid

GOLDFINCH *(Carduelis carduelis britannica)*

Length — 4½ inches (11.5 cm) **Weight** — 1 oz (28.35 g).
Male: Predominantly buff and chestnut on the back and flanks and whitish on the belly with a red face mask, greyish white cheeks, black crown and side stripes. Its wings are black with a broad yellow bar, and white tips, like buttons, on each feather. The tail is also black, with white tips on the upperside of each feather and broad white patches, like half moons, on the underside of the two outer pairs. The long narrow beak is whitish with a black tip. When in breeding condition the beak goes clear right to the tip and the plumage colours become brighter and more intensified.
Female: a little smaller with a less expansive red mask or blaze. In the cock the blaze extends behind the eye, whereas in the hen it only extends to the front of the eye. There are other small differences: the bristles round the base of the beak are jet black on the cock and brownish on the hen and the same applies to the wing butts. These differences are not infallible and a young cock will often show the female characteristics, except that he is generally slightly larger. This is not an easy species to sex without experience: perhaps the best guide is that the hen nearly always has some brown flecking on the crown.
Juveniles: lack the red blaze and black crown but have the wing and tail markings like the adult. They are generally more greyish and known as grey-pates.

Distribution

The goldfinch is a beautiful little bird often called the seven coloured linnet because of the number of colours in its plumage. A very pleasant and consistent singer, it is well distributed throughout the British Isles except the northern half of Scotland, but is more plentiful south of the line from the Wash to the Dee and in Ireland south of Ulster.

It is found on open ground where there are weeds — especially thistles — and it nests in tall bushes or trees on farmland, parkland, orchards, gardens, churchyards, scrub and woodland edges. It is a sociable bird and not very territorial and does not seem to mind others of the same species being close to the nesting site. The pair will quite often go some distance from the nest to feed. In the winter family parties join together into small flocks called charms and forage the waste lands for food.

Nesting

The goldfinch is a somewhat late nester commencing in May. The nest is neat and compact and made of moss, roots and lichens, wool and spider silk lined with the down of thistles and other plants. It is built high on a bough up to 30 feet (10 m) above the ground and its unusually deep cup helps to retain the contents in windy weather. The usual clutch is four bluey white eggs with red–brown speckles. Incubation is thirteen days and the young usually fledge in sixteen days. They are fed by regurgitation and the parents continue to feed them for several weeks after they leave the nest: two broods are normal.

Feeding

The long beak of the goldfinch is particularly suited to feeding on thistles and teazles both of which they particularly like. Their main foods are chickweed, groundsel, dandelion, elm, ragwort, sowthistle, thistles, hardhead, teazel, meadowsweet, burdock, birch and alder, each one being taken as soon as they become available. In wet summers many thistle heads fail to open leaving more food for the goldfinches in the winter months. Some dead seed heads fall to the ground and disintegrate — the birds prefer to take them from the ground as long as they are available — this results in the heads left on the plant being left until later and are often accessible in times of snow. When their favourite foods are scarce the goldfinches will feed on birches and alders and sometimes pines. During the rearing of their young they take a fair quantity of small insects, such as greenfly and gnats, but are particularly fond of groundsel at this period.

Migration

The reference books give a confused picture of some goldfinches being resident but rather more being migratory: our own observations lead us to believe that the British native goldfinch is a resident though some southward movement may take place in severe weather. In winter the goldfinch flocks band together in large communal roosts, old woods heavily planted with rhododendrons being favourite places. From these roosts the birds set out each morning in small parties to forage but each follows the same route — a rough circle — so that the birds arrive back at the woods at roosting time. So fixed is the pattern and the route that one can say to within a few minutes what time the birds will be at a certain place.

There are goldfinches which are summer visitors and it may be these which have led to confusion. These birds are not our native goldfinches and, although not officially recognised as a separate species or sub-species, they are different to our own birds. The visitors come in April and the migration lasts about three weeks; they travel due north and have followed the same flight pattern as long as can be remembered. For the first few days the flock comprises mainly cocks whilst for the last few days almost all are hens. The same birds can be seen at the end of August travelling due south. Where they breed we have not yet discovered but perhaps it could be that these are the birds which account for the spread of goldfinches in Scotland. These birds are continental stock which are much whiter than the British goldfinch: their blaze is a much deeper red, the white buttons on the wings are larger and oval instead of round and they have flesh coloured legs, whereas our birds have dark almost black legs. These continental birds are also slightly larger.

Aviary Breeding and Rearing

The goldfinch is a most adaptable bird for both cage and aviary. It is colourful, a good songster and one of the most popular British hardbills. A reasonably free breeder, it will also hybridise with the canary and other species of British finch — altogether a very desirable bird which may be kept in a small flight as a single pair or in a mixed collection in a large aviary. The goldfinch will not harm other birds and several pairs can be kept together provided that care is taken not to overcrowd and that sufficient nesting places are available.

Being rather late in coming into breeding condition, the goldfinch does not generally nest before the middle of May and young birds just out of the nest may be seen with the autumn flocks in September.

Nesting sites should be placed as high as possible and consist of small bunches of fir or heather with a hollow in the centre to form the base of the nest. They also like a bunch of gorse and will build their nest in the top. Alternatively, the artificial hedge described in the chapter on cages and aviaries can be used, especially if there are several pairs in the aviary. Small twigs, moss, rootlets, vegetable down, cow and dog hair, and cotton wool kept in a roll as well as sizal string teased out and cut into 2 inch (5 cm) lengths are suitable materials, which should always be allowed to become wet with rain. A very neat nest will be constructed in which the four or five eggs are laid, and will take thirteen to fourteen days to hatch.

It is best not to interfere merely for the sake of knowing exactly what is happening: leave well alone if everything appears to be going to plan. Goldfinches easily desert the nest if you show too much interest in it and have an awkward habit of throwing the young ones out of the nest if you even look at them during the first few days of hatching.

The feeding of goldfinches is very important as they will not thrive without a fairly rich diet. A good mixture should contain canary seed, hemp, niger, groats, linseed and a little small striped sunflower. Hemp and niger are particularly important: teazel is also very good but expensive and maw seed is a grand 'pick-me-up'. The rich mixture can be used with a mixed collection provided they are in an aviary which allows plenty of exercise.

Wild seeds and plants should be supplied constantly and especially groundsel when rearing young. Groundsel should be placed in jars of water otherwise it will die quickly and become useless. Soaked seed and egg food will also play an important part in the rearing of young goldfinches as will the minute insects to be found on the plants offered or grown in the enclosure. A small lawn is extremely useful and nettles are also a very good weed for attracting live food. Rotting fruit and piles of manure as already described will help to provide this essential animal protein.

A good supply of mineral grit and fresh water for drinking and bathing must never be forgotten. Goldfinches are particularly fond of salt and are frequently found on council dumps of road salt: a small bag tipped on the aviary floor will be found helpful — the birds will continue to pick it over long after it has disappeared from sight.

Exhibition

An exhibition bird should be well proportioned and bold. A large expansive blaze is most desirable, extending well down the throat and back behind the eye. The blaze must be bright red with clear cut edge and free from black markings. The black cap should be wide on the top of the head and unbroken. The wings should have visible golden flights with well defined markings on wings and tail known as buttons. Well tanned on chest and flanks.

Contributions by: A.C. Wyatt.

Figure 6.2 Group of Finches

CHAFFINCH *(Fringilla coelebs gengleri)*
BRAMBLING *(Fringilla montifringilla)*

These two species are very closely related and in many respects are similar in their habits. By dealing with them together it is easier to show the differences.

Chaffinch — Length 5¾ inches (14.5 cm), weight approximately ¾ oz (21.26 g).

Male: in winter has a greeny–blue head and nape passing to buff–chestnut on the back and thence to olive green on the rump with blue–grey on the upper tail coverts. The cheeks, throat and breast are pinkish, merging to creamy–white on the belly. As the bird comes into breeding condition the crown and nape become slate–blue and the beak steel blue: the back assumes a brighter chestnut and the breast a brighter pink. The wings are mainly brownish black with white bars and the tail mainly black with white on the outer pair.

Female: slightly smaller and much duller lacking the pinky shades. The wing markings are the same as the cocks, and leave no doubt as to her identity.

Brambling — often known as bramblefinch. Length 6 inches (15.25 cm), weight approximately 1 oz (28.35 g).

Male: in winter is mainly orange–buff with flecked flanks and white rump; orange shoulder patches, throat and chest shading to white on the belly. The head and back are mottled black but in breeding condition they become a full bright black and the bill turns from yellow to black. The axillaries below the wing are bright lemon–yellow, the upper tail coverts are black with long brown fringes and the lower ones pale buff.

Female: at all times paler than the cock — a dull orange-brown — with a strongly mottled back, white belly and buff–grey head with a dark stripe round either side.

Juveniles: in both species resemble the hen but are generally paler.

Distribution

The chaffinch is resident and generally not migratory. The brambling does not breed in Britain and is migratory, being a winter visitor to this country. In winter large numbers of migratory European chaffinches visit this country: the cocks generally stay in England and the hens go further on — to Ireland for some reason. Large flocks comprising cocks only can be seen in England in the winter, which is why it is sometimes called 'the bachelor finch'. Our native chaffinches tend to remain around the nesting territory visiting the beech woods to feed.

In Europe the bramblefinch replaces the chaffinch as a breeding bird at the higher latitudes and altitudes, breeding mainly in subarctic birch woods and conifer forests or sometimes in the tall willow scrub on the tundra.

The chaffinch is well distributed throughout the British Isles except in Shetland and the Outer Hebrides. It breeds wherever there are trees or bushes and the most dense populations are in mature broad-leaved woodland but it is also common in scrub, farmland, parks and gardens. Once the most common bird in Europe, numbers declined considerably in the 1950s due to the effects of toxic agricultural chemicals. Fortunately, with later legislations, the decline seems to have been arrested.

Breeding

The chaffinch is generally single brooded, mainly because the caterpillar diet used to rear the young is only available for a limited period. Should anything happen to the early nests the chaffinch will make further attempts to reproduce. The brambling, on the other hand, is generally double brooded.

The chaffinch commences nesting in early May (rather earlier in the south) and builds a beautiful little nest from 4 to 12 feet (1.21–3.64 m) above the ground. This is well decorated and merges with the surroundings making it difficult to find — in a hedge, bush or tree, sometimes against a wall or fence in creeper, made of moss, grass, bark fibres, bits of paper and roots decorated with lichen and cobwebs and lined with hair. The usual clutch is four eggs, greenish blue with dark markings. The incubation is thirteen days and the young generally fledge in fourteen days.

The brambling also commences nest building in May and builds a larger, less well-finished nest usually in a tree up to 30 feet (10 m) above the ground. It contains less moss but more feathers than that of the chaffinch and is made mostly of grasses and bents with bits of bark and lichen on the outside, being lined with feathers and hair. The usual clutch is six eggs which are rather darker and greener than those of the chaffinch. Incubation is approximately two weeks and the young fledge in a similar period. Both species are highly territorial throughout the breeding season.

Feeding

Outside the breeding season the chaffinch is almost entirely a seedeater, the main foods being various brassicas, goosefoots, persicaria and chickweeds plus spilled grain from the fields and stackyards. The weed seeds are obtained from the plants and from freshly-tilled soil. Many weed seeds do not germinate at the first opportunity but remain viable for years and form a vast reserve in the top soil — it is these that attract the chaffinches to any newly-turned soil. In the winter chaffinches are particularly fond of beech-mast whilst in the breeding season they turn from seeds to animal matter and rear their young mainly on small caterpillars and other insects from leaves, as well as flies and moths caught on the wing, beetles and beetle-larvae, earwigs and spiders.

The brambling's main winter food is beech-mast, which it is able to open more easily than can the chaffinch, otherwise their feeding is similar. The young are reared on an insect fare but the adults will also take conifer seeds from the opening cones.

Aviary Breeding and Rearing

Chaffinches and bramblings are excellent species for aviculture but, because of their territorial nature in the breeding season, care must be taken in a mixed aviary. If the aviary is large enough and not overcrowded they will probably settle down alright, especially if introduced in the winter — but individual cocks vary and it may be necessary to provide them with a separate aviary. On no account should more than one cock be put into an aviary during the breeding season: some are very virile, chasing the hen continually so that she has no time to go to nest. With such a bird it is best to have two hens because he cannot be chasing them both at the same time. This arrangement usually works well and both hens will bring off broods suggesting that the species may be polygamous in the wild.

Provided that they are given a good diet, and a suitable environment these birds are not difficult to breed. Ideally, an aviary approximately 6 feet (2 m) square will be best for a pair or trio on their own. This will give a reasonable amount of space for the provision of live food which is so essential to the rearing of these species.

The basic diet consists of a good British finch mixture together with small sunflower, groats and a good wild seed mixture. During winter a good canary condition and rearing food should be fed twice weekly increasing to a daily feed by spring; chopped hard–boiled egg should be added during the nesting period. Live food in the form of gentles (pinkies preferably), moth pupae or mealworms should be fed daily during winter and spring so as to achieve early breeding condition and, of course, must be provided in increasing amounts when the young are hatched. The gentles should be dusted with a good vitamin powder because this will help to prevent deformity in the young. It is important to provide other sources of livefood during rearing: stinging nettles, rotting vegetation and fruit and stable manure, as already described in other chapters, will all help in the successful rearing of strong healthy young. Some chaffinch cocks help to feed the young right from hatching and such birds are an invaluable benefit to successful rearing.

Very little cover is required for nesting although they do like a small fork in a horizontal position, but hens will usually accept whatever is provided in the way of baskets, bowls, pans and other receptacles. Some good cover should be provided so that the hen can get away from the cock during the pre–mating period. Provide plenty of moss, small feathers, hair, white copax, cotton wool and, if possible, some lichen and cobwebs.

A good supply of mineral grit and fresh water for drinking and bathing at all times is essential.

The incubation is twelve to thirteen days and the young will generally fledge in fourteen days but to some extent this will depend on the amount of live food provided. Some hens will be found to be double brooded but these are the exception. Once they have reared young they do not usually go to nest again until the following season. The young can usually be left in the aviary until after the moult, though occasionally an aggressive cock trying to drive the hen to nest again can be troublesome, when the young should be removed.

The brambling requires the same winter feeding as the chaffinch but it is even more important to provide the live and egg food in early spring, otherwise they may be rather late coming into breeding condition. Although they can be bred in an indoor flight of, say, 3 ft (1 m) × 3ft (1 m) × 6 ft (2 m) high, it is easier for them to obtain some livefood for themselves in outdoor flight: 6 ft (2 m) × 3 ft (1 m) × 6 ft (2 m) high is quite suitable. As explained in other chapters, a patch of nettles, a pile of stable manure and some rotting fruit are a great help in this respect.

Evergreen branches, particularly fir and pine, make a suitable nesting site: the nest is rather like the chaffinches but larger and much deeper (probably because they breed in colder areas) and not so neat.

Mr Beckett (joint contributor for this section) reports that he used scrambled egg made with milk, with grated cheese, carrot and added vitamin. This, together with mealworms and blowfly chrysalis, was found to be a very successful rearing diet. The young fledged in twelve days. The young can be ringed at about seven days old.

Exhibition

For exhibition, a chaffinch must be as large as possible with a good upright stance, of reasonable length but full bodied and a good full head to match. Cocks must have a rich even deep-plum body colour. Hens should be a rich grey with a tendency to a slight pinkish fusion on the breast. In both sexes the shoulder and wing markings must be clear and distinct. The fact that cocks are somewhat larger than hens should be borne in mind when assessing their merits.

Colour, markings and size are of prime importance in the exhibition brambling: fuller bodied and bolder than the chaffinch with deep rust coloured waistcoat coming well down the breast and with a good run of colour into the flanks. The flank markings must be as profuse as possible and the spangling on the back even and distinct. Hens are less colourful, lacking the dark head and distinct back spangling but must have good profuse flank markings.

As with all good exhibition birds these points must be coupled with that all-important quality of feather and showmanship to be wholly successful.

Contributions by: Bob Partridge; V.C. Beckett.

BULLFINCH *(Pyrrhula pyrrhula)*

Length — 5¾ inches (14.5 cm). **Weight** — approximately 1 oz (28.35 g).
Male: a beautiful bird with a blue grey back and glossy black cap and bib: short rounded black bill and the rump and ventral regions are white. The white rump is particularly noticeable when flying. The wings and tail are black but the secondary coverts are grey forming a bar across the wings and a pinkish–red breast.
Female: has a browner-grey back and brown breast but is otherwise marked the same as her mate. The bullfinch is an easy species to sex.
Juveniles: lack the black cap and bib and are darker than the female.

Characteristics

The bullfinch is common and widespread over most of Britain with the exception of northernmost Scotland, the Outer Hebrides, the Orkneys and the Isle of Man. It is resident and sedentary, few ever moving more than five miles from where they were hatched. The British bullfinches are darker and smaller than all the continental forms which become larger and brighter towards the north and towards the tops of mountains. Curiously they are much more aggressive than the continental birds. It is often said that bullfinches have no song and only utter the familiar piping whistle like blowing across a key. Both cocks and hens will, however, sing a low creaky, almost squeaky, song when unmated: this song is very quiet and can only be heard at close range. It is never used when the birds have mates — the pair will keep in touch with the short whistle.

Bullfinches are very affectionate and pair for life. They will always be seen together except in the autumn when family parties can be seen and occasionally two families will join together. This does not last long and by Christmas the families have split up, the birds have paired and will fight for their territories. They are said to be double and sometimes triple brooded but there is considerable doubt about this: they do suffer heavy predation especially from the sparrowhawk and no doubt to overcome this are persistent nesters.

Originally a woodland bird they now nest in woodland undergrowth, thickets, shrubberies, hedgerows, churchyards, town and village gardens and young forestry plantations. Commencing in April the nest is in thick cover and always well hidden usually 4–6 feet (1.21–1.82 m) above the ground. This is made of a small but firm platform of thin twigs, frequently birch, on which is built a small cup of fine roots often rather flimsy and generally lined with hair. Four deep blue eggs with dark markings is the normal clutch which are incubated for fourteen days. The young are somewhat slower to develop than the other finches and fledge at about sixteen days.

During the breeding season the adults develop special pouches in their mouths in which food for their young is retained. When breeding is over the walls of the sacks fold and shrink. It is the only British finch to use this method of carrying food to their young.

Feeding

Bullfinches perfer to feed directly from their food plants rather than off the ground and prefer to feed in cover, only venturing into the open when food is short. Their short rounded bills are ideally suited to eating tree flowers, buds, berries and other soft fruits which they take to a far greater extent than do other finches. They raise their young on a mixture of seeds and invertebrates including caterpillars, spiders and small snails which are de-shelled like seeds.

The main foods consist of chickweed, dandelion, elm, dog's mercury, jack-by-the-hedge, buttercups, sowthistle, charlock, birch, dock, fat-hen, meadowsweet, bramble, nettle, ash, also buds and flowers of crab-apple, hawthorn, elm, blackthorn, sallow, oak and fruit trees.

Bullfinches are well known for their attacks on fruit trees and are considered pests by the fruit farmers. The evidence appears to show that they only take the fruit buds when the tree seeds are all gone and attacks are worst when the trees, particularly ash, have a poor crop. This seems to happen every few years, consequently fruit farmers are allowed to trap and destroy bullfinches. It is said that they kill thousands, but nobody appears to be able to put a definite figure to it: one would expect this destruction to so reduce the population that bullfinches would soon become scarce but, in fact, the reverse is the case and the bullfinch is more than holding its own. It has been shown by R.K. Murton in his book *Man and Birds* that limited trapping in the autumn removes the surplus population which nature would otherwise remove by starvation in the winter. There are, therefore, fewer birds to eat the available supplies of food which lasts longer and a greater proportion of birds survive to breed the following year. One wonders whether the farmers might do better if they discontinued trapping and left nature to take her own course. It seems that the trapping is in the best interests of the species though hard on the individuals.

Aviary Breeding and Rearing

Bullfinches are excellent aviary birds, provided that one understands their ways. There must never be more than one pair of bullfinches in an aviary otherwise both cocks and hens will fight to the death until there is only one pair left. The family party can be left together in the autumn while they moult out, but the young ones must be removed at the end of November — no later — as the writer knows from bitter experience. Two pairs can be in adjoining aviaries provided that they cannot see each other, otherwise the cocks and hens will spend all day fighting each other through the wires and never settle down to nesting. Several hens can be kept in a flight together provided that there is no cock within sight or sound. Bullfinches are aggressive and it is not safe to leave them in a flight with one other pair of birds of any species. The bullfinches will drive them to the ground and refuse to let them eat. If they are not separated quickly the other pair will die. On the other hand they will settle down quite amicably if there are five or six pairs of birds other than bullfinches. The reason for this is that they cannot chase them all at once, but it is best to have two feeding stations so that they cannot dominate the food. If possible they are best kept in an aviary to themselves.

The artificial hedge described in Chapter 3 on cages and aviaries suits bullfinches well, but if this cannot be provided ensure that there is plenty of camouflage round the nesting site so that the nest can be well hidden. Supply thin birch twigs about 5 inches (12.5 cm) long, coconut fibre, fine roots and hair which should be on the ground in the flight where they will get wet. Teased out sizal string cut into 2 inch (5 cm) lengths can also be given but these birds usually prefer darker materials. Sometimes the hen bullfinch will build in a wicker basket which helps because they often build very flimsy nests. Perhaps this is because the materials supplied do not take the bird's fancy.

The staple diet is a good British finch mixture with some hemp and a supply of sunflower seed. Soaked seed is also essential in the breeding season. When the young hatch live food must be given and ant eggs, if obtainable, are very useful: dried ant eggs can be obtained from a pet shop and scalded. Maggots which have turned to chrysalis can be given and are better than maggots themselves. Some bullfinches will also take mealworms. If insufficient live food is given the birds may only rear one or two young instead of the full brood. Boiled hemp seed is very helpful: let it boil only for a minute or so when it will be found to have sprouted.

A word of warning — bullfinches must have plenty of exercise if they are to remain healthy. When in cages they are prone to putting on a lot of weight and become breathless and wheezy. While they are in cages hemp should be withheld.

Bullfinches should at all times be provided with all the wild foods that are available: in autumn privet berries, blackberries and black currants should be fed to them and will help obtain that lovely pink breast on the cocks. As explained in the chapter on greenfinches there are yellows and buffs and this is another species where it is particularly noticeable. The yellow is a smaller brighter bird and the buff a larger but duller bird.

Bullfinches are persistent nesters and will continue to build nests, laying clutches of eggs throughout the breeding season until they have reared young ones. The experience of a number of breeders is that they very rarely nest again that year once even one youngster has fledged, but should the nest be lost for any reason they will go on trying until they start to moult. While some finches can be reared under canaries the writer does not know of any case of success with bullfinches. They have however, on occasion, been reared by greenfinches. There is clearly something more we need to know about the foods on which the wild birds rear their young.

Without doubt, bullfinches do pair for life and are very devoted to each other, never being more than a few yards apart and always keeping in touch with their piping whistle. Birds from which it is intended to breed should always be kept together and never parted. If one of the birds should die, care must be taken in providing a new mate. For a time a new mate will not be accepted and will be driven away. Several weeks should elapse before introducing a new mate. When a bird is looking for a new mate the soft squeaky song will be heard: it is generally very difficult to see where it is coming from, but once identified it is very easy to recognise.

As with all finches a constant supply of mineral grit and a suitable receptacle with fresh water for drinking and bathing are essential.

The hen bullfinch will pair with other finches if they are paired up when young and they produce some beautiful hybrids. The cock, however, has never been known to pair with other species. The reason for this seems to be that the cock bullfinch is so slow reaching the point of pairing that the hens of other species do not wait long enough. We do not know if this is the case and perhaps one day the cock bullfinch will yet produce a hybrid.

Exhibition

The exhibition bullfinch is a bird which is cobby and round with a broad expansive black cap well back over the head and with clean cut edges. The wings and tail are short and compact. The body colour is very important and should be a light slate–blue back with a bright even crimson starting from the throat, down the chest and belly between the legs and on the flanks. Well defined wing bar. Good size is also important.

Figure 6.3 Siskin

SISKIN *(Carduelis spinus)*

Length — 4½ inches (11.5 cm)   **Weight** — only a fraction of an ounce (10 g).
Male: a small yellow-green bird with dark streaks on the back and flanks, paler below with blackish bib and crown. Yellow rump, wing bars, sides of tail and lores. A longish narrow beak and short forked tail. The bib and cap vary greatly between individuals: in some the bib is absent altogether and the cap varies between mottled black and a full black cap.
Female: lacks the bib and cap and is paler and greyer but more streaked than the cock.

Distribution

At one time the siskin was more or less confined in the British Isles to the Caledonian pine forests in the North of Scotland but in the last thirty to fifty years has spread considerably, though is still somewhat locally distributed. The increase has been attributed to new afforestation particularly Sitka spruce. It is now found in southern Scotland and in many parts of England and Wales and rather more so in Ireland wherever suitable plantations are found. However it is far better known in England and Wales as a winter visitor when its numbers are considerably increased by migrations from the continent. Nevertheless, it is pleasing to record a species which is increasing and spreading although their numbers fluctuate and depend upon the seed crop.

Breeding

In good seed years siskins commence nesting as early as April but in poorer years this is delayed until late May or June. In the good years they will generally have two broods but in poor years only one. They commence breeding when the main spruce crop is available and nesting is normally finished by the time these run out in July and August when they move into the birches. In winter the primary food supply is alder, the seeds being taken both from the cones and the ground below. Siskins prefer, however, to spend most of their time in the branches where their acrobatic antics are reminiscent of the tits. In winter, when food is short, the birds will forage in fields and hedgerows taking tree seeds and weed seeds.

There is a general migration south in the winter which is joined by birds from the continent in a south-west movement so that quite large flocks can be seen. Occasionally some British-bred birds winter on the continent mainly in France and Spain. Siskins are sociable birds which nest in loose colonies and keep up a constant twitter. In the spring and summer the pair always stay close together but it is not clear whether this pair is maintained in the winter flocks.

The usual siskin nest is towards the end of a conifer branch, about 15 feet

(4.57 m) or more above the ground. A neat nest, rather similar to a goldfinch's, made of twigs, lichen, moss and wool, with hair, fur and plant down for the lining. The normal clutch is four bluish–white eggs with dark markings which hatch in thirteen days, the young fledge in fifteen–seventeen days and are reared on spruce seeds, pine seeds, small insects and seeding weeds. They are similar to the female but are rather more streaked.

Feeding

The main foods of siskins are spruce, pine, dandelion, elm, dock, birch, hardheads, thistles, meadowsweet, mugwort, alder and larch.

Aviary Breeding and Rearing

These charming, lovable and friendly little birds make excellent aviary subjects and can safely be mixed with any of the finches except bullfinches. The pairs are devoted and always stay close together keeping up their continuous twittering. Siskins will always come to you when in the aviary and start feeding round your feet.

It is, however, rather more difficult to get them to go to nest than with most of the finches, though once started they will breed well. This seems to be because of the difficulty in providing their natural food of spruce seeds and their special requirements for nesting sites. Few people can provide an aviary 15 feet high but we can provide bunches of fir and pine wired together in the shape of a growing tree so that the branches hang naturally. We can supply fair quantities of small flies, gnats and the like by the use of nettles, piles of rotting fruit and manure as described elsewhere. Siskins will be seen hanging upside–down on the wires collecting these and there is always a better supply of small insects if the aviary is kept damp, if necessary by watering.

Their basic diet should consist of a good British finch mixture with extra niger and a good wild seed mixture. Blue maw seed is important but because it is so small it is generally best fed separately. Livefood in the form of blowfly chrysalis and small moth pupae should be given as well as canary rearing food. Seeding weeds such as dandelion, milk thistle, chickweed and groundsel should be fed throughout the season as available. Groundsel is best placed in a jar of water otherwise it dies quickly and is useless.

If seeding weeds are in short supply spinach, cabbage or young lettuce will be found useful substitutes, as well as soaked seeds such as teazel and small striped sunflower. A good supply of mineral grit and cuttlefish bone should always be available as well as fresh water for drinking and bathing.

If kept in cages special attention must be paid to the diet as siskins are inclined to become overweight and on occasions stiff legged. In cages hemp should be withheld completely and the maw seed increased.

Siskins will sometimes accept small wicker baskets for nesting and do not seem to need much cover, perhaps a few branches of fir wired round the basket. Small flys, gnats and the like help to reduce the mortality rate in young birds and, as already described, the nettle patch, rotting fruit and manure are a great help in this respect. Maw seed is also particularly important at this time and the birds should have an unlimited supply. The young birds are best left with their parents until after the moult. If removed earlier make sure the young birds are feeding well on their own. It is worth noting that very few siskin cocks make any attempt to feed young though they rarely neglect their mates.

Occasionally chicks may show signs of going light but mortality is usually low after they are fully self–feeding.

Exhibition

The siskin is another species where the yellow and buff forms are easy to recognise. When breeding for exhibition particular attention should be paid to type, purity of colour, markings and size. A good yellow will generally take preference on the show bench though good buff hens will do a deal of winning. It should be remembered when pairing that a good buff is just as essential as a good yellow. Generally speaking it will be found that some pairs will consistently produce quality cocks and others quality hens. It is very rare to find good exhibition cocks **and** hens produced by one individual pair.

Although mutations in the form of pieds, dark eyed yellows and lutinos have been produced, none of these have so far been established. The chapter on colour inheritance will help breeders on how to go about producing strains of new colours.

Exhibition siskins should have a good broad black cap with even lacings and clean–cut bib: well laced flanks and distinct pencilling on the back and a good clear yellow body colour free from smokiness.

Contributions by: Bob Partridge.

REDPOLL

Lesser Redpoll *(Carduelis flammae cabaret)* Length 4¾ inches (12.75 cm), weight less than ½ oz (14 g).
Mealy Redpoll *(Carduelis flammea)* Length 5 inches (12.75 cm), weight less than ½ oz (14 g.)
Hornemans Redpoll *(Carduelis hornemanni)* Length 5 inches (12.75 cm), weight less than ½ oz (14 g).

All three species are very similar and closely related. The Lesser Redpoll is our resident bird, the Mealy Redpoll and the Hornemans or Greenland Redpoll being winter visitors though neither of these latter normally cover the whole of Britain. The Mealy Redpoll is found in Scotland and down the east coast while the Hornemans Redpoll rarely comes further south than the north of Scotland. Apart from this all three species are very similar in their habits.
Male Lesser Redpoll: has a rich brown mantle with darker streaks and whitish underparts, a crimson forehead and black chin or bib and dark brown striations on the flanks. Across the wings are two buff coloured bars.
Female: very similar; they are most difficult to sex. There are differences which can be seen when examined carefully; the female is often slightly larger than the male with a larger and deeper bib and much stronger striations on the flanks: the male striations are poor and sometimes almost non–existent. In addition, there is a faint narrow silver grey line all round the female's bib but one has to examine the bird very closely to see it and it is never found on the male. Most books say that the male has a pink breast and rump but experience in breeding these birds in aviaries has shown that this is incorrect. A slight pink flush is a better description and this is normally only attained when the bird is several years old and, further, both cocks and hens will develop this flush. A deeper pink can be obtained, however, by colour feeding.
Lesser Redpoll: has a stout little yellow beak and dark brown legs.
Mealy Redpoll: very similar to the lesser but slightly larger and paler, while the **Hornemans** is much whiter still.

All three species will hybridise in aviaries and there is evidence to suggest that this sometimes takes place in the wild where the species naturally overlap.

Characteristics

The redpoll is an active little bird and its actions are in many ways similar to the tit family. A much faster flyer than the other small finches, it keeps up a constant, distinctive twittering — otherwise it might well go unnoticed. Indeed, it is well distributed throughout the British Islands and quite common, though few people see or recognise it. Originally a bird of the birch woods the redpoll spread to conifer plantations and now nests in scrub growth, overgrown field hedgerows, parks and suburban gardens. It is very gregarious and nests in colonies, which gather into large flocks in the winter in company with other finches.

Feeding

The main foods are tree seeds, particularly birch and alder, and weed seeds including sallow, chickweed, groundsel, dandelion, grasses, meadowsweet, fat-hen and mugwort: they also fond of sorrel and willowherb. In winter they usually leave the gardens and concentrate on tree seeds as long as these last and in spring they take large quantities of tiny insects such as gnats and greenfly which also form the major element of the food given to their young ones, especially during the first five or six days.

Breeding

A late nester the redpoll commences breeding about May building a small neat nest generally about 4–5 feet (1–1.5 m) above the ground, made of roots and dead stalks neatly lined inside with down, hair and feathers. Four or five eggs, which are blue with dark markings, is the normal clutch and although very similar to other finches in colour they can usually be recognised by their small size. Incubation generally takes twelve to thirteen days and the young fledge in a similar period.

Aviary Breeding and Rearing

The redpoll is an endearing little bird and in spite of its lack of colour is a great favourite with aviculturists. It is hardy and adaptable, easy to cater for, breeding readily in aviaries — though better in colonies perhaps due to difficulty in sexing. Supply bundles of heather, fir and such or a hedge as already described in Chapter 3 on cages and aviaries with nesting materials listed above. Sizal string teased out and cut in 2 inch (5 cm) lengths is also very useful.

A standard British finch mixture with all the wild seeding weeds which can be gathered will form the basic diet. Soaked seed must be supplied during the breeding season and, if the birds can be persuaded to take egg food, so much the better. In an aviary the birds will find quite a lot of small flies and gnats and will be seen hanging upside-down from the wires collecting them. A patch of nettles, a pile of rotting fruit (especially bananas) and some cow or horse manure will greatly help to maintain the supply of these insects.

A constant supply of a good mineralised grit is essential as well as fresh water for drinking and bathing.

Soaked seeds and seeding weeds must be supplied until after the young have fully moulted out.

In recent years a very attractive cinnamon mutation has appeared: although there are only limited numbers as yet they are fortunately in the hands of experienced colour breeders and will, no doubt, soon be established. This is a sex-linked mutation, explained in the chapter on inheritance. Pied forms have also appeared from time to time.

The redpoll is an ideal species for any beginner and one which never loses its appeal.

Exhibition

An exhibition redpoll is a well rounded short cobby little bird. A good red forehead and nice bib. Well defined plentiful lines on chest and flanks and a good rich colour according to species.

Contributions by: A.C. Wyatt; Bob Partridge.

Figure 6.4   Greenfinch (top) and Linnet

LINNET AND TWITE

Linnet *(Carduelis cannabina)* Length 5 inches (12.75 cm), weight 1 oz (28.35 g).
Twite *(Carduelis flavirostris)* Length 5 inches (12.75 cm), weight just over ½ oz (15 g).

These two birds, although different species, are so alike in looks and ways that it is advisable to deal with them together and show the differences. Both have a breeding plumage in the males which is acquired as they come into breeding condition, rather than from an actual moult.

Male Linnet: has a chestnut brown back with black and brown streaks, dark wings and tail with conspicuous edgings of white: there are seven primaries edged with white and the white extends to the shaft. The underparts are buff with fine streakings on the flanks. In breeding condition the male becomes a much brighter chestnut and assumes a grey head which certainly is not discernible in the winter. The male also acquires a pinkish flush on the breast and crown and the beak changes colour from horn to steely blue.

Female: very similar to the male's winter dress but has better markings on the flanks although these vary. In addition, the female has only five primaries with white edgings which do not extend quite as far as the shaft. There is also a difference in the underflue on the breast which can be seen if the breast feathers are lightly blown back as illustrated in the accompanying sketch.

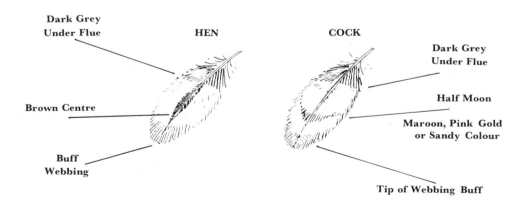

Figure 6.5   Linnet Breast Feathers

Linnets are very difficult birds to sex when out of breeding condition unless one handles them. The young resemble the female.

Male Twite: very similar to the linnet but darker and more slenderly built as shown by the difference in weights. The throat is warm buff, underparts are paler and rump pinkish. The male does not acquire the pink flush on the breast and crown nor the grey head. The twite has a rather deeper forked tail.

Female Twite: very similar to the hen linnet but darker and is more lightly built. The young resemble the female.

Characteristics

The linnet, better known as the brown linnet, is widely distributed throughout the British Isles except the north west of Scotland. In this century it appears to have extended its range and overlaps the twite which has been receding and is now confined to the Pennines and a few isolated areas in Wales, the Highlands and Western Islands of Scotland and the west coast of Ireland.

The linnet frequents gorse-strewn commons, hillsides covered with scrub, coast marshes and sandhills. The twite, sometimes called the mountain linnet, frequents moorland and heather often above the tree line and also heather covered coastal cliffs.

Both birds are residents and are partially migratory: both nest in loose colonies. Migration is similar, there being a westward movement in the autumn and some migrate down the coasts of France and Spain. In the winter birds of both species arrive on the east coast from the continent. The severity of the winter seems to be a factor in how many birds migrate and how far they go. Each appears to return to its own breeding area in the spring and birds which have migrated one year may not do so the next and vice versa. In winter flocks roam the countryside searching the fields, roadsides and uncultivated places for food and sometimes forage in estuaries.

The linnet has a pleasant twittering song frequently rendered. The twite is similar but a little more nasal.

Breeding

The linnet commences nesting in mid-April in gorse and thorn scrub, hedgerows, and young plantations, occasionally on dunes and in heather. Sometimes they will nest on banks and low vegetation, generally near ground level and rarely more than 6 feet (2 m) above the ground. The nest is a substantial structure of grass and moss, lined with hair, wool or fur. Four bluish white eggs with dark markings is the normal clutch.

The twite begins nesting a little later, commencing in May, the location being on the ground or only a few feet up in low vegetation or sheltered cranny. The nest is made of a few twigs, grass and moss, lined with wool and sometimes feathers. Five bluish eggs with dark markings is the normal clutch.

Both birds are very timid and will not stand for any interference with the nest and will very easily desert it. The young are very prone to 'exploding' from the nest when looked at well before they are able to fly and it is quite impossible to put them back: with every attempt they will jump out again.

The incubation is twelve days and the young fledge in a similar period. Two broods are normal in a season.

Feeding

The main foods are chickweed, meadowgrass, dandelion, jack-by-the-hedge, sorrel, buttercup, catsear, persicaria, fat hen, mugwort, meadowsweet, charlock, wild radish and hardheads. Small flies and insects are fed to the young.

Aviary Breeding and Rearing

In an aviary both the linnet and twite are easy to cater for. The artificial hedge with clumps of gorse as described in Chapter 3 will suit the linnet for a nesting site. For the twite pull up a fair sized tuft of heather complete with roots and plant it in the aviary: allow grass to grow tall around it. The heather may not live but it is of no consequence.

A good British finch mixture with some hemp is the main diet and it always helps if the birds are accustomed to egg food made with hard boiled egg as this will provide a lot of the animal protein needed to bring them into breeding condition. They will catch a certain amount of live food themselves in the aviary especially if it is provided with nettles, cow manure and rotting fruit as already described.

A good bath of fresh water must always be available and a plentiful supply of mineral grit. Supply small thin twigs, hay, moss, fine roots and hair for nest building.

With these species leave the birds alone and only watch quietly from a distance. Like the wild birds, they do not like interference. If the young jump out of the nest before they are ready to fly leave them alone — they will hide under the cover of the nettles or whatever else is available. They will be quite all right and the parents will find them and feed them. Do not make any attempt to try to catch them, which, in any case is extremely difficult. It is as well to take the precaution before nesting starts to make sure that there is sufficient cover on the floor, to protect them from the elements and all will be well.

Exhibition

An exhibition linnet should be as nearly cone shaped as possible with a well rounded head, well lined on top: well defined lines on neck under lower mandible and well defined white edges to primaries and compact tail. Small fine even tickings on the chest and down the flanks and underflue.

The exhibition twite should be as large as possible but cobby with neat round and well lined head: clear well defined lines on chest and flanks and a defined white bar in the wing and a good rich nutty brown throughout.

Contributions by: Bob Partridge.

HAWFINCH *(Coccothraustes coccothraustes)*

Length — 7 inches (17.75 cm)   **Weight** — approx 2 oz (56 g).

The hawfinch is unmistakable with its dumpy body, huge beak and its short tail but it has most beautiful colourings of brown, russet, gold and white. The white being most conspicuous when the bird is in flight. On the ground the bird moves in a series of hops with its top-heavy body held very upright.

Male: has upper parts red-brown, underparts peach, black bib and wings with white shoulders, bill horn coloured in winter but steel blue in the breeding season.

Female: rather smaller and much duller. This species is easy to sex.

Distribution

Sparsely populated over most of England and Wales except the south west, the hawfinch is a most shy and elusive bird, seldom seen. For this reason there may be more of them than is generally supposed. They occur mainly in deciduous woodland of wych elm, hornbeam, beech, wild cherry, sycamore and maple and also frequent parkland and large gardens where these trees grow. It is a difficult bird to study and most books on British birds contain little information about its habits. Guy Mountfort's monograph entitled *The Hawfinch*, although out of print, can usually be obtained from the local library and is a must for any aviculturist intending to breed this lovely species.

Feeding

The hawfinch loves the kernels from hard fruit stones such as cherries and damsons and its huge bill is especially adapted for holding and cracking these stones. Although a member of the *Fringillidae* family of hard-billed seedeating finches it does not eat the common weeds to the same extent as the other members of the family and is at all times partly insectivorous. For most of the year it feeds mainly on the seeds of trees and shrubs and is particularly fond of beechmast. In the winter when tree seeds are exhausted it turns to hawthorn berries, hips and haws, yew, ivy and many other berries found on shrubs in gardens and parks. In spring the hawfinch gradually turns to a diet of green caterpillars as these become available in increasing numbers. It does, however, have a liking for young green peas and will raid the gardens in the early morning much to the gardener's annoyance.

Analysis of the stomach contents of young birds has shown that caterpillars of the oak-roller moth (*Tortrix viridana*) and of the winter moth (*Perophtera brumata*) form the bulk of the food of the nestlings but various other green and brown caterpillars have also been found as well as various beetles and occasionally spiders.

Breeding

The British hawfinch is a sedentary bird and does not migrate although some of the continental birds do. In winter hawfinches of both sexes congregate into small flocks (perhaps made up of family parties) feeding together in the woods, but each bird will maintain a small territory about 4 feet (1.22 m) in diameter and drives off any other bird which dares to enter this area.

As spring approaches the cocks temporarily leave the flock and visit the breeding grounds returning to the flock later. After a week or two they bring their mates to settle in the area. Rather loose territories are established and hawfinches prefer to breed in colonies although these are of a somewhat scattered nature. A strict territory does not seem important and the birds often obtain the necessary food for the young at quite long distances from the nest.

Hawfinches nest mostly in woodland, orchards and gardens though more exposed places have been recorded and apple trees, sycamore, pear, oak, hawthorn, blackthorn and birch are particularly favoured. Heights of between 3 feet (1 m) and 65 feet (22 m) above the ground have been listed but the nest is more usually at a height of about 30 feet (10 m) and is frequently built on a horizontal fork, sometimes on the leader. The nest is quite a bulky affair built on a platform of twigs, usually birch and the choice of nest material varies but usually includes twigs, strips of bark, climbing plants such as bindweed, traveller's joy, honeysuckle and grass, lined with closely woven roots, occasionally a little hair.

Laying usually starts during May and is timed so that the young hatch out just when the caterpillar harvest is at its height. The usual clutch is four to five eggs which can vary in colour between bluish-white, greenish-grey and pinkish-buff with dark markings. Incubation is by the hen only and is said to be nearly two weeks and the young fledge in a further twelve to fourteen days depending on conditions and the food supply. Experience in aviaries, however, where of course the food supply is constant suggests a much shorter period for both incubation and fledging. Nestlings are covered in white down until feathered and when fledged are considerably mottled and barred. The cap and black bib are not acquired until the moult.

Predators destroy many nests which are often in exposed positions and perhaps accounts for some of the hawfinch's secretive ways — yet the young in the nest are often noisy and continually clamouring for food. The species is single brooded and perhaps the short incubation and fledging period helps to overcome the high predation rate.

Aviary Breeding and Rearing

Aviary-bred hawfinches are excellent subjects for British bird breeders being hardy, long lived and easy to look after. They can be kept safely in a mixed aviary and will not interfere with other small birds. During the breeding season it is generally recommended that the pair is put in a separate aviary but, if space is limited, they will benefit from the extra flying room in a mixed aviary. They do require plenty of cover and a number of suitably placed nesting sites with forked branches. Wicker nest baskets and wire netting bowls will sometimes be used.

Provide fine birch twigs, rootlets, grasses, some horse hair or coconut matting fibre for nesting. It is very important to leave the birds alone with only the minimum amount of disturbance absolutely necessary to ensure their well being, and adequate supplies of food and water. Hawfinches are thirsty birds and must be able to drink and bath frequently. As hawfinches are naturally colony nesters it does help if there is another pair within sight and sound but there should not be more than one pair in an aviary during the breeding season.

When the young hatch, give live food in the form of mealworms, well cleaned maggots dusted in vionate multi-vitamin powder to combat rickets, together with any smooth green caterpillars that can be obtained. Green peas and soaked sunflower seed should also be available. The species is strictly insectivorous at this time of the year and Colin Clark reported that a pair consumed 6 lbs (2.76 kg) of mealworms while rearing their brood. The cock also fed the hen almost exclusively on mealworms while she was sitting. The incubation took eleven days and all four young left the nest in a further eleven days.

Breeding birds are best kept in an aviary all the year round and can be fed on pine nuts, safflower, sunflower, hemp and radish seed with access to British finch mixture. They are somewhat conservative in their likes and dislikes and individuals will vary in what they will eat. They should also receive daily a limited supply of live food such as mealworms which must be increased as spring progresses. In the autumn and winter supply all berries that can be found, especially rowan, hips and haws and hawthorn together with the tree seeds mentioned earlier. Over-ripe apples make a change and although they eat some of the fruit it is mainly the pips which the birds like.

Exhibition

An exhibition hawfinch is as large as possible with a short body very thickset at the shoulders. A broad bold head and neck with well defined thumb nail shaped bib: well defined, steel-blue glossy wing markings and white edging with rich brown body colour and nut brown tannings on the chest.

Contributions by: Malcolm Taylor; Colin Clark.

Figure 6.6 Hawfinch

CROSSBILLS

Common Crossbill *(Loxia curvirostra)* Length approximately 6½ inches (16.5 cm).
Scottish Crossbill *(Loxia curvirostra scotia)* Length approximately 6½ inches (16.5 cm).
Males: in both species mostly reddish with dark brown wings and tail, large head with the crossed bills and short, forked tails.
Females: in both species female and juveniles are mainly greenish with dark brown wings and tail but otherwise similar to the males.
Scottish Crossbill: has a slightly larger head and stronger bill.

There is a third species which has occasionally visited the British Isles. This is the **Parrot Crossbill** *(Loxia pytyopsittacus).* This species has a larger head and a more massive, more arched bill. Like the Scottish crossbill, this bird feeds mainly on the cones of the Scots Pine. Their eruptions do not usually reach Great Britain but 1962 was a particular exception.

Crossbills are adept at climbing among the branches using their feet and bill to pull themselves about parrot-fashion and often hang upside down.

Characteristics

Crossbills have a rather wider, though sparse, distribution in England and Scotland than is perhaps generally realised. The main areas are the Scottish Highlands, the Kielder Forest in Northumberland, Norfolk and Suffolk and the New Forest, but as post–war plantations of pine and spruce mature new colonies are developing.

The crossbill's life–style is most interesting and has been developed to meet the supplies of fir cones on which it lives almost exclusively. The specially adapted beak, with the tips of the hooked mandibles overlapping, enable the birds to open the cones which they hold in their large feet: the seeds are then extracted with their long red tongue. The mandibles are crossed either to the left or the right. The juveniles do not have the crossed mandibles which perhaps shows that they are a finch which, in the process of evolution, has become specialised to living on fir cones. When the young leave the nest their bills are still uncrossed. By the time the young are a month old the upper mandible is well grown and the lower begins to bend to one side. The young then begin to practice on cones and at about thirty eight days can pull out seeds but are not self-supporting until forty–five days old or thereabouts. The parents may, however, continue to feed them for some time after this. It is not only in the beaks that crossbills show their affinity to the finch family; their courtship displays and general breeding behaviour also follow the same pattern. Hybrids between the common crossbill and the greenfinch have been recorded several times and it is interesting to note that the hybrids did not have crossed bills. No doubt further hybrids with the finch family will be recorded in time.

As the fruiting season of the different conifers varies considerably, it is necessary to explain them since they do have a very direct bearing on the life style of the crossbill family. The seeds of all conifers form in late summer and then remain on the tree until the cones open which, according to the species of tree, is anything from three to twenty-two months later. Crossbills can extract the seeds from cones at any stage of ripeness but prefer them when the cones have begun to open naturally: hence the seeds of different trees become available at different seasons. Crossbills cannot easily pick up seeds from the ground so that once the seeds have been shed they are lost to the crossbills.

The important trees are spruce which retains its seeds for nine months until the following spring, pine holding its seeds for twenty-two months until the spring of the second year and fir and larch both of which retain their seeds for three months until the first autumn. The cones on the larch stand erect so there are still some seeds in the cones for several months after most of them have been shed. Good cone crops are sporadic varying from year to year.

When the food supply in any area runs out or the crop is poor the majority of the crossbill population moves out and may travel long distances until another area with a good crop is found. Crossbills do not migrate in the generally accepted meaning of the term but have developed a one-way movement. These movements take place in mid-summer. It will be seen from preceding remarks that this is when the food supply on which the birds have been feeding will be running out and the new crops will be forming. Having found a new area where the seed crops are good the crossbills remain in the area until the next summer, moulting and breeding in the meantime.

Breeding

It will now be easily understood that crossbills must breed either very early or very late in the year when the food supply is sufficient to enable them to rear the young. In fact they do both but it is not clear whether the same birds breed at both times of the year. There is, however, recorded evidence that young birds in immature plumage can and do breed in the autumn and there is also evidence that crossbills can and do breed during the moult. It seems that they are opportunists taking an opportunity when there is an abundance of food to raise a family and this fact must be remembered when breeding in aviaries. Breeding may begin in August when the cones from fir and larch are coming to their best and it may continue until the following April or even May if the food supply holds out.

In England the breeding season usually commences in December when the cones are sufficiently open to enable the birds to extract the seeds quickly and in large quantities. For this reason their nesting has become independent of the changes in day length which plays such an important part in the breeding of many other species.

The nest of the crossbill is placed high in a tree in thick foliage, usually on the south side — because of their winter breeding they will not be worried by the hot midday sun of the summer. It is built on a base of thin twigs and made of grass, moss, lichens and shreds of bark, lined with lichens, moss, hair and feathers. It is a bulky nest thickly lined. The usual clutch is three to four pale bluish-green eggs spotted with brown and violet. The hen commences to sit when the first egg is laid so preventing them from freezing. Thus the young hatch on different days and vary in size. This gives the young various chances of survival. If food becomes scarce the smallest will quickly die leaving more food for the larger ones.

Incubation takes between thirteen and sixteen days, or even longer, depending upon the weather and temperature. The young grow much more slowly than other finches due to the short daylength in which the parents can feed them. Fledging generally takes between eighteen to twenty-two days. During this period the young can survive temperatures which would kill the young of other finches. When the adults return from collecting food the young may be torpid but after a few minutes brooding are able to lift their heads again for food. As previously mentioned, the young are not completely self-supporting until about forty-five days old and are fed almost exclusively on conifer seeds.

Crossbills are gregarious and nest in loose colonies.

Aviary Breeding and Rearing

In aviaries crossbills are quiet and tolerant birds and can be mixed with other species but will fight with their own species. It is therefore only safe to have one pair in an aviary. On the other hand, as they naturally nest in fairly close proximity to other crossbills, it is a help if there are other pairs in aviaries within sight or sound of each other but this is by no means essential. The size of the aviary is not important and crossbills will breed in large cages more easily than most finches, perhaps because their needs are in some ways more easily supplied. As they naturally build their nests about 20–50 feet (7–18 m) above the ground it is helpful to place bunches of fir branches to provide good cover as high as possible in the aviary to give them a feeling of security. They will sometimes use a wicker basket or even a shelf but many birds prefer to choose their own site. The nesting site should have some cover. Apart from this crossbills are hardy birds but it is as well to give some protection from driving wind and rain.

A good supply of fresh water is essential especially when the birds are breeding. All the materials used for nest building in the wild must be supplied in large quantities and, as it is natural for them to breed in the winter, the hen must be able to build a substantial and warm nest otherwise results are likely to be disappointing.

The seed of cones is the most important part of their diet and this also keeps the birds occupied as well as enabling them to live the life for which nature designed them, therefore large quantities of cones must be collected. Each bird should have about six cones per day, more when young are being fed. These can be supplemented with British finch mixture, hemp and plenty of sunflower seeds. Greenfood such as groundsel, chickweed, persicaria and dock will also be taken.

Ian Newton in his book *Finches* states that the young in the wild are fed almost exclusively on cone seeds and it is difficult to imagine that the birds would be able to obtain much live food during their breeding season in the winter. Surprisingly, the experience of aviculturists is that crossbills will take mealworms, gentles, spiders and caterpillars and it must help rearing if these can be provided while the young are in the nest. Pine nuts can sometimes be obtained from seedsmen and these are also helpful.

Ringing should be carried out with care and will depend on the rate of growth of the youngsters. This depends on the weather and the food supply. If the young are nicely developed then about eight days old would be a suitable time.

Exhibition

An exhibition crossbill should be as large as possible with short body very thick–set throughout with a broad bold head and neck and be of good even colour.

Figure 6.7   Crossbill

CHAPTER 7

Buntings

Order: *Passeriformes*
Family: *Fringillidae* (Finches)

YELLOW BUNTING: REED BUNTING: CORN BUNTING

Yellow Bunting *(Emberiza citrinella)* Length 6 inches (15.25 cm), weight 1 oz (28.35 g).
This species is better known as the yellow hammer. The male has a predominately yellow head, breast and underparts with chestnut brown upperparts and stout grey bill: brown streaks on head and flanks, bright chestnut rump and white sides to the tail. The female is similar but duller with more brown streaks.
Reed Bunting *(Emberiza schoeniclus)* Length 6 inches (15.25 cm), weight ¾ oz (21.25 g).
The male has a black head and throat with distinctive clean white collar: brown streaked upperparts, with underparts varying from white to pale buff-brown and greyish rump. The head pattern is obscured in winter. The female is streaked brown, lighter below with black and white moustache stripe. Both birds have outer white tail feathers.
Corn Bunting *(Emberiza calandra)* Length 7 inches (17.75 cm), weight 2 oz (56.75 g).
Larger than the other buntings, the male is a sandy-brown bird streaked with dusky-brown on the upperparts, throat, breast and flanks and buffish-white underparts. There is no white on the tail as with the other buntings. The female is similar. During the autumn and winter they become yellower.

Distribution

The yellow hammer is resident and well distributed throughout the British Isles except on high ground. Decreases in population were reported in the late 1950s, thought to be caused by the destruction of hedgerows and increased urbanisation — possibly aided by the use of agricultural chemicals. Although badly affected by the severe winter in 1962–63, it seems to have recovered well since but still does not seem as common as when we were young. The yellow hammer inhabits all types of open country — heaths, commons, young conifer plantations, bracken covered hillsides, agricultural land and woodland edges — as long as small trees or telegraph wires and the like are available for song posts. It is strongly territorial although it does often feed outside its territory even with other members of its own species.

The reed bunting is also well distributed throughout the British Isles but shuns high ground even more than the yellow hammer. Originally a bird of the wetlands, the reed bunting is generally on the increase and seems to have profited by the reduction of yellow hammers and in many areas has taken its place. With the reduction of the wetter waste ground on farmland, the reed bunting has colonised drier situations and may now be found in young conifer plantations and hawthorn scrub as well as reed beds, waterside vegetation and farm hedgerows. Reed buntings do not require high song posts and will sing from a reed, thistle or dock stem.

The corn bunting is declining and reducing its range: at the beginning of the century it was well distributed throughout the whole of the British Isles except, again, on the high ground. It is now absent from Ireland and Wales except for a few isolated groups. In Scotland it is very scarce in the north west and is absent from the south west of England except for a stronghold on the north coast of Cornwall. It appears to be withdrawing eastwards with the notable exception of East Anglia, where it is only found on the coast. Basically a bird of arable farmland; coastal regions with low gorse and brambles are much favoured though these birds generally feed among hay, corn and root crops.

Breeding

The yellow hammer is a late breeder commencing at the end of May or early June and nests on rough ground with bushes, roadsides and hedgerows along arable land, heaths, commons and felled clearings in woods. They nest on or near the ground, often in the hedge bottom or long grass growing up into a bush, sometimes in a bush. The nest is made of grass, straw and moss, lined with hair. Four pinkish–white eggs with mauve scribbles is the normal clutch. Incubation is thirteen days and the young fledge at fourteen days old. There are usually two broods in the season. During the winter the yellow hammer is mainly a seedeater, living largely on weed seeds with some grain and wild fruit. In the breeding season they are almost entirely insectivorous feeding on all kinds of insects and caterpillars and small ground animals.

The reed bunting commences nesting a little earlier, generally in late April. The nest is usually hidden in a tussock or bunch of weeds and is difficult to find. Almost always on the ground the nest is made of coarse grass and lined with finer grass and hair. Four pale brown eggs with dark markings are the usual clutch which are incubated for thirteen days. The young usually fledge at twelve days old. There are normally two broods in a season and the reed bunting's food is in general the same as the yellow hammer's.

The corn bunting is a late nester like the yellow hammer. Again the nest is well concealed in long grass, brambles, dense weeds or thistles and is difficult to find. Generally on the ground, but sometimes in low bushes or gorse, the rather untidy nest is made of grass, straw and moss and lined with fine grass or hair. Four dirty-white eggs with purplish and reddish scribblings is the normal clutch. Incubation is thirteen days and the young usually fledge at about twelve days. There are two broods in a season. Feeding is again similar to the yellow hammer. The rearing of the young is done almost entirely by the hen since the cock is polygamous and is usually paired to several hens.

All the buntings leave the breeding grounds in the winter and join flocks which forage the farmlands and wastelands together. There is also some migration to the continent. In the spring the cocks return first, taking up territories, and are followed several weeks later by the hens which remain longer in the flocks. Buntings normally roost on the ground.

Aviary Breeding and Rearing

In general, all buntings are rather aggressive and unsuitable for breeding in mixed aviaries although one does find the occasional docile pair. Outside the breeding season it is natural for them to flock with other species, but during the breeding season one pair must be kept in an aviary on their own. An aviary 6 feet (2 m) square is ideal for the yellow and reed buntings but the corn bunting, being larger, does better in a larger enclosure.

In the wild buntings, as we have already seen, nearly always nest on the ground and it is not difficult to lay out an aviary to resemble their natural habitat. They will, however, often nest in nesting sites similar to those used by finches if the floor of the aviary does not take their fancy.

Feeding requirements for all buntings are the same. All are cereal crop feeders and all rear their young on live food plus vegetable matter. The basic diet consists of plain canary seed with groats and other cereal crops and seeding grasses in season. They will also take chickweed and many other seeding weeds. Small amounts of live food such as 'pinkies', mealworms, and moth pupae must be provided daily and a plentiful supply of grit must always be available. Buntings will generally take canary rearing food with hard boiled egg once they become accustomed to it and this is a great help.

Incubation generally takes thirteen days and as soon as the chicks hatch out live food must be fed ad lib — greenflies, small flies, gentles, mealworms, smooth caterpillars and any other insects that can be found. A good vitamin powder added to the egg food will be very helpful. Young can usually be ringed at six to seven days old and this procedure is explained in a separate chapter. If progressing satisfactorily the chicks will leave the nest between twelve and fourteen days old.

Exhibition

The most promising young birds can be caged at ten to twelve weeks old to steady them down and train them for exhibition. At this stage the live food should be gradually reduced, though they should always have some live food and the canary rearing food must be given daily until the youngsters are well through the moult. Colour feeding is not generally necessary though some fanciers like to give a little to the yellow bunting, by adding *carophil** to the drinking water or rearing food but only enough to make the water or food pink.

The yellow bunting is the most popular and an exhibition bird must have good size, be well built but with good length, of good colour and nice quality of feather. They should be well trained and steady. Cocks must have well defined markings on head and cheeks and strong markings on the flanks

*Registered product

extending into the chest. Exhibition hens are devoid of head and cheek markings and the head should be dark and well lined, but must carry the markings on the flanks like the cock.

Hen reed buntings being easier to train usually do somewhat better on the show bench than cocks. Cocks must be as large as possible. They should be full bodied with a nice full head: colours should be well defined with good pencilling on back and flanks, clear cut black beard and white collar. Hens must be well pencilled on back and flanks extending well into the chest and must not be bearded but should have moustachial markings. The general body colour should be rich warm brown.

The corn bunting is the largest of our British buntings. For exhibition it must be well trained and of good size and colour, full bodied with good broad head and shoulder. The markings must be heavy and profuse. They are difficult to sex but the cocks tend to be larger and with a somewhat richer colour than the hen.

Bunting Varieties

There are a number of other interesting species in the bunting family most of which reside in Europe and all need similar treatment in their diet and their environmental needs. These include the snow bunting, little bunting, rock bunting, ortolan bunting, yellow breasted bunting, meadow bunting, pine bunting, cinerous bunting, rustic bunting, black headed bunting, red headed bunting, black faced bunting and Lapland bunting.

Contributions by: Bob Partridge.

Figure 7.1   Yellow Bunting

CHAPTER 8

Keeping and Breeding British Softbills

PART 1 — *by Ray Allen*

It is often said that softbills are not 'anybody's meat' meaning, I suppose, that they are somehow difficult and a lot of bother to keep. This fallacy I would like to dispel at once. Most of our native softbills are, in fact, very easily catered for. The thrush, blackbird, hedge sparrow, lark, magpie, jay, and such are all very easy with regards to feeding and most are fairly easy to breed. The remainder of the thrush family, either winter or summer migrants, like the fieldfare, redwing and waxwing are also easy to cater for.

The summer migrants present us with a few more problems; however, with food and warmth they can be kept successfully by most enthusiastic bird keepers.

The first essential — whatever the species — is a healthy alert bird with good clean legs, feet and a bright round eye. Secondly, a balanced diet readily available. Thirdly, will the bird eat it? This third query is a very important one, a bird may starve amid plenty, through:

1. Not being able to find it when newly introduced to its quarters.
2. Not recognising it as food.
3. Improper housing and, with some birds, lack of warmth in the winter months.

Warmth is necessary to such birds as willow and wood warblers, both of the white-throats, lesser and common, and the garden warbler. The chiff-chaff, chats and nightingales can get along without it provided that they have snug draught-free quarters.

Feeding

The food requirements of birds in captivity are many, again it is regulated by the variety of species one intends to keep. The larger softbills can be provided with a coarse grade insectile mixture as a staple diet (of which there are a few very good prepared ones on the market) together with the usual live food available, cheese, minced beef, cooked or raw grated vegetables, fresh and dried fruits.

We are still learning and the modern foods for birds, animals and humans have had years of scientific research spent on them in order to get a balanced product, nutritionally suitable to sustain life and health in most living species.

I have found with softbills of highly insectivorous diets, that our softfoods — which obviously we must use as the staple food — are, as a rule, far too high in carbohydrate content and lacking in a sufficiency of animal protein.

69

The small softbills, which feed mainly on insects in the wild, are the ones we are here most concerned with. Large softbills such as jays, magpies and thrushes are fairly easy to keep in good condition with the foods now available. The small ones are not such an easy proposition. At least thirty per cent of their diet needs to be protein. The usual base of softfoods seems to be biscuit meal of one sort or another which makes up the bulk of the mixture. Bulk does not necessarily mean roughage, which I feel is lacking in most mixtures in sufficient quantity to regulate digestion of the content of the food. By roughage I mean the wings, wing cases, legs and other horny parts of insects which act as the mill churning up the food in the bird's stomach, which, in the case of mainly insectivorous birds, acts in the same way as grit does for finches. The finches, however, have an extra internal organ called the gizzard which is lacking in the softbills. Instead of the softbills grinding up all intake into a size small enough to enable it to pass right through the bird in the form of excreta, as do finches, they regurgitate this indigestible material in the form of pellets. If softbills are not regurgitating sufficiently large pellets, they tend to put on an excess amount of fat and become lethargic, less active and sit about a lot, which in turn automatically reduces very essential exercise. This will even happen in an aviary as well as in the close confines of a cage if the diet is wrong.

One often reads about soft natural perches being necessary to keep a bird's feet in good order. This is all very well and quite a good thing if it really does keep the feet in good order, but I suggest that this is not the real reason why the feet remain in good condition. The real reason for sore feet is not the kind of perching used, but the kind of diet supplied. If the diet is right, then the feet, together with the rest of the bird, will be healthy. The proof of this is that wild birds are never seen with sore feet. Sometimes they do have deformities but these are usually due to accidents and not an inborn disease.

Chopped green food such as green cabbage, young rape, and lettuce should be a regular item of diet. Fruit, for those which will take it, also helps to keep a bird in that high condition so necessary for breeding pairs as well as for exhibition purposes. Watery eyes often accompany sore feet and it is my belief that the cause is mainly lack of animal protein from varied kinds of insects, together of course, with minerals and trace elements.

There are many good milk products on the market these days, all of which give a break-down of the nutritional content printed on the side of the packet. Use the ones that show the highest protein content and avoid those that are high in carbohydrates, such as rusk and grain cereal products. If mixing one's own softfood, grated cheese is a very valuable ingredient also. The use of brook water helps give the birds minerals which have been collected by the water on its way through the earth to the rivers. Polluted water must obviously be avoided. It is surprising the amount of small seed eagerly consumed by many softbills if given access to it. This, as well as providing some nourishment, gives the necessary roughage discussed earlier in the form of cellulose. The latter is abundant in various forms of vegetable life, mostly in the outer casings such as the husk of seed which softbills are not able to discard previous to swallowing.

Certain livefoods are also good for birds that do not normally eat them in the wild. This is mainly because they are either too large for them or their way of life precludes access to them. For example, it is now known that tawny owls sometimes eat fish by reason of the fact that a study of a pair rearing young were repeatedly supplying their chicks with a small fish known as the 'miller's thumb' and then only by the male of the adult pair, which shows us that the female had not yet learned how to catch the fish, or did not recognise it as a legitimate food. With human aid our small birds, like the warblers, can enjoy food like the larger grasshoppers which we can dismember and cut up so that they can easily be dealt with by the birds. Some of the larger beetles, grasshoppers and crickets are also eaten with the hard casings removed. The small softbills as well as the larger ones like a little boiled fish also crab meat and shrimps, without the salting of cooking but freshly boiled or raw from the sea. Most fanciers have access to some food or other which can be put to use as a supplementary food for birds.

So much for the feeding notes which are even now by no means complete here, but can be added to by the fancier himself with a little ingenuity and common sense.

Breeding

The breeding of softbills presents us with a lot more problems; space and of course aviaries cost money. We would all like to breed as many species as possible but one or other of the former desirabilities have to be taken into account. It is therefore a wise plan to select those species of bird which are more likely to produce young in the accommodation available. In fairly restricted surroundings birds like the thrush, blackbird, and hedge sparrow are likely to be more successful than jays or longtailed tits.

Finally, the hygiene of all cages and feeding utensils must be a major consideration in the keeping of softbills, as it is for all birds.

Figure 8.1 Jay

KEEPING AND BREEDING BRITISH SOFTBILLS — PART 2
by A. T. Worrall

Softbills do need that little extra attention if one is to be successful, whether breeding or exhibiting.

Cages and Aviaries

Without doubt the best way to breed softbills is to have them in naturally planted aviaries with adequate cover and abounding in live food; but it is not everyone who has the good fortune to have such aviaries and those without must, in consequence, make use of cages. The latter should be as large as space will allow, the length being the main dimension in order to give plenty of wing space. Softbills can be kept in excellent condition, even though caged, as will be seen in some of the excellent specimens on the show bench.

For covering the cage floors the finest thing is fresh leaf-mould or moss in which the birds find a wealth of tit-bits, including various minerals.

Dampened peat makes an excellent covering, especially for ground birds such as larks, wagtails, pipits or wheatears, as many of these species are prone to sore feet or corns by having too hard a floor. This peat, which is used for pot or bulb planting, may conveniently be purchased in bags from horticultural establishments. For the use, however, of softbills generally, several sheets of newspaper cut to size and placed on the cage floor will suffice, a sheet being removed every day to keep the cage tidy. Sawdust has been used for the purpose, but it tends to blow into the water and food pots.

Particular attention should be paid to perches, which should be cleaned or replaced regularly, for with softbills these become very sticky and can easily give rise to eye and foot troubles. Soft resilient wood should be used, or natural branches of birch, pear, apple, hazel or any of the conifers.

Perches should be placed in such positions as to make the bird use its wings; in other words avoid too many perches which permit the bird simply to hop from one to another. Care should be taken to avoid placing water or food dishes under the perches.

Nesting Conditions

Various softbills such as larks, pipits, redstarts, wagtails and the tits, also some of the larger softbills, including blackbirds, thrushes and redwings, have been bred in cages or flights when given seclusion and cover for nesting but many more have been bred in large planted aviaries where there has been an abundance of cover and live food. One should not overlook the fact that although there appears to be plenty of natural live food in such an enclosure, it does not take long for a surprising quantity to be eaten by a few foraging birds and it is a wise man who places dishes of insectivorous food and mealworms, or gentles in the aviary to meet the inmates' fuller needs.

Food Mixtures

Care should be given to feeding, in order to maintain softbills in excellent condition and I firmly believe in regularly changing the diet, much in the same way as nature changes with the seasons and the wildings have to fall in line with nature's rotation.

Although there are some excellent foods for softbills advertised these days, which are quite capable of maintaining a softbill in good order for some time, it is those birds which also have the benefit of live food which usually come out on top on the show bench, and there is nothing better for keeping the natural colour and condition in a bird.

For my own birds I use the various brands of insectivorous foods, blending 50% of the food with 50% of dried insects, including Chinese flies, mayflies, silkworm pupae, ant eggs and shrimp, all of which are mixed together in corn oil. Upon this, which is my basic softbill food, is placed grated cottage cheese daily, with an occasional change of mashed, hard-boiled egg with finely chopped-up mealworms and a dish of gentles. Grated carrot, which is also a mild colouring agent, is given separately every three or four days. Although dried insects are looked upon as nothing more than roughage, I think that the oil does give something to the birds, as careful observation will show that these insects get eaten first.

Mealworms are frowned upon by many people, and blamed for swollen feet (to date I have yet to experience this) but I feel that if it were not for mealworms many of our birds would not have been reared. Increase the quantity of cut-up worms to the birds when they are commencing to moult, as this is when they really need that extra nourishment to help them through. Abidec is also given in the drinking water at moulting time the dose being three or four drops to a drinker for four days, then repeated again in one week's time.

All mealworms should be chopped up for small softbills in cages, as this helps with their digestion. Birds in aviaries should not come to any harm if the mealworms are fed whole, as they are able to exercise more freely.

Another form of live food can be produced by placing over-ripe fruit, especially bananas, in wooden boxes in a reasonably warm place, and it will not be long before there is a good supply of flies. Handfuls of gentles could also be thrown into the box, and within a week you have two types of fly. A wire basket placed in an aviary containing horse manure and watered occasionally, will also produce large quantities of small flies.

There is an almost endless supply of live-food for a fancier who is fortunate enough to live in a rural area, consisting of creatures such as caterpillars, spiders, woodlice, earwigs and various weevils, not forgetting the greenfly. Ant eggs can be collected from ant hills, usually found in conifer woods and forests or under an old tin, stone or log on some waste ground, in July and August — when most needed for young birds. Dried ant eggs soaked in nectar paste will be eaten with relish by most small softbills. The warblers, including the blackcaps and nightingales, will take sponge cake and nectar, pear, sweet apple, elderberries, blackberries, rowan, and similar.

Mixing Birds and Exhibiting

When keeping several different kinds of softbills in one aviary together, it is a wise policy to have plenty of food pots dotted around to prevent a particular individual dominating the supply. Water dishes should be good open vessels to enable the bird to bathe freely but be sure to avoid deep dishes, which could result in accidents.

Many of our softbills have reputations for fighting, especially when the breeding season is approaching. A particularly watchful eye must be kept on birds such as 'starts, 'chats, wagtails and nightingales; much of the trouble may be avoided if the birds are given plenty of room and convenient cover in which to seek refuge, if need be. The nightingale is perhaps the most aggressive and tends to be very 'robin–like' in his attitude towards other small birds. Avoid placing this species in an aviary with blackcaps or garden warblers as there would certainly be trouble of some kind.

When exhibiting softbills a pair always makes a nice attractive exhibit without a divider between the two birds but be sure that both birds agree and each is in tip–top order — so many pairs are spoilt by the inferiority of one of them. Instead of having an unbalanced, unsatisfactory pair it is preferable to exhibit a single first rate bird than have the other undermine the degree of perfection in the better bird.

The decoration of cages should be tastefully done but not overly so, as this will detract from the bird or may hide him from the judge. The fancier should try to depict a little of the bird's natural habitat. Finally, make sure that the water and food vessels are easily accessible to the show stewards responsible for the care of the exhibits.

Figure 8.2 Nightingale

KEEPING AND BREEDING BRITISH SOFTBILLS — PART 3
by Ron McCluskey

Before one starts keeping softbills of any kind a study should be made of their basic requirements. Where better to get this knowledge than from Mother Nature herself.

Take note of the areas that certain species frequent and you will find that softbills do not usually feed in flocks and are territorially minded. During the breeding season they breed in an area that can support them and their offspring with abundant livefood. They use certain materials for their nests, favour certain types of nesting site and note should be taken of their nearest neighbours.

When courting they need a certain amount of space and peace, therefore do not crowd them into small aviaries with unsuitable companions. The best idea is one pair of birds per aviary — a difficult rule to stick to — but one which I try to practise.

It will also be noted that in the wild the cock bird usually takes up residence first and secures his territory and song posts. He then courts several hens coming into his territory before actually choosing one to become his mate. Once a pair have accepted each other they can get down to business right away and it will not be long before they have their nest built and ready for the hen to lay her clutch.

We can simulate natural conditions reasonably well but livefood is a more difficult proposition altogether. I will therefore endeavour to explain my methods, which are by no means perfect, in the hope that from them you may derive some useful hints.

All small softbills I feed on a basic softfood into which dried crushed hens' eggshells is occasionally mixed. This ensures that they get some calcium in their diet and, being a Scot, I find this as cheap a method as any. Feed them grated cheese at least once a week and maggots ad–lib though this livefood should be dusted with *Vionate* multi–vitamin powder at least once a week. There are other vitamins which can be added to their water such as Abidec or Ribena. I use both and, not being an expert, would say that either additive used occasionally will help give the birds the extra vitamins needed to keep fit. Maggots in their cocoon stage are a must for all softbills providing the roughage needed to produce their pellets. Mealworms are a wonderful food rich in protein, but care should be taken when feeding them to some species as mealworms have very sharp teeth and could do internal damage to the birds. It is therefore recommended that the worms have their heads pinched before feeding to most small softbills.

Small flies are a must for breeding wagtails or pipits. Piles of rotten fruit, vegetables, chickweed and such all harbour breeding insects. My aviaries are treated as a dump all the year round for potato peelings, cabbage leaves, leaf mould, horse or rabbit manure — anything in fact that will produce insects or worms to add variety to the birds' diets. If certain areas of your aviaries are kept damp, white worm can be bred at a terrific rate. I also breed white worms in a glass aquarium filled with leaf mould, tea leaves and old bird seed. To provide the birds with white worms all you have to do is fork a small piece of ground over each day, or in the case of the culture breeding in the aquarium, dig a few out as required and place them in a dish or tray in your cage or flight. Moths, stick insects, crickets and locusts can all be bred if you have the time and space.

If there is a river, lake or small pond near your home or, better still, if you live near or at the seaside, there is a host of small aquatic insects, crustaceans and fish that can be gathered to add variety to your birds' diet. Please take care that the water, be it fresh or salt, is not polluted in any way.

Large softbills can be kept in good breeding condition more easily than can the more delicate of our small softbills. A basic diet of poultry layers' pellets, apples, and maggots, plus a few snails and earthworms is sufficient for thrushes, blackbirds, redwings and fieldfares, whilst waxwings relish a few soaked currants or sultanas daily.

The larger species such as jackdaws, jays and magpies will live quite well on a basic diet of puppy meal, minced raw meat with occasional pieces of fruit or eggs. Here again livefood is essential for successful breeding and a multitude of items will be readily taken by the omnivorous adults including: maggots dusted with vitamin powder, locusts in different stages of their growth, wood ants, cockroaches, tadpoles, grasshoppers, elvers, wasps and their grubs, slugs, all sorts of beetles, small fish such as minnows and tame mice bred specially for this purpose.

The greater the variety of livefood that can be supplied to softbills the better the chances of breeding them.

Figure 8.3 Tree Sparrow

CHAPTER 9

Insectivorous Species (Softbills)

Order: *Passeriformes*
Family: *Prunellidae* (Accentors)

HEDGE SPARROW, HEDGE ACCENTOR, DUNNOCK

(Prunella modularis) **Length** $5\frac{3}{4}$ inches (14.5 cm), **weight** $\frac{3}{4}$ oz (21.25 g).

The three names are all used in the reference books, and although it is not a sparrow, hedge sparrow is the name by which it is most generally known. The house and tree sparrow are members of the finch family with the strong beaks of the seedeaters, but the hedge sparrow has a sharp and thin beak like the insect-eating birds. In fact, it seems to be the link between the two because it is almost entirely insectivorous in the summer and feeds almost entirely on small seeds in the winter.

Characteristics

Both male and female look alike. The wings, tail and back are brown, the head, neck and breast are slate-grey with brownish streaks and the underparts are a paler grey.

This quiet little bird which attracts little notice is the second most common bird inhabiting the whole of the British Isles except some of the Islands to the north of Scotland. It is, however, scarce in thick woodland and inhabits hedgerows, copses, spinneys, gardens, churchyards, parks, scrubland and industrial waste-land. It almost always feeds on the ground, hopping about in a jerky manner, and perches in low bushes. It has a strong and pleasant song which can be heard for quite long distances.

The hedge sparrow is a most useful bird to the gardener feeding in the summer on many injurious insects and larvae as well as spiders and small earthworms. In winter it feeds on the various weed seeds.

Hedges and shrubberies are the most popular nesting places as well as low scrub, brambles and the like. The neat nest made of twigs, moss and leaves is well hidden and lined with moss, hair and feathers. Four sky-blue eggs is the normal clutch which is incubated for thirteen days and the young fledge in a similar period. Being an early nester, commencing in April, there are normally two broods in a season.

Aviary Breeding and Rearing

The hedge sparrow is an ideal bird for inclusion in a mixed aviary of finches to give the aviculturist experience with softbills before going on to the more difficult species. Because it is a shy and secretive bird, spending much of its time in thick cover and on the ground searching for insects, the aviary should be well planted with plenty of cover. A good patch of nettles is almost essential.

These birds go about their business very quietly and it may well be found that they have built a nest and the hen is sitting before one realises they have started breeding. The nest is well hidden and never more than 2 to 3 feet (0.6–1 m) from the ground. Coconut fibre, teased sizal string in 2 inch (5 cm) lengths, moss, leaves, hair and feathers should be provided. Some fanciers report that although the clutch is usually four eggs, three young hatched seems to be normal.

Rearing the young is no problem. The parents should have access to a fine grade softbill food, egg food and gentles which they will supplement with live food collected in the aviary — especially greenfly from nettles. Any smooth green caterpillars which can be collected should also be offered. Nettle patches and oak trees are good sources of this food.

The parents will also take British finch mixture and will live quite well on this together with a few gentles in the winter.

The young can be closed-ringed at seven days old and a full explanation of how to do this is given in Chapter 5. The young leave the nest at thirteen to fourteen days old and the parents continue to feed them for another ten days or so. Some of the food is fed by regurgitation.

At close range the hedge sparrow is much more attractive than it at first appears with its varying shades of lavender grey and brown ranging to chestnut on the wings and back. Although the cocks are usually smaller and carry more of the lavender colour on the head, neck and chest when adult birds, they are still very difficult birds to sex; this may have to be done by trial and error when approaching the breeding season. However, if caged separately in the winter, the young cocks will start to sing by Christmas. Hedge sparrows do sing almost all the year round, the late summer during the moult being the exception.

Exhibition

Hedge sparrows do quite well on the show bench but generally do best when shown in pairs. An exhibition bird must have a good gunmetal blue head with the colour extending well down over the front and back of the body: a clean-legged bird with nice round body having plenty of workings and tickings.

Contributions by: Rex Collins; Rob Taylor.

WHITETHROAT AND LESSER WHITETHROAT
Order: *Passeriformes*
Family: *Sylviidae* (Warblers)

Whitethroat *(Sylvia communis)* Length 5½ inches (14 cm), weight less than ¼ oz (7 g).

Lesser Whitethroat *(Sylvia curruca)* Length 5¼ inches (13.25 cm), weight less than ¼ oz (7 g).

These two species are similar in many ways and we will endeavour to show the differences.

In spring and summer the **male whitethroat** has a grey cap which, in winter, becomes grey–brown. Rufous back and wings: the outer tail feathers are bordered in white, a white throat with light buff underparts tinged with pink on the breast and flanks. The pink tinge is lost in winter.

The **female** is browner and has no pink tinge.

The **male lesser whitethroat** has a greyer mantle and whiter underparts especially the throat. The ear coverts are much darker and the outer tail feathers are white. It is slightly smaller than the whitethroat. The male and female are alike.

Distribution

The whitethroat is well distributed throughout the British Islands except in the Highlands of Scotland and the Orkneys. It was the most common and most plentiful of the warblers until 1968. The following year three–quarters of the previous year's breeding stock failed to return and the same happened in many parts of the continent. This sudden decrease has since been attributed to losses in the winter habitat in Africa where severe droughts have been experienced. Since then the population level has been slowly recovering.

Both the whitethroat and the lesser whitethroat are summer visitors coming here to breed though they winter in different parts of Africa.

The lesser whitethroat has a much more restricted distribution and Britain is the westernmost edge of its breeding range. Consequently, it is mainly concentrated in the south eastern half of England extending as far as Devon, the Welsh border and Lincolnshire and locally in parts of Lancashire and along the north east coast.

The whitethroat, sometimes called the common whitethroat, is a bird of commons, heaths, waste-ground with hawthorn thickets, woodland edges and clearings and around lakes and marshes with good vegetation. It likes brambles and nettles in overgrown orchards, untended gardens and uncultivated field corners. Woodland is generally avoided being too thick for its aerial song flight.

The lesser whitethroat likes tall dense farmland hedgerows, it does not have a song flight and tends to stick to thicker cover in trees and dense shrubs.

Both species arrive around the middle of April and are not gregarious but highly territorial. The cocks arrive first and establish their territory. The lesser is very secretive and sings in dense cover, but the whitethroat is more obtrusive and demands an open space for self advertisement though is seldom on view for long. Both species rarely settle on the ground. The hens follow and courtship is hectic and sometimes violent on both sides.

Breeding

The nest of the whitethroat, which is built by both cock and hen, is placed among low bushes, brambles or in a thick hedge bottom and is a deep cup shaped structure made of grass and roots and lined with hair, with some decoration of wool and down. Four or five greenish white eggs with reddish or black spots is the normal clutch. Incubation by both parents takes approximately twelve days and the young usually fledge in thirteen days. Two broods are normal. The young are fed on small insects and larvae. Whitethroats are fond of fruit and berries when these are available.

The lesser whitethroat nests in a dense bush, hedge or shrub usually between 2 and 5 feet (.6 and 1.6 m) above the ground. A rather frail structure of dry stalks, roots and dry leaves the nest is built mainly by the cock with the lining of hair and decoration with spider's cocoons being added by the hen. Four to six creamy white eggs with sepia-brown markings are the normal clutch. Both birds share the incubation which lasts approximately twelve days and the young fledge in thirteen days. One brood is normal but occasionally two are reared. Insects, often captured on the wing, are the main food for the young but the adults are particularly fond of soft fruits especially red currants.

Aviary Breeding and Rearing

Both these species are very suitable subjects for aviaries but must be taken indoors in winter and housed in separate roomy cages unless indoor flights are available. Provision of heat in severe weather is essential and the temperature should be maintained at a minimum 50°F or 10°C. Being strongly territorial one pair per aviary must be the rule.

Cocks should be introduced first into the aviary, about mid–April, to coincide with their arrival in this country provided that the weather is reasonable: if the winter is extended delay putting the birds into the aviary until May. About a week to ten days after the cock has been introduced into the aviary the hen can be introduced but keep a careful watch for a few days to see that they are not fighting seriously. Two separate feeding stations will help to prevent this.

The aviary should be heavily planted preferably to simulate their natural wild habitat. If this is not possible, use plenty of hawthorn branches and brambles to provide cover so that the hen can seek refuge when being chased by the cock. Growing nettles and tufts of grass will help to provide natural nesting sites and enable the birds to find a lot of live insects for themselves. Given suitable conditions the birds soon settle down and are not difficult to breed.

They should be provided with a good brand of fine grade insectile food, varied with grated cheddar cheese, grated carrot, steamed and grated ox heart. Fruit in the form of ripe apple and heavily scored pear and at least ten mealworms per bird each day: also feed stored ant eggs, earwigs, woodlice, maggots and any other form of live food that can be obtained. Clean water for drinking and bathing is essential and must be given daily. Soft fruit when in season should be added to the diet.

When the young hatch the supplies of live food must be increased as the young ones grow, particularly small mealworms, maggots, ant eggs and caterpillars and the like, together with any other live food which can be obtained.

Exhibition

For exhibition the lesser whitethroat must be as dainty as possible, with a nice dark grey hood extending from the front of the head over the back and fading out towards the tail: a good white surround to the eye helps the dainty appearance. A pair which are well matched in size and coloration make an excellent exhibit. The sexes are alike.

An exhibition whitethroat is more robust, stouter and larger. The cock should have a nice grey head continuing down over the back, brown shaded wings and a rough throated white bib. The hen has a similar bib and a nice brown head, the colour extending down the back. Both should show a good clear defined eye.

Contributions by: Malcolm Taylor; Rob Taylor.

Figure 9.1   Whitethroat

BLACKCAP (*Sylvia Atricapilla*)
Order: *Passeriformes*
Family: *Sylviidae (Warblers)*

Length 5½ inches (14 cm), **Weight** ½ oz (14 g).
Male: brown-grey upperparts, much darker towards the tail and a glossy black cap. Buffish-white underparts.
Female: upperparts rather browner than the male and a chestnut brown cap with buffish-white underparts. The blackcap is an easy bird to sex.

Characteristics

The blackcap is one of the finest of our songsters, a summer visitor which is well distributed throughout the whole of England and Wales but more locally over the southern half of Scotland and the western half of Ireland. In recent years there have been a number of reports of blackcaps wintering in England possibly because the birds feed on berries such as ivy if insect food is not available in cold weather. The migrant birds are amongst the early arrivals at the end of March and early April returning to their winter home in the autumn. They are most frequently found in mature deciduous or mixed woodland with a good shrub layer, as well as overgrown coppice, tall hedgerows, medium aged forestry plantations, thorn scrub and even garden shrubberies. In Scotland and Ireland blackcaps frequently use Rhododendrons probably because many of the mature deciduous woodland had ornamental rhododendrons planted in them by the old estates.

The song of the blackcap is sometimes confused with its close relative the garden warbler which, although distributed over much the same area, is far less common. The blackcap's song is loud, rich and beautiful, on occasions rivalling the nightingale. The garden warbler's song, although similar, is not as rich or as loud and has longer phrases.

A shy bird, the blackcap slips in and out of bushes, hedgerows, brambles and briars and is not often seen in the open. It is, however, strongly territorial although territories often overlap with those of the garden warbler.

Breeding

Nesting commences in late April and the nest is usually built low down in thick cover such as nettles, brambles and shrubs about 2 ft (.6 m) from the ground. It is said to be slung by handles, like a basket, but this does not always seem to be the case. The nest is rather flimsily made of stems, grass and roots and lined with fine grass and hair, the rim often decorated with cobwebs. The eggs laid in May vary in colour but are generally whitish with a brown marbled effect. The usual clutch is four and there are sometimes two broods. Both cock and hen take turns at incubation which lasts about thirteen days. The young fledge in twelve days and resemble the hen but are rather darker.

The blackcap feeds on flies, caterpillars and other insects as well as fruit and berries.

Aviary Breeding and Rearing

The blackcap is a very popular small softbill and a good aviary subject. Although territorial it will not object to other species which do not compete for the livefood. While there must be only one pair of blackcaps in an aviary, a few pairs of finches can be included provided the enclosure is large enough. The breeding quarters should be well planted with elder, nettles and brambles with rough grass to provide the deep cover necessary.

In the winter the birds should be housed in a large cage or small flight in the birdroom which should be heated to a minimum of 50°F or 10°C. Feeding is simple: a good small grade insectivorous mixture with ripe fruit — apple, pear, soaked currants, elderberries and such with a variety of livefood. Clean water for drinking and bathing must be supplied daily.

When the wild birds return in the spring they have a light moult like many small softbills but do not undergo a change of colour in the process. Pairs of blackcaps should be released into the breeding flights in April to coincide with their normal arrival date in this country, providing the weather is not harsh: as they will have been housed in sheltered conditions careful judgement is required at this time.

Care should be taken over the birds' release as, although they have been living quite peaceably together during the winter, the near natural conditions of the flight may stimulate them into an aggressive mood and one may seriously injure the other. Two feeding places some distance apart are essential with plenty of fresh water for drinking and bathing given daily.

If the cock seems aggressive put him into the flight first so that he can establish his territory and introduce the hen about a week later when all should be well, but a careful watch should be kept on the birds for the first few days. Once settled they will soon get down to nesting, but the supply of livefood — caterpillars, mealworms, maggots and such — must be given in ever-increasing quantities whilst the young are in the nest. They will be found to be good parents.

Albert Wyatt gives an interesting account of the courtship display which can be observed so much better when the birds are in an aviary than can be in the wild. The cock bird follows the hen with tail fanned, black cap raised and body puffed out with the wings carried high over his back: during this display the cock can be heard warbling softly. At this point mating takes place.

If it is intended to ring the young it should be done at six to seven days after hatching. Ringing is explained in Chapter 5. The young leave the nest at twelve days old but remain in thick cover. They will rarely be seen but will be heard calling for food and usually being answered by the hen. At four weeks old the young begin to fend for themselves and very shortly afterwards begin to moult into adult plumage.

Birds in aviaries will often live a lot longer than those in the wild and some will continue to breed even at five and six years old.

Exhibition

For exhibition blackcaps should be steady, large and richly and evenly coloured. A large show-cage which is tastefully decorated but not overdone will enhance their chances even in strong competition.

Contributions by: A.C. Wyatt.

NIGHTINGALE *(Luscinia megarhynchos)*

Order: *Passeriformes*
Family: *Turdidae* (Thrushes)

Length 6½ inches (16.5 cm), **weight** 1 oz (28.35 g).

The nightingale's song is so well known that it is surprising how few people have any idea what the bird looks like. It is, in fact, a very sober-looking, almost insignificant bird and both sexes look alike. The upperparts are russet-brown, shading deeper on tail and tail coverts: the underparts are pale greyish-brown showing whiter on the throat and belly. The juveniles are very similar to young robins with the same mottled plumage. Many of the nightingale's habits are very like those of the robin except that it does not share the robin's tameness and liking for human society. On the contrary, it is an extremely shy and secretive bird.

Characteristics

The nightingale is a summer visitor which nests in the south east corner of the British Isles from the Wash to the Severn, generally excluding Devon and Cornwall, and is found in Lincolnshire and Shropshire. It arrives in April and leaves again in August or early September for its winter quarters in tropical Africa. The cocks arrive first, taking up territories where they were bred the year before and are followed about a fortnight later by the hens. Although the nightingale's distribution has not changed much in this century, their numbers have declined. This is generally attributed to the destruction of suitable habitat, due to scrub clearance, the drainage of damp places, tidier hedgerow management and the decline in rotational cutting of coppiced woods. Former coppice with standards, when neglected, become quickly overgrown and quite unsuited to the species' requirements. Between five and ten years growth is the most suitable habitat for the nightingale. After that growth shuts out too much light. This clearly illustrates that it is useless to designate a piece of woodland as a sanctuary unless active steps are taken to manage the area thus providing suitable habitat with food supplies for the various birds.

Well known as a beautiful singer at night, the nightingale also sings just as well in the day, usually from a low tree or bush. It sings to advertise its territory and the song does play some part in courtship. It will continue to sing while the hen is sitting but once the young hatch it has no more time to spare for singing and by June is silent.

Breeding

The nightingale is essentially a bird of woodland copses, spinneys, thickets, and woods with dense vegetation. It always nests on or close to the ground amid dense undergrowth. The nest is well hidden and difficult to find: a rather loose and deep structure of dead leaves, grass and hair built by the hen

84

alone. Often the nest is located in brambles or nettles with long grass growing up into them. There is only one clutch of four or five olive green or olive brown eggs laid in May. Incubation is by the hen for thirteen days and the young fed by both parents fledge in twelve days but sometimes longer presumably depending on the food supply.

Insects of various kinds are the chief food with spiders, small worms and some kinds of berries. Oak trees are never far away from the breeding area: it is the green caterpillars of the oak roller moth which forms the main bulk of the nestlings' diet. This caterpillar crop coincides with the hatching of eggs during the first week in June. If the first nest is lost for some reason the young miss this abundant food and take a few days longer to fledge.

Very often the location of a nest is given away by the noisy clamour of the fully feathered young when being fed by the adult birds. In cool, damp weather the young feather very quickly. On leaving the nest they spread out and keep low in the undergrowth for the first few days. Both adults in an effort to locate the young utter soft 'croak' and 'tace' notes. The nightingale, in common with many summer migrants, has just sufficient time to rear one brood of young before leaving for a warmer climate at the end of July and early August.

Aviary Breeding and Rearing

In aviaries, when well fed and looked after, migratory birds such as the nightingale do not appear to be aware of the seasons of migration which suggests that the food supply is the main reason for their leaving our shores.

Nightingales are not birds for the novice and should not be kept until the aviculturist has had plenty of experience with softbill species which are easier to look after. Being highly territorial one pair per aviary is the rule. The aviary must be heavily planted with dense low cover such as brambles and nettles both of which are easy to grow.

Particular attention must be paid to the birds' needs throughout the winter and during the moult. Juveniles do not moult wing or tail feathers until their first spring moult when first winter birds can be distinguished from older ones by pale buff spots on the tips of the greater wing coverts. Young male nightingales become very aggressive on completion of their first moult, which commences when they are six weeks old. At this time they have to be housed in large separate compartments, preferably in the bird room. In the colder months the bird room should have some form of heating to maintain a minimum temperature of 50°F or 10°C.

The males commence to warble quietly at three weeks old when they are just self supporting. Females can generally be housed with other female nightingales.

They should be fed on a good brand of fine grade insectile food with grated cheese, grated carrot and grated ox heart, together with chopped or minced greenfood, maggots and mealworms. Also acceptable are berries such as elder, rowan, currants, ripe apple and pear heavily scored, with perhaps a few well soaked raisins. At least ten mealworms per bird per day, together with stored ant eggs, earwigs, woodlice and any other form of livefood that can be obtained. Finely chopped nettles can be used as greenfood: rose-hip syrup and blackcurrant syrup (such as Ribena) can be given in fountains with a small aperture to ensure that the birds cannot get these sticky substances on their plumage. Ant eggs, of which they are particularly fond, are a most important part of their diet which must at all times be varied. Clean water for drinking and bathing is essential and should be given fresh daily. As the birds are coming into breeding condition the live food must be increased and be almost unlimited when the young are being reared. Dust all live food with a multi-vitamin powder which, apart from being beneficial to the birds, will prevent rickets.

When spring arrives it is always difficult to obtain compatibility between male and female as the birds selected as breeding pairs are not the mates that they would probably choose themselves. If possible, place each bird in a separate aviary or one aviary which is divided into two and, providing that the weather is reasonable, the third week in April is the right time. Usually it is only a matter of a week or two before one sees the female carrying a leaf about the flight. It is then generally safe to introduce the male. The enclosure should be planted with plenty of shrubs to form a dense undergrowth with sufficient shade so that it has a similar appearance to the birds' natural breeding habitat. This helps to ensure successful breeding and assists in the study of the species. There should be two feeding areas out of sight of each other.

If it is intended to ring the young this is best done in the late evening when they are about seven or eight days old. Overnight feather growth is rapid and the chances of the adults ejecting the young will be lessened.

Apart from the wonderful song which is this bird's main distinguishing feature, it is possible with practice to sex nightingales. Male birds are larger than females, have flatter heads, whiter throats and give the appearance of having longer legs by showing more of the tibia than does the female. Males tend to carry their wing tips lower than the root of the tail which is 'cocked' higher than that of the female. Males also tend to croak more deeply although other call and alarm notes are similar to the females and both sexes tend to rock momentarily when stationary. Young males do not inherit the beautiful song but learn this while in their winter quarters in Africa which are heavily populated with wintering nightingales.

Exhibition

The exhibition nightingale is bold, stout and pleasantly round: clean at the vent, steady and a good showman. A bird of good rich rufous brown colour with a good eyelet and a nice light fading colour on the breast.

Contributions by: Ray Allen; Malcolm Taylor; Rob Taylor.

TREE CREEPER *(Certhia familiaris)*

Order: *Passeriformes*
Family: *Certhiidae* (Creepers)

Length 4¼ inches (10.75 cm), **weight** approximately ½ oz (14 g).

The treecreeper is a most inconspicuous little bird with a brown mantle having paler shadings and a long, curved, slender needle-like beak. Its wings are barred in buff and its tail is graduated. There is a white eye stripe over its eye and its underparts are silky white. Both sexes are alike.

Distribution

Being entirely dependent on trees the treecreeper is well distributed throughout the British Isles wherever there are trees but is absent from high ground and fenlands where there are no trees. It is, in fact, quite a common bird, but because of its dull colours and quiet habits is often overlooked. Originally a bird of the pine trees, it spread to and colonised the deciduous woods when these first spread to this country from the continent. Sometimes called the mouse bird, it starts low down on the trunk of a tree and quickly creeps upwards on a circular route aided by the stiff feathers of its tail. Its specially adapted beak fits into the narrow cracks to secure the lurking insects. When reaching the top of one tree it will fly down to the bottom of another tree and start again. This bird is very much a loner and is nearly always seen on its own even in the breeding season, except when a brood has recently fledged. It roosts in a small crevice in the bark of the tree. Unfortunately it is a bird which suffers very badly in severe winters, being residential and needing large numbers of small insects each day to subsist. Although its losses are high in a bad winter, it usually recovers its numbers within a few years. For all its quiet ways the tree creeper is not a timid bird and will take no notice of human beings even when one is quite close to it.

Breeding

Breeding does not commence until late April or early May. The nest — made of twigs, moss, grass, bark fibres and lined with hair and feathers — is always well hidden in a crevice or behind loose bark on a tree, or behind the trunk of ivy and sometimes in a hole in a building or stone wall. Six to seven white eggs with reddish brown spots is the normal clutch and there are usually two broods a year. Incubation takes thirteen days and the young fledge at thirteen to fourteen days old.

Feeding

Tree creepers feed mainly on spiders, woodlice, beetles, earwigs and their eggs as well as weevils and small caterpillars.

Aviary Breeding and Rearing

In an aviary tree creepers should be provided with natural conditions and at least one side should be completely covered in bark allowing places for nesting. They will use a nest box but it should be covered in bark. If the opposite side of the aviary can also be covered in bark the birds can follow their natural inclination to run up to the top of one and then fly down to the bottom of the other.

The main problems are first to sex the birds to ensure a true pair and secondly to obtain enough small live food to enable the birds to rear a nest of young. Small caterpillars and house fly maggots are a great help, the house fly being better than the blue bottle. Piles of manure and rotting fruit will help to provide a supply of small flies.

In exhibition a tree creeper should be well developed with good colour and clear markings with nice quality and condition of feather.

Exhibition

An exhibition tree creeper must be well developed and neatly proportioned with good strong legs. Well trained and steady with good feather condition brown tinged with golden buff striped with ashy green. Bold round eye.

Contributions by: A. T. Worrall.

Figure 9.2   Tree Creeper

WREN *(Troglodytes troglodytes)*
Order: *Passeriformes*
Family: *Troglodytidae*

Length $3\frac{3}{4}$ inches (9.5 cm), **weight** less than $\frac{1}{4}$ oz (7 g).

The male and female are almost identical. The warm red–brown mantle, wings tail and flanks are all barred and the underparts are buffish. This small dumpy little bird with a cocked tail is extremely well known and will be recognised by everybody. It has a thin brown beak, flesh coloured legs and a light eye stripe.

Distribution

The wren is well distributed throughout the whole of the British Islands with separate races on some of the Scottish Islands. It is one of the most adaptable species and can be found in almost every habitat except the centres of cities. It will be found on the sea shore and on boulder–strewn mountains, but the preferred habitat is woodland with waterside vegetation. For such a tiny bird it has an incredibly loud and forceful song, some of it at such high frequency that some people are unable to hear it at all. It has an almost exclusively insect diet which it finds in crevices in dry stone walls and the crevices in the bark on trees, much of its food being so small as to be invisible to the naked eye.

Breeding

The choice of nesting site is very varied and it may be a hedge, a tree hole, a bush, a thatched roof or a creeper or any place which will accommodate the domed nest with a side entrance. The cock builds, but does not complete, several nests within his territory. The hen selects one and lines it. There are usually two broods.

In our own garden we watch the wrens working over the dry rockery several times a day at all times of the year and they always seem to find something to eat. The cock built several nests — in the ivy on an oak tree, inside the garage where a brick is missing, in a hedge which is thickly overgrown with a creeper and another elsewhere which we have never discovered. Over the years we have found that each nest is used in turn, being repaired and relined. The cock always roosts on top of the nest when the hen is sitting. A nest will only be used once each year, the second clutch being laid in a different nest. The nests, especially the one in the garage, are frequently used for roosting during the winter and as many as ten wrens have been seen coming out in the morning. Providing that they are not interfered with the wrens are most confiding and take no notice of the car being driven in and out, even at night. It is easy to tell when the nest has been repaired and is in use, the entrance hole being rewoven with new moss. All these nests are around 5 feet (1.6 m) from ground level. When first fledged the young ones stay close to the nest for a few days and then disappear — where they go to we have never discovered.

The nest is made of moss, grass, leaves and bracken beautifully woven together with cobwebs and, for all their apparent frailty, are remarkably strong. Nesting starts in April and there are usually said to be five or six white eggs spotted with brownish red. In our experience the usual brood is eight or nine but this may be dependent on the amount of food available. The young are fed on small insects and their larvae, particularly moth larvae and spiders. Both parents feed the young and the cock continues to feed them for a time when they fledge. The juveniles are like the parents when fully grown.

The wren is constantly on the move and requires a continuous food supply to make up for so much spent energy — small wonder that it has difficulty in storing up enough food in its body in the winter to maintain them through the long night. No doubt this is why they roost together in old nests — to help them keep warm. Unfortunately many do die in severe weather and their pathetic little bodies are found by the nests. The prolonged and severe winter of 1962 almost wiped them out: luckily with milder winters since, the wren population has fully recovered but they were very scarce for several years.

Aviary breeding and rearing

Being so adaptable the wren is a very suitable species for aviculture and has always been popular with softbill enthusiasts. It has a magnetism all of its own and, given that little extra attention, is most rewarding.

Like most of our softbills the wren is extremely territorial and the rule is only one pair to an aviary, although the odd pair of hardbills or even another species of softbill will be tolerated provided that they have dissimilar habits and are not seen as a competitor to the wren's environment.

The aviary should be well planted with vines, honeysuckle and plenty of low cover shrubs and grasses to suit the wren's natural inclination to 'skulk' and, at the same time, to attract a natural supply of live food. The aviary must also be protected against our winter weather as, although it is a hardy little bird, it cannot stand prolonged cold as we have already seen.

Providing that a liberal supply of live food can be maintained wrens are extremely good parents though the broods tend to be smaller than in the wild, four being the average.

Though not easy to sex visually, cocks do tend to be larger, bolder and richer in colour and more distinctly marked than the hens. If they are carefully watched it will be found that cocks come into the open more often and will continually show off, display and sing. Hens are more secretive and shy. Although it is said that the cocks in the wild build the nests, this has not been found to be so with aviary-bred wrens. In fact cocks do help with the initial building, but the greater part is done by the hen and moss, leaves, fine grass, feathers and hair will all be used.

Incubation is thirteen days and the young can be closed ringed at seven to eight days, but great care must be taken not to enlarge the entrance hole too much. A bent teaspoon will be found useful to ease the chicks out of the nest. Fuller details on ringing are given elsewhere. In some cases the situation of the nest makes it impracticable or almost impossible to closed ring the young. In this case the British Bird Council split rings should be used. Chicks leave the nest at about sixteen days and are independent at about twenty-five days old: they can usually be left as a family group until after the autumn moult.

The wren's basic diet should consist of finely grated cheese, nuts, hard boiled egg, biscuit and meat meal to which should be added a little finely grated carrot, greenfood and dried fruit. Small feeder gentles (pinkies), small or chopped mealworms and moth pupae must always be available. Live food needs to be fed liberally during rearing and should be dusted with a good vitamin powder. Wrens also have a liking for nectar and honey-water.

Exhibition

When training young wrens for exhibition make sure there is the minimum amount of decoration as the birds will hide if given half a chance. Although so small, they are forever active and the minimum size for a show cage is 30 × 12 × 18 inches (76 cm × 30.5 cm × 46 cm). The exhibition wren must be of good size, rich rufus brown in colour, well marked around eye and ear coverts with distinct barring on wings, tail and flanks. The bird must be steady in the cage but with good 'action'.

Contributions by: Bob Partridge.

Figure 9.3   Wren

SKYLARK *(Alauda arvensis)*

Order: *Passeriformes*
Family: *Alaudidae* (Larks)

Length 7 inches (17.75 cm), **weight** $1\frac{1}{2}$ oz (42.5 g).

The male and female skylark are very much alike with brown plumage, light and dark mottlings on the head and mantle and a buff eye stripe. The underparts are whitish with some streaks on the breast. There is a short crest, often quite prominent and the outside tail feathers are white.

Characteristics

This well known bird sings on the wing as it rises vertically over the nesting area until it disappears out of sight and continues singing as it comes down again, but it is not so generally known that it also sings on the ground and sometimes on a fence or bush.

The skylark is well distributed over the whole of the British Isles. It inhabits farmland, chalk downland, scrub, salt-marsh, sand-dunes, heaths, moorlands, meadows, marshes and mountain pastures. It is absent from wooded areas, as its essential need is to have areas of short vegetation in which to feed.

Although a resident species some British birds emigrate in the autumn, but large numbers arrive on the east coast from the continent at the same time. Outside the breeding season it is very gregarious, congregating in large flocks, sometimes in company with meadow pipits. Apart from its song-flight the skylark is a ground bird, feeding, nesting and roosting on the ground.

Breeding

The skylark's nest is always built in a well concealed depression in the ground amongst grass or growing crops and is made of grass, sometimes lined with hair. Breeding commences in April and there are usually two, sometimes three, broods. The average clutch is three or four eggs which are greyish white heavily marked with brown speckling. Incubation lasts for thirteen days and the young fledge at about twelve days old but are not fully grown until about ten days later.

Skylarks feed on the seeds of charlock, chickweed, sow thistle, sorrel and other weeds, as well as the leaves of clover and other plants. They also consume earthworms, caterpillars, beetles and their larvae, spiders and small ground animals. Also acceptable are some grain and seedlings such as lettuce, peas, and root crops including sugar-beet.

Aviary Breeding and Rearing

From the above notes it might be supposed that the aviary for skylarks would have to be about 1000 feet (300 m) high but this is not the case and an ordinary aviary is quite suitable. A perch or log will serve quite well for a singing post and the skylark will fill the air with melody from dawn to dusk from March to August. The most difficult part of breeding skylarks in an aviary is sexing the birds. The hens will warble at times and this can be most misleading, but once a cock bird comes into full song in the spring there is no mistaking him. The aviary must of course, include a patch of rough grass which is not allowed to become too rank. If possible it should be kept as if it is being grazed by animals with the odd tuft left to grow naturally and leaving some depressions.

Supply hay for the hen to line her nest. The eggs take thirteen days to hatch and the young can be ringed at five days old. The young grow fast and at eleven or twelve days old they leave the nest. At this stage care must be taken to prevent stepping on them when entering the aviary as the young 'freeze' and are most difficult to see. Any large water vessels should be emptied and small ones substituted to prevent accidents.

At all stages of nesting protective coloration plays an important part. The sitting hen is very difficult to see and when the young hatch they are covered with a coarse down which closely resembles dead grass in appearance.

Skylarks are easy to feed but it must be remembered that they are ground feeders and food supplies should be placed accordingly. Provide fine grade insectivorous mixture together with live food such as gentles. Seeding weeds which can be placed in a jar of water buried in the soil, sprouted seeds and finch mixture thrown on the ground, together with greenfood, remembering that they are fond of seedlings. When the young hatch, gentles and mealworms and any other live food obtainable should be fed ad lib.

Mealworms must be severely curtailed once the young ones are independent and the diet modified to substitute egg food. Experience has shown that mealworms have been the cause of trouble during the moult when young were lost.

Skylarks are long lived in aviaries and have been known to be still breeding at ten years old. It is interesting to note that A. C. Wyatt reported that one four year old hen changed sex and mated with her grand-daughter: every egg produced was fertile, but the young did not reach maturity in two breeding seasons. However in the third season a young hen was reared.

Contributions by: A.C. Wyatt.

REDSTART AND BLACK REDSTART
Order: *Passeriformes*
Family: *Turdidae* (Thrushes)

Redstart *(Phoenicurus phoenicurus)* **Length** 5½ inches (14 cm), **weight** ½ oz (14 g).
Black Redstart *(Phoenicurus ochruros)* **Length** 5½ inches (14 cm), **weight** ½ oz (14 g).
Male Redstart: blue grey head and mantle, black throat and cheeks and white forehead in summer: bright red rust breast, rump and tail. In winter the male is duller with browner underparts and paler throat.
Female: like the male in winter plumage: **Juveniles** are like the female but more mottled on their upper and lower parts, but they do have the characteristic red tail.
Male Black Redstart: has the chestnut coloured tail of the redstart but has much darker plumage, almost black. It is greyer with a clear white wing patch and no orange colour on the breast.
Female: less dark, more a smoky-grey colour, with the reddish tail.

Distribution

Both species are summer visitors who come here to breed. The redstart is well, though sparsely, distributed throughout England, Scotland and Wales except in the eastern counties and Cornwall, but is rarely found in Ireland. The black redstart is quite rare with us and is mainly confined to the south east although there are some signs that it is slowly spreading.

The redstart is a bird of open woodland, clearings and woodland edges. The black redstart originally lived on sea cliffs, mountain screes and boulder strewn slopes, but on the continent has become more of an urban bird both in gardens and around large industrial plants. Its preference for rocky ledges is shown in its use of ruins, building sites and bomb sites, where there are plenty of suitable ledges.

Feeding

Both species are territorial and not gregarious even in the winter. They are active birds constantly on the move with continual tail quivering. Much of their food is caught on the wing, the redstart darting in and out of the branches after passing insects. The black redstart is generally more in evidence flitting from perch to perch catching insects — more like the flycatcher.

Breeding

Nesting starts early April and the redstart chooses any place which provides old timber for nesting holes such as woods, parklands, heaths, commons, gardens and orchards. The black redstart, with its preference for ledges, chooses farm sheds, under eaves and in crevices and holes in rocks and cliffs. In towns any hole or crevice in buildings will suffice. Where old timber is not available the redstart will nest in holes in stone walls and readily takes to suitable nest boxes. Both species use the same materials — grass, moss, roots and line the nests with hair and feathers. The black redstart's normal clutch is four eggs and the redstart more often averaging six. The eggs are different, the black redstarts' being white, occasionally faintly marked, whereas the redstart lays greenish–blue eggs which are also occasionally faintly marked. Incubation by the hen only lasts thirteen days and the young fledge in fourteen to sixteen days depending on the availability of the food supplies. Redstarts and black redstarts feed almost entirely on insects and the nestlings are reared mostly on caterpillars. While the redstart is usually single brooded, the black redstart often has two broods.

Aviary Breeding and Rearing

Redstarts or 'firetails', as they are sometimes called, are ideal species for those who are taking up insectivorous birds or softbills as they are known by aviculturists, for the first time. Management for both species is the same.

In the winter they should be housed indoors in roomy cages or flights. While in some parts of the country they can be kept without heat it is generally better to maintain the temperature between 45° and 50°F (8°–10°C) especially in severe weather. The temperature should not be allowed to rise above this otherwise there will be difficulty in transferring them to an outside flight in the spring, because they are early nesters. Both cock and hen can be kept together. Care must be taken, however, when putting them into breeding quarters because they may fight like demons for territory with disastrous results. It is best that the flight or aviary be divided with wire netting until the birds are ready to pair up. There should always be two feeding places, screened from each other. It is, however, natural for the cock to chase the hen before pairing. An aviary 6 feet × 3 feet × 6 feet (2 m × 1 m × 2 m) high with a removable partition is ideal but if necessary smaller flights can be used. On no account should more than one pair be put into an aviary. Redstarts can be bred in cages or indoor flights, but the natural supply of insects which the birds can obtain from an aviary will supplement their food and be a great help in rearing the young.

The aviary should be protected from the prevailing wind and rain and as thickly planted as possible. Bare branches high up round the aviary should be provided for song posts. Nest boxes should be sited in the foliage to resemble holes in trees. For the black redstarts provide sheltered shelves. Budgie nest boxes with bark nailed to the outside are useful and similar boxes with half the front cut away will also be attractive. Hollow logs with one end blocked off should be sited horizontally and bricks arranged to leave a cavity or stone walls can be built with rockery stone. A patch of nettles will help to provide live food and cover for the young when first fledged. A pile of stable manure will also attract flies which the birds will relish. Clean water for drinking and bathing must be supplied fresh daily.

For the nest supply grasses, fine roots and moss — some pairs will also use dead oak leaves — also hair and small feathers for the lining. When the hen starts nest building it is best to leave the birds alone with as little disturbance as possible, and watch their activities from a distance. Only enter the aviary to provide food and water and do not attempt to look at the nest. When young have hatched, eggshells will usually be seen on the aviary floor at the opposite end to the nest.

Redstarts, being insectivorous almost exclusively, require a good fine grade insectile food with plenty of varied livefood. Hard boiled egg, grated cheese, grated carrot, finely chopped lettuce, dandelion and nettle leaves can be added as well as dried flies which have been scalded or soaked in oil and free access allowed to maggots and a few mealworms each day. Some fruit will be taken — small pieces of ripe apple and pear and some berries such as elderberries. Clean water for drinking and bathing must be supplied daily.

When the chicks hatch the supply of livefood will have to be continually increased. Ant eggs, greenfly, spiders and anything else which can be obtained as well as green caterpillars. The last mentioned are the natural rearing food and those of the wax-moth which feed on oak leaves are especially useful.

The young redstarts have a tendency to stay on the ground when they first fledge and it is important to have plenty of ground cover to protect them from the elements.

In the black redstarts' nests some young will be found to be darker than others and they generally turn out to be young cocks.

The young should be ringed at six to seven days old.

Exhibition

For exhibition a redstart should be a nice chubby shape with a rich russet brown breast, well frosted: clear eye markings and head shield: well frosted and in nice condition with good quality feather.

Contributions by: A.T. Worrall; Malcolm Taylor.

STONECHAT *(Sacicola torquata)*

Order: *Passeriformes*
Family: *Turdidae* (Thrushes)

Length 5 inches (12.75 cm), **weight** ½ oz (14 g).
Male: in summer has a black head and throat, black mantle and tail. The underparts are chestnut shading to buff with conspicuous white patches on neck, wings and rump. In winter it is rather drab looking.
Female: brown with darker streaks.
Juveniles: similar to the hen.

Distribution

The stonechat is a resident species although a few do migrate. It is unfortunately very susceptible to severe winters which do reduce their numbers considerably, from which they only recover slowly.

Like the whinchat, the stonechats are birds of rough country with a combination of close-cropped grass and gorse; heather or bracken and coastal heath and common are their favourite haunts; inland heaths, commons, downs, hillsides and cliffs are also used. The cock will perch prominently on the tops of bushes or posts and if disturbed utters his alarm call which sounds like two pebbles being sharply knocked together — a call which is quite unmistakable.

The stonechat is mostly found in the coastal area of England, Wales and Scotland except for the east coast of England: inland in Devon and Cornwall and, locally, inland in England and Wales and rather more in Scotland. In Ireland it is more widely distributed over most of the country. After a succession of mild winters when the numbers have built up there is an increase in the colonisation of inland heaths. Man's activities in reducing available habitat, together with the species' susceptibility to severe weather, accounts for its westerly and coastal distribution, where the weather is milder and there is less disturbance to its habitat. As several successive severe winters could easily reduce this species to danger point it is most important that stocks of aviary-bred birds should be built up and anyone who has the space and facilities to breed stonechats should have a pair of these lovely little birds.

Breeding

The stonechat is not a sociable bird but usually remains in pairs although it is said that they may change mates in both spring and autumn and that they are frequently polygamous.

The nest is on or near the ground in a well concealed nook at the foot of a gorse or other bushes: it is built by the hen with moss, grass and roots and lined with fine bents, fur, hair, wool or feathers sometimes with a tunnel runway to the nest. Five pale blue-green eggs with reddish speckles is the usual brood. Two and sometimes three broods are normal as the stonechat is an early nester commencing in late March or early April. Incubation is approximately thirteen days and the young leave the nest after another thirteen days.

Feeding

While some seeds are eaten, insects are the stonechat's chief diet.

Aviary Breeding and Rearing

This species does extremely well in confinement and is not difficult to keep, probably because of the more sheltered conditions afforded by an aviary. They should be provided with a good brand of fine grade insectivorous food together with a few mealworms and maggot pupae. A pair should be housed in an outside aviary or flight. If the aviary is in a sheltered position in the southern part of the country they can be wintered outside, but in severe weather or in more northern areas provision should be made to keep them in a roomy cage or flight inside the birdroom in winter.

They will not bicker when kept together and can be housed with other birds of similar size except during the breeding season when, in common with other species of insectivorous birds, the golden rule is one pair to one aviary. Both birds of a pair of stonechats become very dominant over other similar sized birds, particularly members of a related species. To encourage a pair to nest the aviary should be not less than 6 feet × 3 feet (2 m × 1 m) with part of the roof area covered and sheltered from the prevailing wind and rain. The aviary can be set out to resemble their natural habitat with some short grass, a bunch of gorse or bracken fixed with a post as if growing in the ground. A box bush with the grass allowed to grow all round it is a good substitute. Try to arrange it so that the potential nesting site is protected from heavy rain. Another post about 3 feet (1 m) high at the other end of the aviry will provide the cock with a look-out and singing post: this is quite important. Increasing the livefood will help to bring the birds into high breeding condition.

The cock bird will select the nesting site and the female will build the nest. Provide dry grasses, moss, rootlets, rabbit fur, dog hair and small feathers. When the eggs hatch the nestlings will require livefood in the form of ant eggs, small maggots (pinkies), mealworms, moths, caterpillars and anything else that can be obtained. The supplies must be continually increased as the young stonechats grow. It will generally be found that the parent birds will only feed livefood to the nestlings.

Clean water for drinking and bathing must be supplied fresh each day.

At about fourteen days old the young stonechats will leave the nest and remain in the undergrowth for several days until they can fly. The chief reason for this is that being a ground nesting species the brood has a greater chance of survival by leaving the nest before they can fly properly. At least two broods can be expected in a season. Ring the young at approximately six to seven days old.

When the young are on the wing they can be easily sexed: the cocks having white wing patches. Altogether, stonechats are delightful little birds to keep.

Exhibition

For exhibition the stonechat must be very upright and bold with head as large and jet black as possible, with good rich rufous breast markings and good lacings on the back: a short tail, bright eyed with nice clean legs.

Contributions by: Malcolm Taylor; Rob Taylor.

Figure 9.4   Whinchat (left) and Stonechat

WHINCHAT (*Saxicola rubetra*)

Order: *Passeriformes*
Family: *Turdidae* (Thrushes)

Length 5 inches (12.75 cm), **weight** under ¼ oz (7 g).
Male: the mantle is brown with darker streaks and with a white eye-stripe. The underparts are buff with deeper shading on the breast: the chin is white and there is a broad white patch on the wings. The tail is dark with white at the base. The male is somewhat duller when out of breeding condition.
Female: resembles the male in winter being duller with less conspicuous eye-stripe and wing patch.

Distribution

The whinchat is a summer visitor which winters in tropical Africa. Arriving in the latter half of April it is well distributed throughout the north of England, the whole of Scotland and Wales but is very local south of the line from the Humber to the Severn estuary and across the centre of Ireland. It is not now common anywhere, yet sixty years ago it was common in southern and eastern England. The reason for its decline is not fully understood and several factors seem to be involved one of which could be the loss of habitat, especially roadside verges. The modern mechanical method of cutting the hedges in spring and spraying the verges with weed killer is one of the causes and it has been shown that where the hedges and verges are allowed to grow wild until August the whinchat is more successful.

A combination of tussocky grass and suitable song posts such as wire fencing, gorse bushes, heathland, rough ground and waste land is whinchat country. Roadside verges, railway embankments, bracken covered hillsides and young forestry plantations are all favourite places, though its main distribution nowadays is in the uplands except in Ireland where it is mainly found in the lowlands — possibly because the land tends to be rather wilder than in England.

Feeding

The whinchat is not gregarious. It is an active little bird which flits from perch to perch, occasionally darting out to seize some passing insect. In many of its ways it is like the stonechat and the redstarts to which it is related and is basically a ground feeder, insects and their larvae being the principal food.

Breeding

A late breeder, the whinchat starts nesting in May. The nest is well concealed at the foot of a bush, among meadow grass or under bracken. It is built by the hen and made of grass and moss and lined with finer grass and hair. Five to six bluish green eggs, speckled with rusty-brown, form the clutch. Incubation by the hen alone is thirteen days. The cock is nearly always close to the nest singing on his favourite perch while she is sitting. The young fledge in thirteen or fourteen days. One brood is normal but sometimes two are reared.

Aviary Breeding and Rearing

In the winter whinchats should be kept in roomy cages or flights in the birdroom which should be maintained at a minimum temperature of 50°F (10°C). They can be released into the outside aviary in late April if the weather is reasonable. Like most small insectivorous birds, they will not tolerate others and the rule is one pair per aviary for which 6 feet × 3 feet (2 m × 1 m) is the minimum size. The aviary should be allowed to grow wild: a small bushy shrub like box is very useful, especially if the grass is allowed to grow up round it. Arrange suitable song posts such as bunches of gorse some 3 feet (1 m) above the ground and there must be some cover under which the food can be placed and some protection from wind and rain.

The birds should be watched quietly from outside, causing as little interference as possible with the daily routine of feeding and watering. They should be fed on a good brand of fine grade insectivorous food with a few mealworms and maggot pupae. When the young hatch the livefood must be increased — ant eggs, small maggots (pinkies) mealworms, moths, green caterpillars and any other insects which can be obtained. Clean water for drinking and bathing must be supplied fresh daily. A pile of cow or horse manure will help attract flying insects which the birds will relish.

The young should be ringed at six or seven days old.

It is natural for the young birds to leave the nest and hide in the undergrowth before they can fly properly. In the wild this helps to reduce losses by predators. The parents will continue to feed them and in a few days they will begin to show themselves.

Exhibition

An exhibition whinchat has similar characteristics to the stonechat but is rounder, showing plenty of dark biscuit coloured spangles on the back: a very light eye-stripe and a nice light tan from beak down to the legs.

Contributions by: Rob Taylor.

Figure 9.5 Pied Flycatcher (top) and Spotted Flycatcher

SPOTTED FLYCATCHER AND PIED FLYCATCHER

Order: *Passeriformes*
Family: *Muscicapidae* (Flycatchers)

Spotted Flycatcher *(Muscicapa striata)*
Length 5½ inches (14 cm), **weight** just under ½ oz (14 g).
The spotted flycatcher is an inconspicuous bird with greyish–brown upperparts and whitish underparts having some dark streaks on the head and breast. The male and female are alike and are not really spotted at all: the name seems to refer to the spotted juveniles.

Pied Flycatcher *(Muscicapa hypoleuca)*
Length 5 inches (12.75 cm), **weight** just under ½ oz (14 g).
In summer the male is a beautiful bird with black above and white below. His forehead is white and a broad white wing bar contrasts with the black mantle. In the female brown replaces the black and she does not have a white forehead and a smaller white wing patch. In winter both male and female are alike.

Both these species have very similar habits; they winter in tropical Africa and are summer migrants to these Islands, being the latest of the summer visitors and some of the earliest to leave.

Distribution

The spotted flycatcher is well distributed throughout the British Isles in woodland, by streams, lakes, farmland, copses, orchards, farmyards, gardens, churchyards — areas where abundant insect life can be found. They are only absent from industrial areas and places where there is an absence of trees.

The pied flycatcher is much more restricted and prefers deciduous woodland in upland valleys: alder and birch woods, along rivers and lakes where there is an abundance of caterpillars, dead branches for perching and holes for nesting. Previously restricted mainly to Wales, it has been increasing during this century especially where nest boxes have been provided. It's range now includes south west England, the Welsh border counties, the Lake District, north east England and southern Scotland. In recent years it has extended further north in Scotland but is still rather scattered.

Feeding

The spotted flycatcher lives exclusively on flying insects which it is adept at catching: it chooses an observation post, or sometimes two, on which it will sit for hours ready to dart and seize any passing insect, returning back to the same post. It rarely goes on the ground. It is unsociable and outside the breeding season generally resides alone. Its song is rather shrill and squeaky.

The pied flycatcher also takes flying insects and generally uses dead branches for observation posts. Unlike the spotted flycatcher, it does not return to the same branch after making a catch. It also makes use of defoliating caterpillars when rearing young and it has a tit-like habit of clinging to a branch. It will also feed on the ground and take berries in the autumn. The pied has a loud and pleasing song.

Breeding

The spotted flycatcher's nest is frequently built in a shallow niche or opening or against a vertical surface, often within some concealing vegetation and in gardens, a position on a wall behind some climbing plant but open-fronted nest boxes without any concealment may be used. The nest is slightly constructed of moss, wool and hair woven together with cobwebs. Nesting commences in late May and the usual clutch is four greenish-grey eggs with brown spots. Incubation takes fourteen days and the young fledge in a further fourteen days. One brood is normal but occasionally there are two.

The pied flycatcher nests in loose colonies but is dependent on suitable holes in old trees or in a wall and frequently uses the old nest of a woodpecker. As such locations are rather restricted in its natural habitat, it readily takes to nest boxes when these are provided. The nest is loosely put together with grass, moss, leaves and hair. The usual clutch is five to six pale blue eggs, again laid about the end of May. Incubation takes thirteen days and the young fledge after another twelve to thirteen days. One brood is normal.

Aviary Breeding and Rearing

Flycatchers need a well planted aviary which will attract a lot of winged insects. This can be helped by the inclusion of piles of ripe manure and rotting fruit. Jars of maggots in bran with a small hole in the lid so that the flies can escape as they hatch are very acceptable. A number of jars with maggots in various stages will be needed to ensure a continuous supply. Any other winged insect which can be obtained should also be supplied, as well as caterpillars for the pied. An observation post — such as a fence post — should be suitably placed for the spotted and a number of bare projecting branches for the pied. Both species readily take to nest boxes, although this is more of a shelf in the case of the spotted and, provided there is sufficient live food available, there is no difficulty in persuading them to nest.

Supply fine insectivorous food, maggots and mealworms as well as fresh clean water daily.

Exhibition

Exhibition flycatchers must be nicely proportioned with an upright watchful pose. Good feather condition, well trained and steady, and bold round eyes.

The spotted flycatcher must have a nice ashy brown plumage with spotted crown and lightly streaked whitish breast.

The pied flycatcher should have a nice brown and white colour with clear wing patch.

MEADOW PIPIT AND TREE PIPIT

Order: *Passeriformes*
Family: *Motacillidae* (Wagtails and Pipits)

Meadow Pipit *(Anthus pratensis)*
Length 6 inches (15.25 cm), **weight** ½ oz (14 g).
Tree Pipit *(Anthus trivialis)*
Length 6 inches (15.25 cm), **weight** ½ oz (14 g).

These two species are so much alike that it is difficult to distinguish them. In both cases the sexes are similar. The upper parts are warm brown streaked darker, whilst the underparts are much paler and the white outer tail feathers are very conspicuous in flight. The meadow pipit is generally more olive-brown and slightly smaller than that of the former. The tree pipit has pinker legs and perhaps rather brighter plumage and the meadow pipit has more flesh-brown legs. The main difference is in their songs.

Distribution and Habitat

The meadow pipit is a resident species although there is a two-way migration both to and from the continent in both autumn and spring. The tree pipit is a summer visitor only. The meadow pipit is well distributed throughout the British Isles but the tree pipit is unknown in Ireland and the more northern Scottish Islands. Although there is some overlap in habitat, the tree pipit is more dependent on trees and is less numerous than the meadow pipit.

The breeding habitat of the meadow pipit is rough grasslands, heaths, moors, sand-dunes and it is also found in more cultivated districts, particularly on river margins though it tends to avoid those areas of the country which have the heavier clay soils. It has been suggested that the rather low rainfall in these areas may have some effect on the insects on which the pipits feed. The tree pipit breeds in a wide variety of habitats with tall bushes or trees from which the males can make their distinctive song-flights — open woodland, scrub areas, heathland, parkland and pasture with scattered trees are all used.

Both pipits have song-flights similar in some respects but not comparable with the skylark: the pipits only rise to a maximum of about 100 feet (30.5 m) and they do not have the sustained length or power of song of the skylark. The meadow pipit, being very much a ground bird, will make his song-flight from the ground whereas the tree pipit will make his from a tall tree or pole. Both generally return to the same place.

The meadow pipit, outside the breeding season, is gregarious and moves about in flocks with wagtails and the like over low pasture lands, marshes and sewage farms and generally does not suffer too badly in severe weather.

Breeding

The meadow pipit is an early nester commencing in late April. The nest is on the ground, beside or under a tussock and is usually invisible from above but nests in banks have also been recorded. The nest is made of grass and lined with finer grass and sometimes hair. The eggs vary in colour from mainly whitish to brownish with dark markings. The clutch is generally four or five and incubation takes thirteen days. The young fledge in twelve to thirteen days and there are normally two, sometimes three, nests in a season. The meadow pipit is frequently used by the cuckoo as a host and many nests are lost in this way.

The tree pipit starts to breed later and nests are built in May — again on the ground, hidden under a tussock, sometimes in a bank with a 'mouse hole' entrance and is made of grass and moss, lined with grass and hair. Again the eggs are variable in colour from reddish–brown to grey with dark markings. Incubation is thirteen days and the young usually fledge at twelve or thirteen days old. Tree pipits generally have only one brood in a season although sometimes two are reared.

Feeding

The food of both pipits is similar, consisting mainly of insects and their larvae — beetles, flies, grasshoppers, spiders, carne-flies, blow-flies, caterpillars and small earthworms and, occasionally, grass seeds.

Aviary Breeding and Rearing

Although the meadow pipit can be wintered in an aviary, it is better to bring both species indoors during the bad weather because it is easier to cater for them in this way. They should be provided with a good sized cage at least 36 inches (1 m) long × 18 inches (0.5 m) deep, fitted with a natural branch for a perch: they do sometimes use them in spite of the fact that they are mainly walking birds and spend a considerable time on the ground. Fine sand at least 1 inch (25 mm) deep can be provided in one half of the cage and horticultural peat or moss in the other. This arrangement helps to keep their feet clean but it is most important that the cage is kept clean and fresh. The birds must have an opportunity to bathe every day — as with all insectivorous birds this is essential.

Provide a fine grade insectile mixture together with mealworms, maggots and their pupae and any other livefood that can be obtained. Ripe fruit or a few washed currants will be appreciated. During the winter pipits will eat an appreciable amount of wild seed to which can be added maw seed.

The breeding aviary should be of reasonable proportions so that at least part of it can be allowed to grow wild to resemble the wild habitat in which they nest. A pile of farmyard manure, and a pile of rotting fruit will help to provide a supply of flies. It also helps to construct a small pool of static water which will attract a lot of insects. This can easily be made out of a piece of polythene, but it is important that the pool is saucer-shaped with shallow edges to prevent accidents.

During the breeding season pipits are almost entirely insectivorous and large quantities of insects must be provided. Fortunately crickets can now be bought from commercial supplies and this is a great help and time saver.

Pipits are always good parents and if given a fair chance will always rear their young — perhaps this is why the cuckoo so often makes use of them as foster parents.

Exhibition

Exhibition pipits must be well developed with a full chest tapering to the vent and bold round black eyes. Must have good feather condition and be well trained and steady.

The meadow pipit must be a nice olive brown colour striped with black and have a sandy buff cere.

The tree pipit must have upper parts brown streaked blackish and creamy buff underparts.

Contributions by: Ray Allen.

Figure 9.6   Meadow Pipit

WAGTAILS
Order: *Passeriformes*
Family: *Motacillidae* (Wagtails and Pipits)

Wagtails, running along the ground with their long tails wagging up and down as if it is fastened to a spring, are so well known and as different from any other family as to be unmistakable. There are three species which breed in Britain: the **Pied,** the **Grey** and the **Yellow** and it is these with which we are concerned in this Chapter.

The grey and the yellow are sometimes confused as they both have bright yellow underparts. There are five sub–species of the yellow wagtail spread throughout Europe but we are dealing only with the sub–species which visits Britain to breed. All wagtails are closely related and will readily hybridise in aviaries. In the wild hybrids have been reported between the sub–species of the yellow wagtail.

A resident species, the pied wagtail is frequently known as the water wagtail. This is rather a misnomer as the pied is less dependent on water than the grey and the yellow.

Pied Wagtail *(Motacilla alba yarelli)*
Length 7 inches (17.75 cm), **weight** only a fraction of an oz (10 g).
Male: forehead, cheeks, and underparts are white. The crown, breast, mantle and tail are black, but the outer tail feathers are white. The wings have a double wing bar.
Female: greyer on her back and less black on her crown and breast.

The pied wagtail is well distributed throughout the British Isles, although in the autumn many of the more northern birds migrate to the southern counties and some cross the channel. It is gregarious and, outside the breeding season, will often participate in communal roosts of hundreds of birds in trees, city buildings and commercial greenhouses. Whereas the pied used to be common around farm yards, the changes in farming techniques — cleaner yards, fewer livestock and the filling-in of many farmyard ponds — have reduced the insect population so that there is no longer a living for the birds and they have had to move to other habitats. This may in part account for the slow recovery of this species after the severe winter of 1963 and they are not as common as they used to be. The pied frequents the banks of rivers and streams as well as grasslands, particularly where there are cattle and they can be found in city centres and on the seashore. They breed in every county of Britain and Ireland.

Pied wagtails nest in a cavity or ledge on a building, bank, cliff or pile of stones, dry stone walls and banks of streams with hanging vegetation being particularly favoured locations. Breeding commences in mid–April and the nest built by the hen is made of twigs, moss, grass and leaves and is lined with hair, wool and feathers. The normal clutch is five greyish–white eggs with grey markings. Incubation is approximately thirteen days and the young fledge in a similar period. There are frequently two broods.

The pied wagtail feeds entirely on insects, especially winged insects of all sorts including small moths and also beetles.

Grey Wagtail *(Motacilla cinerea)*

Length 7 inches (17.75 cm), **weight** only a fraction of an oz (10 g).

This species is also a resident but in winter moves from hilly places to lower ground and some migrate. It is well distributed throughout Britain and Ireland except in the eastern counties where there are fewer suitable habitats.

The male is blue-grey on both head and mantle and the underparts are a brilliant yellow; the dark brown wings are tipped with white and there is a white stripe above and below the eye. In breeding condition the male has a black throat which is replaced by white in the winter.

The female has less brilliant yellow colouring and her throat is always white.

The grey wagtail is not gregarious and is usually seen alone or in pairs. It is primarily found along fast flowing, rocky upland streams and rivers, but is also found beside lowland streams especially where there are fast-flowing stretches. It is much more dependent on water than the pied wagtail.

A dainty and elegant bird, with a slender tail 3 inches (7.5 cm) long, the grey wagtails suffer badly in severe winters when the streams and rivers are frozen and on these occasions will often be found at sewage farms, water-cress beds and on the sea shore.

Breeding commences in late April or early May. The nest is cleverly concealed in a crevice in rocks, on a ledge or in a hole of the river bank with overhanging vegetation, almost always close to water. Roots, moss, leaves and grass are used to build the rather untidy nest which is lined with hair and occasionally a few feathers. Four or five stone-coloured eggs with brown mottling form the normal clutch. Incubation and fledging are each approximately thirteen days duration.

The grey wagtail feeds entirely on insects, mostly the flying varieties, especially those found near water such as flies, small beetles, and dragonfly nymphs.

Yellow Wagtail *(Motacilla flava flavissima)*

Length 6½ inches (16.5 cm), **weight** ¼ oz (7 g).

The yellow is a summer visitor and a member of a species complex which shows extensive geographical variation in head pattern and colour in the males. It arrives in April from West Africa and leaves again at the end of September.

The male has greenish-yellow on the top of his head and ear-coverts with vivid yellow chin, throat, sides of neck, eye stripe and underparts. The wings are blackish-brown with two whitish wing bars. The mantle is greenish yellow and the dark tail has white outer feathers. In autumn the male resembles the female who is much duller. The juvenile's throat is bordered by a kind of black bib.

The yellow wagtail is not nearly as common as it was at the beginning of the century and is now only locally distributed throughout England except Devon and Cornwall where it is only found in a few isolated places. It is almost entirely absent from Ireland and most of Scotland and the western coast of Wales. There is no apparent reason for its shrinking range.

The yellow wagtail is almost always associated with water but, whereas the grey wagtail favours the upland streams, the yellow wagtail prefers the damp water meadows and marshy fields along river valleys, sewage works, reservoirs, flooded gravel pits and waste ground. It perches freely on fences, bushes and trees and likes to follow the plough or mingle with cattle in the fields collecting insects which have been disturbed.

Breeding commences in mid–May. The nest is built on the ground, usually in a slight hollow sheltered by herbage and consists of grass and roots, lined with hair. Five greyish or pale brown eggs with yellowish–brown markings is the normal clutch. Incubation is approximately thirteen days and the young fledge in a similar period. Two broods are usual.

The yellow wagtail is entirely insectivorous and feeds on flies, small insects and larvae, beetles and sometimes caterpillars.

Aviary Breeding and Rearing

If one is attempting to breed wagtails in cages these must be of very generous proportions. All wagtails have a nuptial display on the wing and therefore the chances of breeding are much greater in an aviary. Although wagtails can be mixed in the same aviary with other birds such as finches, it is wiser to have only one pair of wagtails in any aviary. Ron McClusky reported that he had both grey and pied wagtails breeding in a range of aviaries which were all interconnected and had no trouble; this arrangement is not recommended especially where the space is limited. A planted aviary is naturally best, with plenty of suitable nesting places similar to those used by wild birds as described earlier.

Livefood in most forms is essential to bring the birds into condition and even more so for feeding the youngsters. A good nettle patch is most useful in this respect and it can also be sited in front of a dry rock wall to give privacy to the birds and encourage them to use the wall for nesting.

A heap of horse or cow manure will help to attract flies as will a pile of rotting fruit especially bananas. An elderberry bush is also useful. Aquatic insects are eaten in large quantities by wagtails and we must try to supply these. A good plan is to have an old bath or large tin in the aviary full of static water and rotting herbage which will produce a constant supply of food. Deep water can, however, be dangerous, so a wire tray should be fixed just below the surface of the water to prevent accidents. An even better arrangement can be made, if space permits, with a series of trays having a drip feed from one to another and if the first tray can be connected to a fresh water supply so much the better, but again beware of deep water — birds can be drowned. Ron McClusky reported that he used to fetch bucketfuls of water daily from a small river and pour these into a dish. The water contained minnows, water boatmen, dragon fly nymphs and a host of other aquatic insects which the wagtails used to rear their young and indeed other birds in the aviary also took to this livefood. To anyone who has a convenient stream close by, this is a most useful piece of advice.

Plenty of nesting material in the form of dried grass, roots and hair should be supplied and the birds should not be disturbed any more than is absolutely necessary to supply their needs.

In addition to the livefoods already mentioned wagtails should be fed on a good brand of fine insectile food together with maggots, mealworms, stick insects and moths. All birds, and especially softbills, must bathe every day, sometimes several times in the day. It is therefore essential that a good supply of clean water for drinking and bathing be supplied fresh daily.

Exhibition

An exhibition pied wagtail must have a nice clean cut cone shape with well defined black and white colours, good quality feather and nice size.

The yellow wagtail should also have clean cone shape with olive yellow back, pure yellow breast shading off to a light yellow, good size and quality in the feather.

The grey wagtail should be a dainty but clean cut cone shape with a jaunty action: good blue grey back and lemon breast shading and have quality of feather.

Contributions by: A.T. Worrall; Ron McClusky.

Figure 9.7 Yellow Wagtail (top) and Grey Wagtail

WHEATEAR *(Oenanthe Oenanthe)*
Order: *Passeriformes*
Family: *Turdidae* (Thrushes)

Length 5¾ inches (14.5 cm), **weight** approximately ½ oz (14 g).
Male: (in summer) has a blue grey back with white rump and black wings, white tail coverts and a prominent white eye stripe above the eye and over a black patch on the side of his face. Underparts are various shades of buff. In winter the cock resembles the hen. The white rump on both birds being very noticeable.
Female: much less colourful with sandy brown back, mask and wings and light buff below.
Juveniles: resemble the female but are spotted on the body.

Characteristics

The wheatear is a short, dumpy little bird with a stubby tail and looks rather larger than its weight suggests. It is a summer migrant visiting these Islands to breed. Being one of the earliest arrivals, generally early March, it is well distributed throughout the north of England, the whole of Scotland and Wales and western Ireland; elsewhere it is rather local. At one time common in south England, its decline in these areas is attributed to lack of suitable habitat, generally due to the reduction in sheep farming which kept the grass on the downs short.

A bird of the heathers and downlands it is also at home on the more remote uplands — almost anywhere that the grazing of sheep or rabbits keeps the grass short. This seems to be essential to the species, so coastal cliff tops are also used since winds and temperatures keep grass growth to a minimum.

A restless bird, the wheatear is constantly on the move, flitting from stone to stone or tussock to tussock, bobbing and bowing with spreading tail. Essentially a ground bird it perches on walls and fences but very rarely on trees. It roosts in holes among the rocks or low vegetation and sings with great vigour while standing on a stone, fence or wall and sometimes from the ground. While the hen is sitting the cock will take up a position opposite the nest to sing and to wait for her to leave the nest when he joins with her to feed.

Wheatears nest in holes in the ground, in crevices in stone walls or rocks and in sheltered nooks of all kinds — rabbit holes are frequently used. The nest is built mostly by the hen and made of grass and moss lined with fur, feathers and hair. Six pale blue eggs is the usual clutch which are incubated for fourteen days mostly by the female, but the cock sometimes takes short spells. The young fledge in about sixteen days and there are frequently two broods.

Insects of all kinds and especially beetles are their main food.

After our migrant wheatear has come and settled down in his territory a second migration arrives. These birds are, however, the Greenland wheatear which is a larger species and much paler. The Greenlands stop only to rest and pass right through the British Isles on their journey north.

111

Aviary Breeding and Rearing

Because it winters in tropical Africa the wheatear must be kept inside during our winter months and a minimum temperature of 50°F (10°C) should always be maintained. They settle down well in a roomy cage or small indoor flight.

It is a highly territorial bird and great care has to be taken when introducing them into an aviary. Generally it is better to delay this until April depending on the weather conditions. On no account should there be any other wheatears or other birds which will compete for food supplies and the hen should be separated from the cock with wire netting. Being ground birds a pair or two of finches can be included, provided that the aviary is of sufficient size. There must also be provision for the young birds which should be removed from the parent's aviary as soon as they are fully self-supporting, especially the first brood.

As short grass seems to be so important, a patch of grass should be included with large stones dotted about to simulate their natural surroundings. A dry stone wall can easily be built from rockery stones allowing suitable crevices for nesting. This should be sited so as to be protected from the prevailing wind and rain. If necessary, build a bank of earth behind it. 4 inch (10 cm) field drainpipes can be used to simulate rabbit holes. These should be fixed into a bank of earth forming a small chamber inside with bricks. With grass growing over the top and a tuft of grass to hide the entrance, it will make an ideal nesting place. The drainpipe should slope slightly downwards from the nesting chamber to prevent rain from running into the nest. A patch of nettles and a pile of cow or horse manure will all help to provide a natural supply of live food.

When the cock is seen displaying to the hen through the wire and she appears to be responding the separating wire can be removed, but keep a careful watch for a day or two to see that all is well. Moss and hay, together with small feathers, fur and hair should be provided and the birds left alone with as little interference as possible.

Feed the birds on a small grade insectile food with grated cheese, cooked ox heart and liver which has been minced with a little finely chopped greenfood: spinach and dandelion leaves are very useful. A daily ration of mealworms and maggot's chrysalis must also be given. While breeding, insects of all sorts including green caterpillars, must be provided in increasing quantities for the rearing of the young. Clean water for drinking and bathing must be provided daily.

Ringing may be a problem because of the difficulty of getting to the nest but if it is intended to use closed rings they should be put on at six to seven days old. If the nest cannot be reached, the young can be ringed with the Council's split rings when fledged.

Exhibition

An exhibition wheatear has a bold upright appearance with as bright colour as possible on the breast: plenty of blue on the head and down the back towards the rump, with good darkness on the wings, nice white rump and clear black ear patch.

Contributions by: Rob Taylor.

NUTHATCH *(Sitta Europaea)*
Order: *Passeriformes*
Family: *Sittidae* (Nuthatches)

Length 5½ inches (14 cm), **weight** 1 oz (28.35 g).

The nuthatch is an unusually shaped bird with a plump, short tailed body which is easily recognised, though not so often seen. It has greyish-blue upperparts with buff underparts and the flanks are tinged with a rich chestnut. There is a dark line running through its eye extending towards its neck with white cheeks and throat. The sexes are alike, but the juveniles are duller and lack the chestnut colouring.

Distribution

The nuthatch is well distributed, though somewhat sparsely, throughout the southern half of England except in Lincolnshire and the fenlands where there is a scarcity of woodland. It is also resident in Yorkshire but not in the industrial belt. Prior to the nineteenth century it was much more widespread but disappeared from the northern parts of England at which time they also left the inner London parks. It has been suggested that increased atmospheric pollution might have been the cause. Since 1940 it has spread throughout Wales, Cheshire, Lancashire, Durham and Northumberland.

The nuthatch never flys far and prefers to stay close to trees. It climbs with short jerky movements along the tree trunk and, although it never uses its tail like other climbing birds, it can move with equal agility — upwards, sideways or head downwards. It is the only bird which habitually descends trees head downwards. The nuthatch is a resident, very sedentary and not gregarious.

Woods, parks and hedgerows with scattered mature trees and even large gardens are favourite places but the nuthatch most often occurs in mature woodland, both deciduous and mixed, especially where there are beech, oak and sweet chestnut. Apart from the food it finds on the bark of the trees it also eats hard foods such as chestnuts, beech masts and hazel nuts by inserting them into crevices in bark and hammering them with its bill to open them. It is this habit which has given it its name. It usually roosts in a hole in a tree.

Breeding

Breeding commences in late April and is usually in a hole high up a tree at a height of anything from 10 to 30 feet (3 m to 10 m). The hole is plastered with mud, reducing the size of the entrance so that the nuthatch can just pass through. The hole is then lined with bark fibres and dead leaves. Sometimes quite large quantities of mud are used. Seven to ten eggs is the average clutch. These are white, spotted with reddish-brown. Incubation is approximately sixteen days and the young fledge at three weeks old. There is only one brood.

Feeding

The young are fed entirely on insects, caterpillars, beetles, earwigs and flying insects.

Aviary Breeding and Rearing

The nuthatch requires an aviary similar to the tree creeper with bark nailed on the sides — rough bark, if possible, since the nuthatch needs to be able to wedge nuts into it. Feed on a good, fine grade insectile food in the winter with a few mealworms each day, together with beech masts, hazel nuts, walnuts, acorns and chestnuts. Good supplies can be gathered in the autumn and stored to last through the bad weather. In the spring the livefood must be considerably increased with gentles, caterpillars and anything else that can be obtained. When young are in the nest the supplies of livefood must be unlimited.

The nuthatch will take readily to a nest box provided that it has a large hole which they can plaster up. The box should be covered with bark and securely fixed so that it does not face south and is well protected from driving rain. A small dish of sloppy mud must also be provided as well as fresh water for drinking and bathing.

Exhibition

An exhibition nuthatch should be as large and stout as possible. With good air force blue and rich chestnut colour extending from the throat well down under the legs and on the flanks. It should have a good sized cage well lined with bark so that the bird can show itself well.

Contributions by: Rob Taylor.

Figure 9.8   Nuthatch

MISTLE THRUSH AND SONG THRUSH
Order: *Passeriformes*
Family: *Turdidae* (Thrushes)

These two birds are very much alike in many ways and are therefore included together in the same chapter.

Mistle thrush *(Turdus viscivorus)*
Length 10½ inches (26.5 cm), **weight** 5 oz (141.75 g).

The sexes are alike, grey-brown above, very pale beneath with round chestnut spots and white outer tail feathers. The mistle thrush is distinguished from the song thrush by its larger size, bolder spots and the white tail feathers seen when flying.

Song thrush *(Turdus philomelos)*
Length 9 inches (22.75 cm), **weight** 3 oz (85 g).

Again the sexes are alike — brown above, breast buff with slight reddish tinge on the breast and flanks; the breast is covered with dark brown spots. The golden brown underwing can be seen in flight although this is not always easy. It is distinguished from the mistle thrush by its smaller size, warmer brown plumage and lack of white tail feathers.

Distribution

Both species are resident although there is some movement to and from the continent in the autumn, and in severe weather there is a general south westerly movement.

Both species are well distributed throughout the British Isles except for the Orkneys and Shetlands, although the mistle thrush is rather more sparsely distributed, requiring a rather large breeding territory. Formerly the mistle thrush was restricted to the south and west, but has been increasing its range and numbers throughout the century. The song thrush, on the other hand, has declined in numbers. Both species suffer badly in severe winters and this has been attributed as the main cause of the reduction in the numbers of song thrushes although its competition with the blackbird must also have had some effect.

The song thrush is a beautiful singer and can be distinguished from the mistle thrush and blackbird by its habit of constantly repeating its notes. The mistle thrush has a wilder song which gives rise to its other name 'stormcock' — due to its habit of singing from the top of a tall tree in the teeth of a March gale. The mistle thrush is best heard in the first three months of the year. After that it gradually reduces its singing whereas the song thrush will continue singing throughout the summer.

Mistle thrushes are birds of woodland edge and open country with scattered trees and bushes and are found in farmland, large suburban parks and gardens and like to feed on lawns and grassland. Song thrushes breed anywhere with trees and bushes, woodland edges, farms, hedgerows, bushy commons, suburban gardens and parks, but are not found in bare moorland or mountain habitats. The song thrush is generally sedentary, but in autumn the mistle thrush is found roaming over moorlands and wild open country in small flocks or family parties.

Breeding

The mistle thrush is a very early nester commencing in February before the leaves appear on the trees if the weather is not too severe. There are normally two broods and breeding is finished by June. It builds its nest high up in the fork of a tall tree. The nest is made of bents, roots and moss lined with dry grasses and often decorated with wool and feathers. At this time the parents become very pugnacious and will fiercely drive off any intruder near their nest — especially predators — as well as animals and even man.

The song thrush commences nesting in April. Two or three broods are reared in a season. Hedgerows, bushes, trees, wall ivy and sometimes buildings are favourite places, always less than 6 feet (2 m) above, but not on, the ground. The somewhat bulky nest is made of grasses, roots, leaves and moss which are solidified with mud mixed with bits of wood and horse dung.

The four bright blue eggs with small black spots of the song thrush are well known, but the greenish–blue eggs blotched with brown and violet markings of the mistle thrush are not so often seen. In both cases incubation is generally fourteen days and the young fledge in a similar period.

Feeding

There are considerable similarities in the diets of these two species. Worms form a most important food during the early part of the year and during the breeding season. These, together with beetles, weevils, wireworms, caterpillars, craneflies and spiders, are the main foods fed to the young, the proportion of caterpillars being higher than generally appreciated. Snails and slugs are also taken when other foods are short, but the slugs are always wiped on the ground to get rid of the slime before being fed to the young. The song thrush is adept at smashing the snails' shells by banging them on a stone but the mistle thrush will only take the smaller snails. In autumn and winter both species turn to wild fruits and berries and will also take soft garden fruits — yew, holly, haw, ivy and elder being great favourites.

Aviary Breeding and Rearing

Aviaries need to be lengthy rather than wide, but should be large enough to be able to enter in comfort when tending to the stock: 10 feet (3 m) long × 4 feet (1.5 m) wide × 6 feet (2 m) high is a convenient size. If the aviary is planted with some privet and honeysuckle it provides a superb garden decoration especially if the aviary is constructed with rustic wood. It is best to plant at the far end and cover the top with boards, but leave the sides open. Thrushes prefer the wind and rain across the nest. After the nest has been built a slight cover on the cross wind side will be an advantage. Natural branches only are needed at the front end so that the birds are able to make a direct flight from front to rear. The floor covering should be soil and peat, with plenty of nettles and grass to give floor cover during the spring and summer when the young leave the nest. Water should be provided in a shallow dish in the middle of the

116

aviary so that it will not get fouled with droppings. Thrushes like to bathe daily.

Food is best served from the outside through a small serving hatch. This prevents disturbance in the aviary. Make sure that the dish containing the food is covered from the rain and the sun. A small box with a felt roof and a door on the outside attached to the aviary will do the trick. Thrushes seem to eat a large quantity of food and then rest so it is important that they are fed frequently. If they are only fed in the morning they have a long time to go before going to roost.

During the non–breeding season the birds will have to be kept separately otherwise fighting will occur. If kept in a large cage inside, plenty of length is the main point to consider. A good deep tray is needed, so that plenty of sawdust can be used as floor covering. If pressed down firmly it makes a solid base to absorb the droppings. Perches of natural branches are preferred to dowelling and they provide a firm foothold for the bird. Water is best provided in a clipper type fountain which is easily cleaned daily and does not get fouled up so easily. The bird should also be given an opportunity to bathe. Under these conditions thrushes will live up to seven years and sometimes longer.

Sexing thrushes is very difficult indeed and although it is sometimes said that there are differences in the markings, the best way is to listen for the cocks singing — they will start to sing at about six months old. The song is broken and out of tune at first but after the annual moult the song becomes more in sequence.

Breeding will commence during late February, early March. When put together the pair of song thrushes will bicker for a while but will not fight. Mistle thrushes may be a bit more troublesome but once they have settled down they will mate. The hen makes the nest using fine grass, rootlets, moss and thin twigs, the inside is lined with fine grass and mud. A mixture of soil, sawdust and water made sloppy must be provided in a small dish. About four days after the nest is finished the hen will commence to lay. The eggs are laid daily and incubation commences when the full clutch is laid and takes fourteen days.

Just before the eggs are due to hatch the hen will be observed to bathe regularly so it is important that the bath is kept full at this time.

Once the chicks hatch the pair will feed the young in turns or sometimes the cock will feed the hen and the chicks. Food must be plentiful at this stage and during the next four weeks. Ringing must be done at six to seven days old.

The hen will start another nest at the closing stages of rearing and possibly lay leaving the cock to carry on the task of feeding the first brood. Sometimes the hen will wait until the young have left the nest and use the same nest for the second round. There are nearly always two or three clutches. However, first year birds sometimes have clear eggs in the first round.

Once they have left the nest the young birds must be observed daily and should begin to feed themselves ten days after leaving the nest. As soon as they are self-supporting they should be removed from the aviary because the cock can become very aggressive towards them, especially the young males. If brought in at this stage, they can be trained in a stock cage and colour feeding can be commenced.

The basic food for thrushes is soaked chick crumbs, minced morsels or puppy biscuit (Viscan contains cod liver oil) to which should be added on alternate days grated cheese, hard boiled egg and raw minced beef. In addition livefood must also be supplied such as worms, maggots, beetles, bluebottles, mealworms (up to about twelve per day) crickets and ripe fruit such as apples and grapes. During rearing large quantities of livefood must be given, especially worms, although these should not be too large. Snails are also appreciated sometimes.

Instead of the chick crumbs or puppy biscuits a soft food can be supplied. This is a cake consisting of flour, sugar, eggs — plus the egg shells — mixed with peanuts, sultanas and cheese, all ground up and mixed with honey, Delrosa syrup and beef dripping, all mixed together finely and dried off with soya flour and P.Y.M.

Exhibition

Thrushes should be exhibited in a roomy black cage with white interior; moss or peat provides an excellent floor covering. Thrushes are never shown in pairs — always single cock or hen as they can prove quite vicious if confined together in a small cage. Condition, size and large spots are the major points when showing. The feet must be clean and all toe nails present. One of the biggest problems with the thrush family is that they have delicate toe nails and if the nail receives a slight knock it can result in the nail coming out. Plenty of daily bathing can help to keep a thrush in good condition and a shallow bowl should be put in the cage each day.

Contributions by: Eric Peake; Judith Domin.

Figure 9.9 Mistle Thrush

REDWING AND FIELDFARE
Order: *Passeriformes*
Family: *Turdidae* (Thrushes)

Redwing *(Turdus musicus)*
Length $8\frac{1}{4}$ inches (21 cm), **weight** $2\frac{1}{2}$ oz (70.87 g).
  Both the male and female are olive brown above with white eye stripe, much paler below with spotted neck, breast and flanks. Chestnut flanks and underwing.

Fieldfare *(Turdus pilaris)*
Length 10 inches (25.25 cm), **weight** 4 oz (113.4 g).
  The male and female both have a bluish-grey head and rump and a golden brown mantle: a rich chestnut breast spotted in black with light-buff underparts heavily speckled with black. Undercover wing covers are white and a blackish tail. In summer the male has an all-yellow beak and the females beak is yellow with brown on the upper mandible. In winter the females upperparts are browner and the mantle paler, the blotches on the flanks are browner and the throat and breast less rich.

Distribution

  Both these species live in the same regions mainly Norway, Sweden, Russia, Siberia and Germany and both come here as winter visitors. They may be described as the northern song thrush and the northern mistle thrush. Both appear to be extending their range into Britain and the redwing has been breeding in the north of Scotland in small numbers for the last fifty years. Fieldfares on the other hand have only been reported breeding in Britain in the last ten years, though over a rather more scattered area than the redwings. In England there are recordings of breeding in Derbyshire and Staffordshire. Both species are normally gregarious and in winter can be seen in open pastures, farmlands and woodlands especially where there are berry-bearing trees which form a large part of their winter food. Hard winters often drive the birds into city parks and gardens. Both species wander about in flocks often in company with each other. They roost together, mostly on the ground, among the bushes and vegetation, in furrows of ploughed fields and similar places.
  The redwing is a bird of the birch woods and scrubland, whereas the fieldfare is more a bird of park lands and city gardens. Neither has the singing ability of our native birds though the redwing has a pleasant but rather restricted song. Fieldfares, like the mistle thrush, are very aggressive during the breeding season.

Breeding

  The fieldfare's nest is in many ways similar to the blackbird's, being constructed of grass and mud with a grass lining and the eggs are very similar too. Four to five eggs is the normal clutch with both species. Incubation is fourteen days and the young fledge in a further fourteen days. There are usually two broods. Their main foods in the breeding season are worms, caterpillars, beetles and their larvae, leatherjackets, other insects and occasionally snails. In the winter wild fruits and berries in addition to worms and the like.

Aviary Keeping

In aviaries both these species require exactly the same treatment as the mistle thrush and song thrush as already described in the previous chapter.

Exhibition

For exhibition the redwing should be slightly smaller than the song thrush and have a good rich colour with more striations than spots, a warm buff breast, clear buff eye-stripe and a dark brown back and rufous red under the wings.

A fieldfare should be bold and strong with pale grey head and rump and chestnut back: rusty yellow throat and breast which are streaked with black and mottled flanks.

Contributions by: Rob Taylor.

Figure 9.10   Ring Ouzel

BLACKBIRD AND RING OUZEL
Order: *Passeriformes*
Family: *Turdidae* (Thrushes)

Blackbird *(Turdus merula)*
Length 10 inches (25.25 cm), **weight** 4 oz (113.4 g).

The male blackbird, with his jet black plumage and bright orange bill, is so well known that it needs no description. The female has a dark brown mantle, wings and tail with lighter and rather rufous–brown underparts with indistinct mottled markings on the breast and a blackish beak. Juveniles are browner and more mottled than the hen.

Ring Ouzel *(Turdus torquatus)*
Length 9½ inches (24 cm), **weight** 4 oz (113.4 g).

The male ring ouzel is very like the male blackbird except that he has a conspicuous white crescent patch on the breast and his wings are much paler. The female is browner, the light wings are more conspicuous and her white crescent is rather indistinct. Juveniles are very like young blackbirds and do not have the white crescent.

Distribution

The blackbird is found throughout the whole of the British Isles except on mountains and moorland and have been increasing and extending their range throughout this century. They are now far more common than the song thrush which it seems to some extent to have pushed out. There is at any rate a considerable overlap in habitat and feeding habits in these two species. Originally a bird of woodland edge the blackbird has been extremely successful in colonising farmland, hedgerows, parks, suburban and urban areas, in spite of the fact that they suffer heavy predation from cats and a heavy toll on the roads. Although generally blackbirds are sedentary and can be seen in our gardens throughout the winter, there is some movement southwards from the north in severe weather. Our native population is also augmented in the autumn by continental birds, many of which winter in Britain. The blackbird is not gregarious and can usually be seen in pairs. They are said to mate for life. It must surely be our finest songster with its rich flute–like song which is easily distinguished from the song thrush by the fact that it does not repeat its notes.

The ring ouzel is a bird of mountain and moorland and, being very wary, is not often seen. It is the mountain blackbird and takes over on the higher ground where the blackbird does not penetrate. Even so, in more recent years the blackbird has started to colonise the lower parts of the ring ouzel's range and one wonders how long it will be before the ring ouzel is pushed out altogether. There is clearly a good case for building up stocks in aviaries before this species becomes endangered. Ring ouzels are well but sparsely distributed throughout the high grounds of Scotland and Wales as well as the Pennines, Dartmoor and Exmoor. In Ireland there are isolated pockets on the

121

north west and south east coastlines.

Ring ouzels have a rather disjointed song and penetrating whistle which can be heard over long distances and they do not compare with the blackbird as songsters. They are summer visitors only arriving in mid–March and April after having spent the winter in south Europe and North Africa.

Breeding

The blackbird's breeding season begins in March, sometimes earlier in mild winters, and bushes, hedges, wall ivy, gardens, parks and even buildings are favourite places. The nest is rarely more than 5 feet (1.5 m) from the ground. Three and sometimes four broods are reared in a season. The nest is a bulky cup of stems, grass and moss, plastered with mud and an inner lining of grass. Four greenish eggs with dark markings are the usual clutch which is incubated for fourteen days: the young fledge in a similar period. The young are fed mainly on worms with caterpillars, beetles, spiders and other insects which are obtained by turning over dry leaves. They will also take fruit, especially in dry weather.

The ring ouzel, being a migrant, commences nesting rather later than the blackbird and the first nests are usually built towards the end of April. They are generally well concealed in clumps of heather in wooded valley or rocky ravine, sometimes on a ledge of rock. Usually on or close to the ground, nests are somewhat untidy and made of heather, bracken and grass. Four greenish blue eggs with dark markings rather similar to those of the blackbird, form the usual clutch. Incubation is fourteen days and the young being fed on similar foods to the blackbird also fledge in fourteen days. There are usually two broods in a season.

Aviary Breeding and Rearing

Blackbirds and ring ouzels are easy to look after in aviaries and cages and should be treated in exactly the same way as described for the mistle and song thrush.

Exhibition

An exhibition blackbird must be bold with a rich glossy black colour and rich crocus yellow beak and eye cere and be of good clean feather.

The ring ouzel should look bold and fearless, with good eyes, beak, legs and feet: a good clear whitish gorget, with whitish tips to the lacings on the belly and back. The hen is similar but of a browny black and with a faded gorget.

STARLING *(Sturnus vulgaris)*

Order: *Passeriformes*
Family: *Sturnidae* (Starlings)

Length 8½ inches (21.5 cm), **weight** 3½ oz (99.25 g).

The male and female starlings are alike with variations in the plumage at different times of the year. This bird is so well known that it needs no description but, seen at close quarters in the summer sunshine, it is most beautiful with variegated iridescent colourings of brown, purple, blue and green. In the winter the adults are duller and the juveniles are a smokey brown.

Distribution

Starlings are well distributed throughout the whole of the British Isles except in the more exposed highlands of Scotland. They have colonised all kinds of habitat and will nest almost anywhere if there is a hole large enough to accommodate it.

Few people realise that the starling was not always so common as it is today. About 1800 the starling was confined to little more than the south of England: at around 1830 it began to expand and colonise the north of England and later Wales and Scotland. West Cork in Ireland was reached in the 1930s but some parts of Ireland were not reached until the 1960s. This expansion is probably still continuing. Although changes in agricultural activity have had some bearing on their expansion of range it is felt that climatic conditions have also played a considerable part.

The starling was once an entirely migratory bird and even now great numbers arrive from the continent each autumn to winter here. The birds' habit of roosting in vast numbers on buildings and trees in the centres of cities has created difficult problems and nuisances which many authorities have tried in vain to remove. The damage they do is considerable.

Springtime sees the birds, still in flocks though much reduced in number, chasing each other round possible nesting sites in trees, on buildings, in wall ivy, haystacks, nesting boxes, cracks and crevices in cliffs, quarries — even woodpeckers' nests. The starling is a good singer and a great mimic: it will imitate other birds' song as well as many local noises such as dogs and cats.

Breeding

A rather untidy nest, made of straw and hay, lined with hair and wool or anything soft, is usually built in April. Five pale blue eggs is the normal clutch and both parents brood. The incubation period is approximately thirteen days, but the young do not fledge until nearly twenty days old. Generally they are single brooded but if anything should happen to the first nest they will usually try again. For a time the family stick together, eventually joining into larger flocks as winter approaches.

Feeding

Starlings are voracious feeders, always on the move. They consume large quantities of leatherjackets, worms, spiders, snails, slugs and other insects but in the autumn they also eat fruit and berries, as well as roots and seeds.

Aviary Breeding and Rearing

Starlings are an easy species to keep in aviaries and cages though being such active birds need plenty of room. It is important to give thought to cleaning because being heavy feeders they produce copious droppings which are rather loose. Apart from this they are not fussy and almost any accommodation can be used. Any nest box or crevice will serve for nesting, provided that it is large enough for the birds to enter.

Basic food is puppy biscuit (preferably one containing cod liver oil), grated cheese and hard boiled egg or raw minced beef for a change, together with available livefood daily. Maggots, worms, beetles, spiders, crickets and such. Mealworms should be limited to about twelve per day. Fruit — apples, grapes and berries — when in season is acceptable. When young are in the nest the livefood will have to be considerably increased and the use of a home made softfood will also assist. This can be made from flour, sugar, eggs — together with the eggshells — mixed with peanuts, sultanas and cheese all ground up finely and mixed with beef dripping, then dried off with soya flour until of a cake–like consistency. P.Y.M. can also be added.

Starlings must have a plentiful supply of clean fresh water every day for drinking and frequent baths.

As the sexes are so much alike the main difficulty will be in obtaining a true pair. While the cocks are usually slightly larger and brighter than the hens, the best way to sex starlings is to watch for the cocks singing.

Exhibition

For exhibition a starling should be as large and as bold as possible with a nice sharp featured head, heavily spangled with a metallic hue.

Contributions by: Judith Domin, Rob Taylor.

WAXWING *(Bombycilla garrulus)*

Order: *Passeriformes*
Family: *Bombycillidae* (Waxwings)

Length 7 inches (17.75 cm), **weight** 2 oz (56.7 g).

The waxwing is a beautiful bird. Both sexes are alike having a general colour of soft buffish-brown, much darker on the mantle and much paler on the underparts, a prominent chestnut crest and black throat. The lower back and rump are grey. Yellow, white and waxy red markings on the wings give it its name. The dark tail has a bright yellow tip. From the forehead a black stripe runs to behind the eye. It has the build and size of a starling. Juveniles are duller with shorter crests and no black on the throat.

Characteristics

The waxwing is a winter visitor to the British Isles and does not breed here in the wild. It inhabits the conifers and mixed woods in the coldest and most northern parts of Europe and Asia. In October the birds move south to central Europe and in severe winters or after a good breeding season some come further west as far as the British Isles. The numbers reaching this country vary considerably from year to year. They usually congregate in flocks and may be seen in tree-lined avenues and in parks and gardens.

In the winter waxwings feed on berries and will take rowan, cotoneaster, pyracantha, viburnum, juniper and hips and haws. Like the starling they have voracious appetites and spend most of the day hunting for food. These birds are inquisitive and quite fearless by nature and may be approached closely without taking wing.

Leaving in March the waxwing breeds in the Arctic summer, that is, in June and July. They build a cup-shaped nest of twigs and moss on the branches of the trees. The normal clutch is four eggs which are greyish-white with light and dark spots all over. Incubation is fourteen days. The young fledge at seventeen days. The nestlings are fed entirely on insects and larvae. After nesting the birds join together into large flocks.

Waxwings also occur in North America where they are known as the bohemian waxwing, sometimes referred to as the bohemian chatterer but the name is a misnomer as the species is almost silent, having only a weak call note.

Aviary breeding and rearing

Waxwings are more for the experienced aviculturist. When only one or two birds are kept they tend to be rather inactive and are prone to obesity. Ideally they should be kept as a small colony of say five to seven birds in an aviary about 20 × 10 × 7 × or 8 feet (6 m × 3 m × 2.5 m) high. A small colony of waxwings is a hive of activity. The birds are continually on the move calling to one another with a trilling call rather like a ringing of bells.

In the breeding season the cocks continually display to the hens, often carrying a morsel of food which is offered to the hen usually prior to mating taking place. Cocks tend to be slimmer built than hens and raise their crest much more frequently: the waxwings are more developed in cock birds.

Waxwings will nest in large trays, approximately 9 inches (23 cm) square and 3 inches (7.5 cm) deep, or similar nesting sites, secured high in the aviary. For nesting the birds should be supplied with fine twigs, roots, coconut fibre and fine grasses.

The diet should consist of a good coarse grade insectile food plus turkey pellets and dried or soaked currants, chopped sultanas, diced fruit such as apple, together with a varied supply of berries in season and livefood such as blowfly chrysalis, mealworms, wasp grubs and the like. The livefood must be fed ad lib during the rearing period. These birds are great bathers and it is essential that a good bath is always available.

Exhibition

For exhibition the waxwing should be as large as possible and of good colour. The feather must be perfect including a full set of developed waxwings.

Contributions by: Bob Partridge.

Figure 9.11   Waxwing

CHOUGH, JACKDAW, JAY, MAGPIE
Order: *Passeriformes*
Family: *Corvidae* (Crows)

These four members of the crow family have many similarities and require almost similar management and for this reason they are included in the same chapter.

Chough *(Pyrrochorax pyrrhocorax)*
Length 16 inches (40.5 cm), **weight** 13 oz (368.5 g).

The male and female of this gentle and delightful bird are alike, having black plumage with a green and blue sheen, a long curved red bill and red legs. Juveniles have an orange bill.

The chough formerly had a much wider range than at present which included the east coast of Scotland, Yorkshire, cliffs of Sussex, the Isle of Wight, Dorset, Devon, Cornwall, Wales and the coasts of Ireland. During this century there has been a continual decline in numbers and range and it seems that a long run of cold winters has badly affected this species. This was especially noticeable in the severe winter of 1962–63. Nowadays the chough is confined to Skye and Mull, the Isle of Man, Wales — particularly the coast, but also inland in quarries — and the north, west, and southern coasts of Ireland. There are very few left in Cornwall and none in the rest of England and Scotland. Ireland is now its main stronghold where it appears to be holding its own.

Choughs nearly always nest in very high, inaccessible places on ledges in caves, or cavities and crevices on sea cliffs, quarries and such like. Breeding commences in April and the nest is a bulky pile of sticks, heather and gorse and is lined with hair, wool, grass and feathers. Four to five whitish–green eggs with dark markings form the usual clutch. Incubation is seventeen to eighteen days and the young fledge at about five weeks old although the parents continue to feed them for some time. Only one brood is reared each year.

The chough's main foods are insects and larvae, worms, spiders and small animals. In the breeding season they rely very largely on ants and their larvae, being well adapted to obtain these in areas where the turf is close–cropped. It follows that they do best where sheep and rabbits are continually grazing.

Although the pairs stay close together the chough is a sociable bird and feeds in flocks in the summer. These flocks include a fair proportion of young birds which, although they may have paired, are not actually breeding and they do not commence nesting until they are three years old.

Jackdaw *(Corvus monedula)*
Length 13½ inches (34.25 cm), **weight** 9 oz (255.15 g).

The jackdaw is at all times gregarious and both the male and female are alike having glossy black plumage with an overall blue tinge, but the nape and the back of its head are a contrasting silver-grey — the only black bird with this characteristic.

It is well distributed throughout the whole of the British Isles except the north-west of Scotland where it is rather local.

Jackdaws breed in a variety of habitats including woods, parkland, hedgerows, trees, sea cliffs, inland crags, quarries and town centres. They breed colonially, several pairs sometimes occupying the same tree or cliff face.

These birds spend a large part of their time feeding on grassland, often in company with rooks but, unlike the rooks, the jackdaws are surface feeders, taking larvae of moths, butterflies and flies as well as spiders. They will also take young birds and eggs, small animals and carrion, together with some grain and weed seeds. In the breeding season they depend largely on caterpillars obtained from oak and elm trees.

Breeding does not commence until the caterpillars are plentiful in late April. The nest is built with large quantities of sticks, wool, hair and rubbish and is sometimes built on top of old nests of other species. The usual clutch is four eggs which are bluer and less marked than other members of the crow family. Incubation is eighteen days and the young fledge at four to five weeks old. There is only one brood each season.

Jay *(Garrulus glandarius)*
Length 15 inches (38 cm), **weight** 7 oz (198.45 g).

Both male and female are similar in this beautiful bird. It has a brown-pink or wine coloured body with an erectable white crest having black streaks. Brilliant blue wing-coverts barred with black, a white rump which is especially conspicuous when flying and dark flights and tail with broad white bar on the wings.

The jay was formerly persecuted by landowners and gamekeepers because of its liking for young birds and eggs and this may, in part; account for its shy and wary habits and for the fact that it was formerly restricted in its range. Today, with far less persecution, the jay is expanding and is now well distributed in England, Wales and Ireland, wherever there are suitable woods and plantations but is still absent from some of the counties of south Scotland. It is also absent from the highlands and upland sites like the north Pennines. It is sedentary and secretive, liking thick cover and rarely strays far from trees. Although a restless bird, it is not easy to find or see; easily alarmed, it flies away at the first sign of danger. It is characteristic of the oak woods but also occurs in beech, chestnut and other woods, coppice, suburban parks and Scots pine and spruce plantations. The jays in Scotland and Ireland are considered a sub-species, though there is little visual difference.

Jays feed extensively on large insects, caterpillars, beetles and especially the winter moth. They also favour varius fruits and seeds including acorns, beech and hazel nuts, pine seeds and some grain. They will also take garden soft fruits as well as the eggs and young of gamebirds and song birds.

Breeding starts in April and the nest, though bulky, is always well concealed in thick cover and anything from 4 feet (1 m) to 30 feet (10 m) above the ground. Sticks and twigs are interlaced to form a deep bowl lined with rootlets and sometimes hair. The hen sits very tightly and only flies off when the tree is climbed.

The usual clutch is five greenish-brown eggs with delicate markings. Incubation is sixteen to seventeen days and the young fledge after three weeks but may not be fully on the wing until about twenty-five days old. There is only one brood each season.

Acorns are particularly important to jays as winter food.

Magpie *(Pica pica)*
Length 18 inches (45.75 cm) including 10 inches (25.25 cm) of tail, **weight** 8 oz (226.8 g).

Both male and female are alike having black with green and violet sheen on head, neck, breast and long tail: this contrasts with the pure white underparts and back — a most striking and beautiful bird.

The magpie is another bird which was extensively persecuted in game bird areas because of its fondness for young birds and eggs, but it has recovered considerably since the war and is now quite a common sight. It is now well distributed throughout England, Wales and Ireland and some parts of Scotland with notable exceptions in areas where there are no trees or hedges. Grassland with thick hedges and some trees, thickets and the outskirts of woods is the typical habitat although it has now penetrated into town parks and gardens.

The primary diet is insects, small mammals, carrion, cereals, fruits, berries and, during the breeding season, the young and eggs of other birds.

The magpie usually builds its nest in a tall tree but sometimes in thickets, overgrown hedges and thorn bushes. In woods the nests are usually located on the fringes and conifers are sometimes used. The bulky nest is often built in February but the eggs are not laid until the end of April and it is built of sticks strongly lined with mud and a layer of grass roots, usually with a dome which is often thorny. The usual clutch is six greenish eggs with dark markings and incubation is seventeen days. The young fledge in approximately three weeks but the parents continue to feed them for some time afterwards. There is only one brood each season.

Aviary Rearing and Breeding of Crows

Owing to their size and habits these four species all require larger than normal aviaries, a minimum of 12 feet (3.65 m) long is recommended. Height, too, is important and particularly in the case of the chough 8 feet (2.5 m) is the minimum — 12 feet (3.65 m) would be much better. There is insufficient space for them to breed in cages. They are noisy birds with harsh cries and may cause complaints from neighbours if located too near other habitations. However, for those who have the space and facilities, they are easy birds to look after and are well worth while. The main problem is the difficulty of ensuring that the birds are a true pair. The chough is on the decline in the wild and is a fully protected bird therefore it is all the more important that anyone who has the facilities should help to build up the stocks of aviary-bred choughs before they disappear from our countryside for ever. We should ensure that the species will be perpetuated for future generations to watch and admire.

All four species are comparatively long lived and it should not be too difficult to build up good strains if enough fanciers take them up. Both the jay and the magpie are excellent mimics and make interesting pets. For all the jay's natural shyness it soon gets to know the hand that feeds it and becomes quite tame with a little patience.

For breeding it should not be difficult, in a good sized aviary, to simulate the birds' natural surroundings: for the chough a small artificial cave, large enough for the birds to walk in, situated high up; for the jackdaw ledges like cliff or quarry faces or an old tree trunk with branches; for the jay, heavy cover with conifer branches used as screens, and strong lateral branches to hold the nest — and for the magpie, an old thorn tree.

Feeding is much the same for all of them. A good coarse grade of insectivorous food, mealworms, maggots, beetles, worms, raw minced beef or liver. Cheese, soaked dog biscuits such as Saval. Feed crickets when available and dead mice, dead birds and rabbits which can often be picked up on the roads. Some milk and raw eggs can be provided — especially for the magpies and jays and day-old chicks from hatcheries when available especially in the breeding season. They can also be given from time to time, cooked potatoes, cooked green vegetables as well as apple, orange, grapes and sultanas. Variety being the keynote, as it is unnatural for these birds to live on the same diet continually.

Exhibition

For exhibition the chough should have bright dark red beak and legs, a nicely curved and uncrossed beak, a good broad width of head and a lovely jet black colour, as deep as possible.

The jackdaw should be a good thick sturdy bird, having a stout beak and good compact wings and tail: jet black colour with nice blue eyes and clear silver grey nape and hood.

The jay should be a stout bird with good colour and chestnut tannings, carrying a clear crest on well defined head and plenty of coloured workings on the wings.

The magpie must be bold and fearless, as large as possible, with good bright blue–black colour and good clean white patches: jet black feet and bill with plenty of whiskers and a tail as perfect as possible.

Contributions by: Judith Domin; Rob Taylor.

CHAPTER 10

Mules and Hybrids
by Walter Lewis

Mules and hybrids although named in this way are, of course, all hybrids. Mule is the fancier's term for offspring raised from a canary and a British seedeater.

The hobby of mule breeding has been going on for possibly the best part of 100 years, perhaps even longer. In the first place these crosses were no doubt bred for their hardiness, longevity, and power of song. Later, the mule breeders became fanciers, and bred these birds for their beauty and eventually exhibited them. Many years ago there were numerous fanciers who concentrated on breeding light mules by using the most popular finch, the goldfinch. Other species of finch were used but the goldfinch was the favourite which produced these lovely hybrids.

Light Mules

The light mule which all fanciers hoped to produce was the clear, followed in order of merit by the evenly marked and the lightly marked. For many years now light mules have been extremely rare. It is surprising to note, however, that in 1899 no fewer than twenty eight light mules were exhibited at the National British Bird and Mule Clubs Show held in London. During the past forty-five years we have not seen more than perhaps half a dozen at a time in the adult classes and two or three in the unflighted class at our large National Shows.

Since 1945 a new light mule has appeared although, in a sense, it is not a normal light mule — the Lutino greenfinch mule produced by either a Lutino carrier greenfinch cock or a Lutino greenfinch cock. Mules produced in this way are always hens. Like all Lutinos they are much smaller than the normal specimens, even when they are produced from the same type of Norwich hen that the standard dark mules are bred from.

The Lutino carrier cock is produced from a Lutino hen, or a Lutino greenfinch cock: these two cock finches will definitely produce Lutino mules if they can produce fertile eggs. Sometimes a carrier cock is produced by a carrier cock paired to a normal hen but only by trial can this be proved. Unfortunately, the cock greenfinch is not a reliable 'filler of eggs' when paired to a hen canary. From my own practical experience it is the least reliable of all the British finches as a mule breeder. If the greenfinch cock was as reliable as the goldfinch cock, I am sure we should see many Lutino mules.

The Lutino greenfinch × canary hybrid, although it often competes at our smaller exhibitions with light canary hybrids, is an entirely different hybrid from the normal light hybrid, its coloration deriving entirely from the Lutino greenfinch cock or carrier cock. Yellows and buffs occur in Lutino hybrids as well as the normal light canary hybrids but the yellows are much rarer than buff as is usual in all varieties and species of birds.

My thoughts on the breeding of normal light mules are that I consider that sometimes the canary is responsible and at other times the finch. Having talked to many old fanciers and read many old books on the subject, I believe that if any fancier possesses a canary hen which produced mules more light than dark, it should be used to produce young canaries which may carry this desirable factor. An author, writing years ago, said that he had never known a fancier who had produced a strain of canaries from scratch, to breed a single light mule. The successful fancier was the one who, by mere chance, had happened to own a hen which had produced a light mule. He then bred canaries from that hen which, in turn, passed on this desirable factor. I advise any enthusiast who possesses a canary hen which has produced a mule carrying more light feathers than dark, to use it and breed more canaries. Some years ago Mr Phillip John of Llanelli and Mr Grosvenor Ridgway of Shrewsbury, produced a number of light goldfinch mules which were the result of using a particular finch — a cheveral goldfinch cock, the bird with a white mark running through the under blaze. These two fanciers produced light mules from different hen canaries.

In Mr John's case, he bred from the same goldfinch cock for two seasons with the same results. Unfortunately Mr Ridgway's finch died before the next breeding season. Mr John and Mr Ridgway did not produce any more light mules after their finches had died. I think in their particular cases the goldfinch cock was the key to success.

Standard Dark Mules

I have concentrated on mule breeding for some years, and I have had a reasonable amount of success in producing good exhibition mules — but they have all been the standard dark specimens. Good exhibition mules are produced from the Norwich type canary and occasionally from crossbreds. I prefer the long barrel type Norwich which the Norwich fancier despises and have produced good mules from the Norwich × Yorkshire cross. Always use the yellow hens because these produce the most desirable mules, the Jongues and, in my opinion, the buff mules bred from these yellow hens are the best quality. Good mules are not easily bred but with luck they will live for many years. Some years ago I bred a siskin mule which had eight consecutive wins at the Hounslow All British Show and seven consecutive wins at the National Show when held at Olympia.

The best method of breeding mules, in my opinion, is to use large double breeding cages.

In the early spring I have my muling finches running with the canary hens. I very often change a canary's partner if I see the finch is unsociable or sometimes I change the hen canaries around. It is surprising how attached some finches become to their partners and this is an excellent sign that the pair will produce fertile eggs. You can, of course, use a good muling goldfinch with two or three hens but employ a little discretion if a canary hen does not take to the finch or, conversely, if the goldfinch appears not to accept the hen.

If squabbling takes place it may upset the goldfinch and could result in infertile eggs when being used with its favourite partner. I have come to the conclusion that the brightest and purest coloured mules, particularly goldie mules, are bred from clear or lightly marked hens. When trying for siskin mules it is always desirable to use the best type of canary you have. Please do not think you will produce good siskin mules from Border type hens. For some years we have seen very few Redpoll mules. If any fancier has a proven muling redpoll cock, run him with the best type *Norwich* hen you can spare.

In recent years **Twite mules** have become quite popular and I have been responsible, in a small way, for their appearance in increasing numbers having bred quite a number of good ones which has stimulated fanciers' interest. Always use the yellow Norwich hen for this cross — the larger the better, even if the hen's quality is not too good — the finch will have his influence in this direction, and put quality in the feather of the mules.

Linnet mules have always been bred in good numbers but, as in all mules, good ones are not easily bred. A really good Jongue linnet mule is a delightful bird. The linnet cock is a reliable muler once fit and if he does take to a canary hen he is most fertile and will fill every egg. The more linnet mules you breed — the more likely you are to produce good ones.

The **dark greenfinch mule** is not an easy mule to produce as I said previously. Most fanciers who try for this combination come to the conclusion that the most likely way to produce this cross is to mate a hen greenfinch to a canary cock. In this particular cross it is more important than ever to use the best Norwich type cock you have. Size, as in an exhibition greenfinch, is the most important point in an exhibition greenie mule.

Some years ago, the **crossbill × canary** was bred by Mr J. Dalrymple and what a wonderful bird it was. If any fancier possesses a nice kindly crossbill cock, this is a cross which should be tried. I consider that the crossbill × canary was the finest example of all the canary hybrids I have seen. The majority of mules bred do not come up to expectation even when you pair first rate specimens; if they did we should have many wonderful mules at our shows.

Methods of Mule Breeding

My method of mule breeding was the one adopted many years ago by Mr Ralph Pearce of Barnstaple. In the first instance run the finch with the canary hen during the early months of the year: towards late March or early April the canary will show signs of wanting to go to nest. When it is obvious that the canary hen is in breeding condition I run a cock canary with her leaving the finch in the double breeder. The cock canary does not usually concern itself with the finch's presence but, if squabbling does take place, you should remove the finch for the time being.

If all goes well the hen canary will go to nest and will produce young canaries in due course. I separate the finch when the hen canary is about to lay just leaving the cock canary with her. When she lays her clutch of eggs and settles down to incubate, after a few days I take the cock canary away. I then introduce the finch — but do separate them by a wire slide for safety reasons. As soon as the hen hatches her young canaries, I introduce the finch and I have found that the finch becomes interested in her and the young, sometimes helping to rear the young canaries. By this time, in early May, the finch could be ready for breeding but not always; it is a matter of experience in telling if the finch is ready and even experienced mule breeders can be mistaken. Generally mules are produced from late May onwards. If you can delay your muling as long as possible you are most likely to get results.

If canary hens were rather later in coming into breeding condition than they usually are I am sure we should be more successful in our mule breeding. What happens to so many fanciers who start mule breeding is that the first clutch, and very often the second clutch, is infertile. Half the season's eggs have been wasted. Run a cock canary with the hen first so that her breeding operations are delayed as far as mule breeding is concerned.

I realise, of course, that there are exceptions to every rule — some finches are ready very early and mules are produced in April and earlier but generally this is unlikely. Always separate the finch from the hen the night before you think she will lay. In the morning collect the egg, replace it with a dummy and re-introduce the finch so that he is running with her all day. When the hen canary has completed her clutch of eggs and starts to sit replace all her eggs and replace the dividing wire slide in the cage so that the finch sees his mate but cannot disturb her. When she hatches her young mules allow the finch freedom to take part in rearing them if he will. In any case he seldom does any harm and very often a lot of good by feeding the hen canary food which she in turn passes on to her young. When the young mules are a fortnight old, introduce a clean nest pan in to the cage — usually I place it in the other end of the cage. She will soon start nesting again. As soon as you see the young mules begin to pick up food remove them from the breeding cage into a nice large cage and provide them with plenty of soft food and water. Always colour feed your mules, starting with a little about early July.

Hybrid Types

Canary hybrids have been produced from the goldfinch, linnet, greenfinch, siskin, redpoll, twite, and the crossbill cock. Only one crossbill × canary has been bred and exhibited in this country so far.

The canary hybrid bred from the bullfinch is *always* produced from the bullfinch hen. Many canary hybrids bred from the greenfinch are bred from the hen of this species, but of course are also bred from the greenfinch cock. Practically all canary hybrids bred are dark specimens, their coloration being similar to their finch parent. Mismarked mules do also occur, however, with odd light feathers in the body, wings and tail.

The most popular seedeater hybrid is without doubt the **bullfinch hybrid**. Its coloration is so attractive and the quality of feather is good. The rarest bullfinch hybrid is the redpoll × bullfinch, followed by the canary × bullfinch, greenfinch, linnet, and goldfinch. These are the only bullfinch hybrids we have seen so far. The bullfinch cock has never produced a hybrid.

The greenfinch hen, also the cock, produce hybrids when paired to other species of seedeaters. The rarest hybrids the cock greenfinch has produced are the **grenfinch × crossbill**, and **greenfinch × brambling.** The **greenfinch × chaffinch** is also a rare hybrid and is difficult to breed. Usually an odd one or two appear each year and it is a popular hybrid usually doing well on the show bench. Many years ago it was considered by many fanciers to be impossible to breed.

The greenfinch hen has produced hybrids when mated to the siskin, redpoll, twite, goldfinch, linnet, and crossbill cocks. Hybrids are also produced from the matings of goldfinch × siskin, twite × siskin, goldfinch × redpoll, greenfinch × twite, and redpoll × siskin. Both sexes of the above will produce the above crosses and the linnet cock and hen will also produce hybrids with any of these species. Chaffinch and brambling hybrids are rare with the possible exception of the hybrid between the two species, although in recent years this hybrid has not been seen often.

As already mentioned, the greenfinch × chaffinch is now produced fairly often but not in any numbers. The **goldfinch × chaffinch** and **redpoll × chaffinch** have been bred — but are extremely rare and the examples we have seen have not been quite what we would expect. The redpoll × chaffinch were hens, and the goldfinch × chaffinches, if cocks were not as colourful as one would expect.

The **greenfinch × brambling** has been bred to my knowledge three times, each of the progeny I have seen being undoubtedly hens: we have seen one redpoll × brambling and that was a hen. Great possibilities are open to hybrid breeders to breed cocks of the above crosses. No hawfinch or bunting hybrids have to my knowledge been bred so far.

When attempting to breed the canary × bullfinch and canary × greenfinch, the use of a small aviary or flight may be more desirable but these hybrids are often bred in cages.

Breeding Conditions

British bird hybrids are usually bred in small aviaries, others in large cages. The average British seedeater does more readily go to nest in an aviary. The rearing of any hybrids is sometimes difficult: some pairs behave in a perfect way if supplied with all the natural food we can possibly gather whilst others, for various reasons, do not rear their young. Bullfinch hens are sometimes tricky. Many years ago the average hybrid breeder would never think of leaving a bullfinch hen to rear any hybrids she may have hatched. The bullfinch's eggs were usually transferred to a reliable canary hen if one was available. In recent years many bullfinch hybrids have been reared by the bullfinch hen. One most successful bullfinch hybrid breeder, Mr Syd Humphries of Northampton, is full of praise for the bullfinch hen as a parent.

Greenfinch and other true seedeaters usually make excellent parents if supplied with the right diet but, as with everything else, there is always the exception. Chaffinch and brambling hens make good parents if supplied with plenty of live food as extras to their usual seed diet.

The diet of canary hens rearing young hybrids is the same as if they were rearing canaries. The usual softfood should be provided, if possible, three times a day with the addition of seeding weeds and grasses such as chickweed and dandelion seeding heads and the like.

Rearing

When the young hybrids leave the nest they should not be removed from their parents until they are *eating well for themselves*. When weaned they should be provided with soft food and the usual seed mixture and natural food and a *shallow* dish of water so that they can bathe. Start colour feeding when the young hybrids are about six weeks old. The Ready Mixed Colour food plus *Carophyl* Red* is very good. I always add *Carophyl* Red* to the drinking water. Make the solution by dissolving a small teaspoonful of CR in a cup with boiling water, making half a cup of solution, stir it well and leave for fifteen minutes. Pour into a pint bottle and add water to fill. The mixture is now ready for use and a small quantity can be added to the drinker. Change the drinking water every other day. Always allow your young hybrids to bathe but remove the bathing water afterwards so that they drink the *Carophyl* Red solution. Colour feeding should be continued until the young hybrids have completed their moult and do not be in a hurry to discontinue.

Exhibition

The mule and hybrid section of the British Bird Fancy has always attracted enthusiasts who are interested in the exhibition side of our hobby. Many years ago fanciers who were wealthy travelled the length and breadth of the country when they heard a particularly good mule or hybrid was to appear on the show bench.

Good light canary mules were sought after and high prices were paid: these were the mules which usually took the major awards at our exhibitions eighty years ago — may we see these varieties again.

HYBRIDS KNOWN AND UNKNOWN

Canary Hybrids

Goldfinch Cock
Linnet Cock
Siskin Cock
Redpoll Cock   } **Canary Hen**
Twite Cock
Greenfinch Cock
Crossbill Cock

It is possible to breed canary hybrids from the hen of the above species with a canary cock. Only one crossbill × canary has been produced so far in this country to the best of my knowledge. A rare **Red Factor Canary Cock** × **Chaffinch Hybrid** has also been produced once. The canary cock has hybridised with the bullfinch hen, but not the bullfinch cock with the canary hen.

*Registered trade mark

Bullfinch Hybrids

Goldfinch Cock
Linnet Cock
Greenfinch Cock } Bullfinch Hen
Redpoll Cock
Canary Cock

Possible bullfinch hybrids yet to be produced are the siskin, twite, hawfinch, and crossbill cocks using the bullfinch hen.

Chaffinch Hybrids

Brambling Cock
Greenfinch Cock | Chaffinch Hen
Goldfinch Cock
Redpoll Cock

Possible chaffinch hybrids yet to be produced are the linnet, twite, siskin, canary, hawfinch and crossbill cocks, using the chaffinch hen. Only three goldfinch × chaffinch hybrids have been produced as far as is known. The redpoll × chaffinch has only been bred twice maybe three times.

The chaffinch cock has only been successful with the brambling hen, producing the well-known chaffinch × brambling hybrid.

Brambling Hyrids (known to have been bred and exhibited)

Chaffinch Cock
Greenfinch Cock | Brambling Hen
Redpoll Cock

The greenfinch × brambling has only been produced on two or three occasions and have been hens. No doubt a number have been hatched but have died before reaching maturity.

The redpoll × brambling has only been bred once — the breeder being Mr R. C. Tout. Possible brambling hybrids using the brambling hen, are: goldfinch, linnet, twite, siskin, canary, hawfinch and crossbill.

Greenfinch Hybrids

Goldfinch Cock
Redpoll Cock
Siskin Cock
Linnet Cock } Greenfinch Hen
Canary Cock
Twite Cock
Crossbill Cock

Possible greenfinch hybrids using the greenfinch hen are hawfinch and chaffinch and brambling and there is a possibility of the bunting family being used. I personally have not got a lot of faith in the last two cocks mentioned for crossing with true seedeaters.

Goldfinch, linnet, twite, redpoll and siskin of both sexes have all hybridised with each other.

The hawfinch cock and hen, the bunting family, have not yet produced hybrids, at any rate none which reach maturity and the show bench. I have heard reports of hawfinch hybrids hatching which, unfortunately died at an early age.

There is without a doubt great scope for the perservering fancier in the hybridising field. The hybrids which I should like to see and which I am surprised have not been produced yet are the siskin × bullfinch and the canary × chaffinch using the Norwich type canary. The crossbill cock is now a proven hybridiser and one crossbill canary has been produced. The chaffinch and brambling hens are also interesting subjects for hybridisation and could produce lovely hybrids especially if young could be produced from the canary cock.

Breeding Mules — An Old Method

Walter Lewis mentions in his notes that claims have been made that fanciers used to breed a special strain of canaries from which to breed clear or lightly marked mules. He says there used to be good numbers of light mules exhibited whereas there are only a few today. For those who wish to try it, this is what the old books say ....

A Strain of Canary Hens for Breeding Mules

The basic stock to form the strain was selected from Norwich type canaries with good shape, plenty of girth round the shoulders and chest, neatly coned off tail, with size and quality of feather. Yellow greens were considered ideal for the purpose of breeding good deep coloured, dark mules. It is said variegated yellows could be used, but clear yellow hens have a tendency to throw light feathers in the young. Green or heavily variegated buff hens can be used for breeding dark buff mules, but clear buffs rarely produce show specimens, most of the youngsters having light feathers on the neck and in the wings or tail.

For clear mules, clear canaries known as 'sib' hens were specially bred for the purpose in the following way; Norwich canaries, of the same type as for dark mules, being recommended.

First obtain some cinnamon variegated canaries or these can be bred from a cinnamon paired to clears. The variegated canaries are paired together and the young selected until you have at least two pairs of clears with pink eyes, that is to say, they are clear cinnamons — these then are the foundation stock.

Inbreeding is used to form two lines which are intercrossed in succeeding years. The yellows are especially valuable: two yellows paired together will produce some young canaries which are pale buff. These buffs are paired together but they should not be brother and sister. From these pairs some yellows will be obtained. The hens are the ones which will throw very light and clear yellow mules. They are the 'sib' hens. The cock yellows can be used to pair to buffs and so start another line.

Warning is given that double yellow pairings should not be used more than every other year otherwise size will be lost and the feathers eventually become wiry. Two buffs paired together will generally not produce any yellows unless they are themselves bred from double yellow pairs.

It takes at least five years to produce a strain of canaries which will consistently throw clear or lightly marked mules and considerable patience is required.

As the canaries needed are clear cinnamon birds with pink eyes the strain will be spoiled if crossed with normal canaries and they should be kept separate in the breeding room.

The explanation of the cinnamon and lutino inheritance in greenfinches in Chapter 4 may be found helpful in understanding this sex-linked character.

Figure 10.1   (from left) Greenfinch Canary, Redpoll Canary, and Linnet Canary

CHAPTER 11

Feeding

PART 1 — *by A.C. Wyatt*

Birds are divided into roughly two categories regarding their food requirements:
1. **Hardbills** — those which consume seeds of various kinds.
2. **Softbills** — those which eat mainly insects and fruit.

Hardbills, especially during the breeding season, will often partake of quite a substantial amount of insect fare for feeding their young ones. Softbills will in some cases eat a little seed which is not de-husked as in the case of hardbills, but is swallowed whole. Fresh fruit and greenfoods are sampled by almost all species.

Seed mixtures may be purchased to suit all requirements. They come under the headings of 'Canary mixture', 'British Finch', 'Foreign', for example. In an aviary of mixed birds these seeds may be all fed with advantage as it will be found that many birds will take seeds which are not in their normal mixture. In cages a little discretion may have to be used as, although variety is a good thing, some birds will gorge on the richer seeds such as hemp, resulting in over-fatness and maybe early death.

For rearing young birds soaked seed is essential. There are many methods of doing this, and my method is simply to place a quantity of seed in a bowl and cover it with water. Place the seed in a sieve under the cold tap about every twenty-hour hours and in warm weather it should be ready in two or three days having just started to sprout. The time varies of course according to the conditions. Begin another bowl of seed as you start to use the first one. You will find, by this method, that seed will be used in all stages of sprouting and will not smell or turn sour if fresh water is run through it occasionally. As with all things, trouble comes with neglect, but experience will show the amounts of seed needed for your requirements. Also used for rearing are canary rearing foods, hard-boiled egg and biscuit.

Collect wild plants such as chickweed, dandelion, sow-thistle and all others in season, along with various fruits and berries. Be certain that contamination has not occurred through spraying or fouling by dogs.

In the case of insectivorous (softbills) birds one's ingenuity may be put to the test, as a great variety of food may be bred or collected besides the branded foods on the market. These packet foods contain all the basic requirements for softbills, but, depending on the types of bird one is keeping these may be varied in many different ways. The egg-biscuit food, already described will be taken, also a little bread and milk occasionally. Add also a little grated cheese, minced meat, chopped fruit, such as apple, pear, grape or soaked currants and raisins. To these may be added the fruits of the hedgerow in season, blackberry, elderberry and hawthorn.

Greenfly and other small insects will be found on stinging nettles, and it is a good plan to have these growing in a well planted aviary. Plants may also be grown over the flights and these will attract much livefood. Rambler roses and kidney beans are especially good for this purpose while the honeysuckle makes a very valuable contribution by also adding its berries.

Livefoods which may be purchased, include mealworms and gentles (maggots) though the former must be used sparingly as they can cause trouble in young birds, which should be weaned off them as soon as possible after reaching independence, and thereafter fed as a tit-bit only. Softbills confined to cage life may also suffer from obesity caused by a surfeit of mealworms.

Gentles (maggots) obtainable from fishing tackle shops should be well cleaned in bran, or sawdust for a few days before feeding them to your birds to allow the putrid food to be passed through their bodies.

Figure 11.1   Gentle Pupae

Courtesy: Arthur Hissey

PART 2 — REARING YOUNG FINCHES

It is now more generally accepted that finches in their wild state rear their young in the early stages on insect life, and in some species up to ten days old, gradually weaning them onto half ripe milky seeds. The insects most commonly used are small flies such as greenfly, blackfly and gnats. Maggots and mealworms are not a good substitute for these insects. The small insects give the young birds a high animal protein diet, but as it is difficult to provide these in sufficient quantities substitutes have to be found. The best of these are hard boiled egg, milk and cheese (cheddar cheese being the best for our purposes). It is fairly easy to get the parents to take these foods, but difficult to persuade them to feed them to their young. Canaries can be used to help and birds reared in this way are more likely to rear their own young on these substitute foods, in time. Egg-biscuit food can be used, but it should always be mixed the night before which allows it to swell before being fed to the birds, otherwise there is a risk of the young birds being choked. Crumbled stale white bread with a hard boiled egg mixed into it is the easiest to prepare and is well liked by the birds. Grated cheese can be added to it. It is sufficiently moist on its own and it should not have any moisture added. Mixed in this way it will last all day without going sour. Milk can be given in the water pots but it should be diluted with at least equal parts of water. Alternatively a teaspoonful of dried milk per egg can be added and mixed' with the hard boiled egg and crumbed bread. A continuous supply of greenfood is essential, for most finches.

*Abidec** is a very useful vitamin supplement and is best supplied in the drinker. One drop to a jam jar full of water being quite sufficient. A weak mixture of *Nectar Paste** is helpful during rearing. Half a teaspoonful mixed in a jam jar full of warm water is the right quantity. The birds like the sweet taste and take it readily. Seed treated with cod liver oil can be given throughout the breeding season and the moult. If given as soon as the frosty weather is over it will help to bring the birds into good hard breeding condition quickly. The treated seed is not as hard as the dried seed and is more easily digested by young birds. Care should be taken with all supplements not to exceed the recommended dose, as in excess they can do more harm than good. P.Y.M. yeast and also mineral mixtures can be mixed with the seed in almost any quantities and are a great help.

Piles of manure and rotting fruit, especially bananas, in the aviary do help to attract the right type of insects and are a great help in rearing.

Carophyl Red* mixed in the drinking water so that the water is just pink can be supplied throughout the breeding season without any harmful effects, and will enable the birds to assimilate it in more natural small quantities which will bring out their natural colour when they moult. This will not be sufficient, however, to colour feed a bird for exhibition.

**Registered Trade Mark*

Mortality in Young Finches

The high mortality in young finches, especially greenfinches often worries breeders. This is generally more evident during the moulting period. There is now no doubt that the commonest cause of the trouble is inadequate feeding in the early stages of growth, but feeding after weaning is also very important. There is abundant evidence that birds reared on hard boiled egg, develop more quickly and are larger and stronger birds which breed more easily and live longer. It is necessary to include with this a constant supply of greenfood. Any greenfood can be used but grass is available anywhere at almost all times of the year. If this is provided in the form of turves the birds also seem to find a lot of goodness in the soil.

Birds in the wild never have to eat hard dried seed until the severe weather arrives when they are fully mature and well through the moult. They feed on the soft ripening seeds which are available in abundance, together with a good deal of greenfood. It follows that we should try to avoid hard seed. Many fanciers provide seed which has been soaked in cold water until it sprouts. This generally takes several days and the water has to be changed frequently. A better way is to boil the seed for a few minutes. It might be expected that this would kill the seed, but in fact it splits the case and sprouting follows, showing that a chemical change has taken place. The actual quantity required can quickly be prepared daily. After boiling the seed should be washed under a running tap.

Supplies of egg food and boiled or soaked seed should be provided when the birds have commenced to breed and kept up continuously until the heavy frosts start, together with unlimited greenfood and free access to maw seed. Unlimited supplies of hemp seed also seems to be essential for all young finches and is not fattening if it has been boiled.

Grits and cuttlefish are essential at all times as aids to digestion and for calcium requirements. Trace elements and minerals are also obtained from various foods and methods of feeding as will be noticed when birds are watched searching freshly dug earth. Hardbills will take their grit and cuttlefish as provided, and some softbills will peck at cuttlefish, a little of which may be scraped over their food occasionally.

Vitamin supplements are not normally required as, with a varied diet, these should be well covered. Water-soluble multivitamins are available which may be used in regular, small amounts for your birds, during the moult, for example. Mineral grit may also be purchased which contains most of the trace elements. Careful observation of your birds will soon tell you if anything is wrong with the diet, and experience (which cannot be bought at any price) will soon teach you how to put matters right. There should rarely be any need to reach for the medicine bottle.

The Importance of Grit

As birds have no teeth with which to chew their food, a special digestive system has been evolved. Insect eating birds feed on the soft parts of the insects which generally do not need to be masticated. Owls and other predators cast up pellets of the parts of their prey, such as bones and fur, which they are unable to digest.

The seed–eating birds such as finches are able to dehusk the seeds they eat, but are still unable to chew them so, in the wild, they continually take small particles of stone and earth while collecting the seeds on which they live. This serves two purposes, first they obtain a lot of minerals which are important to their health and secondly the small pieces of stone pass through to the gizzard where they help this organ to grind to a pulp the seeds which the bird has eaten. These small pieces of stone are gradually worn away and eventually pass through the bird's system and are replaced continually by a fresh intake. A bird's intake of grit does seem to be rather erratic but, no doubt, they take it when they need it. Most hens will be seen to be taking quantities of grit a few days before laying; whether this is to help with the production of the eggs, particularly the calcium needed for the shells, or whether it is to ensure that she has plenty of grit in her gizzard while she is sitting is not quite clear.

Birds can obtain some grit particles from sand, but generally this is not quite large enough for British seedeaters. Good quality grit is obtainable from pet stores in packets generally marked suitable for canaries and budgerigars. The best grit mixtures are sold as mineralised grit, which contains blended quantities of minerals such as calcium, phosphate, sodium chloride, magnesium, iodine and potassium. These mixtures are much nearer to what the birds would take in the wild and are recommended.

Grit is best supplied in a small pot or dish and should be available for all seed–eating birds at all times, so that the birds can help themselves whenever they want to. It is essential for the birds well being and to keep them in full health.

A mineral mixture can also be supplied, and one which contains iodine is especially useful for young birds while they are moulting. It does help to overcome some of the problems with young greenfinches going light, though it is not a complete cure.

Figure 11.2 Chaffinch (left) and Goldfinch

PART 3 — FEEDING SOFTBILLS
by P.W. Beauchamp

All British softbills feed from the first rays of daylight until dusk in their native haunts, flitting from place to place, always hunting for insects. A few, such as warblers, partake of berries and fruits in season. It will be easily seen, therefore, that variety and 'little and often' will fulfill nature's demands, provided we study such essentials as cleanliness and exercise.

First we must prepare our stock food, this to be of two grades: fine for all small softbills and coarse for the larger birds. All ingredients must be mixed dry and kept in a cool dry place, preferably in tins with lids which fit but are not air-tight.

Basis of Stockfood

No.1 Grade: for small softbills I prefer a basis of fine biscuit meal four parts, fine oatmeal one part, maize germ meal one part, crushed buckwheat one part, ground nuts one part, ant eggs one part. When procurable substitute dried flies for crushed buckwheat, and add silkworm pupa one part. Mix all dry ingredients together and keep in a tin as mentioned. If possible, moisten sufficient for each day's use only with beef dripping or just a little melted suet; vary this by moistening the mixture with grated raw carrot, finely chopped lettuce or watercress leaves only. For variety add a little finely grated, cooked liver and a little hardboiled or dried hen's egg.

No.2 Grade: for all softbills the size of the song thrush and larger use a coarse biscuit meal and add any stale home-made cake, even fruit cake, before adding the other items in proportion as for No.1 Grade; vary the mixture in similar manner but leave out hen's egg.

From the above two grades of stock foods it will be seen that variety is in the order of nature, but a keen lover of British birds will soon observe that very few of the ingredients mentioned would be sought by our insectivorous birds in the wild. All contain, however, nature's vitamins, which for our purpose keep the balance of health, with the addition of livefood and fruit for certain species.

Rearing and Livefood

Livefood is essential from the first, as parent birds feed their young on this diet alone; in the wild the insectivorous cock and hen make about 300 sorties a day to bring food for a nest of four youngsters and, perhaps, for twelve in the case of certain tits. Nature demands a little and often; a youngster is never crammed but can digest each small feed.

The beginner will find no difficulty in making up his stock food, but with livefood the seasons vary and there may be a scarcity during certain months of the year; hence our old standby the mealworm, which can be bred and so a supply kept up all the year round.

Most small softbills seem to find mealworms very indigestible, but they are ideal for all larger birds such as starlings and upwards. I advise cut-up mealworms in moderation for small species, when other livefood is unobtainable. Gentles, wasp grubs and ant eggs are only available from May to September, but it will be explained later how these can be kept for use up to the end of December, provided sufficient quantities can be gathered in the season. It will be noted that most of the best livefood is procurable during the breeding season of our softbills; at this time smooth caterpillars, woodlice and small red earthworms are also plentiful followed by earwigs, green fly and various garden pests.

From three weeks of age youngsters will begin to pick up insect food life, so offer gentles and the like, as these will move and so attract in nature's way. At a month old place a little moistened stock food in a china dish with livefood on top; the softbill will soon partake of a little softfood with its usual insects. Proceed to cut down the livefood gradually but make sure the youngsters are actually eating some softfood, not just scattering it on the cage floor.

Having explained my method of feeding I would point out that this is practicable for all species, from the smallest to the largest softbill, as all must be weaned gradually from livefood only to a certain amount of softfood. The main factor to bear in mind is that all insectivorous birds have a tendency to fatness in captivity, especially if kept in cages.

Fruit

All warblers, whitethroats, the lesser and the greater, need a certain amount of ripe fruit daily in their diets, combined with a little soft stock food and a few insects. The blackcap is another lover of soft fruit, but also enjoys livefood. Useful fruits include: banana, obtainable all the year round; ripe pear, a valuable addition — those fanciers fortunate to be able to obtain or grow a quantity and store them will have an advantage; sweet apple — preferably over-ripe and not sharp, as these contain too much acid and so are not suitable for softbills; all soft fruits, such as strawberries, raspberries, currants — blackberries can be bottled and so kept for autumn and winter use.

Amongst the large birds needing fruit in their daily diet is the waxwing; my greatest success resulted from feeding with soaked shop currants plus No.1 grade softfood and, as a variety, with ant-eggs and wasp-grubs added. Actual livefood is not relished.

Wild Berries

Softbills which thrive on the berries of our countryside include: blackbirds, mistle and song thrushes. In addition, starlings and the redwing enjoy berries such as rowans, elder, privet, ivy, which should be ripe. Bunches of these can be hung up in a dry place and so be useful when the season ends.

Nuts

Many small softbills require various nuts as an addition to the daily diet; this also applies to such birds as the nuthatch. Monkey nuts, hazel and filberts are ideal and fanciers should endeavour to secure a stock for all the year round feeding. All tits enjoy nuts and it is advisable to add a little crushed nut occasionally to No.1 grade softfood for these birds.

The Moult

Once we have reared our youngsters successfully and been rewarded by having kept these exquisite specimens in perfect health and feather, up to the time of the moult, we are apt to satisfy ourselves that we know enough about the feeding and keeping of British softbills. It is necessary to point out, however, that to bring up insectivorous birds and keep them healthy for the first few months of the year is only the first achievement; to attain the second even extra care will be needed, as the period of the moult is *the* severe test for these birds.

Live insect food becomes scarce just at the time of the moult, for most species in captivity, but provided a good supply of ant-eggs has been stored and plenty of gentles put in a tin with sand and placed under soil, to prevent them from turning too quickly into flies, we shall have assured an acceptable supply of food for our special variety to bring them through the moult — a test of stamina. The smaller the softbill the greater is the risk of surviving the moult. With our larger softbills, from the redwing upwards, less difficulty will be experienced in getting them through the moult, as these birds will partake of meal and earthworms, also over-ripe stored apple mixed with their stockfood. I always find that those birds which have a quick, even moult will be the show specimens, and above all, the sheen and bloom of their plumage, denoting health and contentment, will prove that they have been fed and kept correctly and as naturally as possible.

Bathing

From the time when the softbill can feed itself, put a bath on the front of its cage; a dish of water placed inside is not advised, as the floor will become wet and soil both the food and the bird. Train your birds from the first to use an outside bath, preferably a roomy one. Through the birds' life offer the bath as often as you can, certainly not less than twice a week, paying particular and daily attention during the moult, as a bath is a great conditioner to assist nature.

Floor Covering

The excreta from an insectivorous bird contains acid and so care must be taken with the floor covering to combat any damage to the birds' feet. I prefer to use granulated peat as a cover, this being both pleasant to handle and absorbent, so taking up the excreta. If excreta is allowed to acccumulate it clogs the feet and in a short time the acid softens and rots the toes. Should fine sawdust be used there is the danger of it getting into the food and water, while coarse sawdust may inflame the feet, and so allow acid to penetrate.

Ailments

One of the most common disorders which occurs in young softbills is known as *Going Light*, symptoms being listlessness and looseness of feather, caused by wrong feeding; indigestion results and so loss of stamina. Variety being the remedy, offer a spider at intervals, and cut out all hard insects; feed with ant–eggs soaked in milk. With adults, watch out for obesity, as blood pressure will follow and cause fits, especially if too many mealworms are given to small species and too much meat to the larger birds. Syrup of buckthorn is a handy remedy, six or eight drops in a small drinker for the smallest bird, increasing the number of drops according to size. Remember that loss of tightness of feather always indicates that something is wrong with a softbill: syrup of buckthorn should be given occasionally all the year round.

Figure 11.3   Wax Moth

Figure 11.4   Stick Insects

PART 4 — FEEDING YOUNG SOFTBILLS
by Ray Allen

When the aviculturalist is forced to take over from the parents through some mishap to either or both birds, hand rearing becomes an important science to the breeder: it is probable that all breeders have had a go at it at some time or another with varying degrees of success. My aim has always been to keep as near to the natural diet as possible; livefood all the time and no sloppy soft food at all for migrant softbills. Birds of thrush size and above may be permitted to have an occasional feed of softfood, but even then animal protein must be available in plenty to make a good strong bird. If using just mealworms and maggots, mashed greenfood, to supply what would normally be in green caterpillars, is the only other food needed. The principle is little and often and increasing as the birds grow.

When hand feeding is no longer necessary it is still a wise precaution to feed them up occasionally, especially last thing at night. Softfood together with what livefood (killed) they have been having can then be put before them at all times. The birds automatically sample the softfood if their insect food is placed on the top of it. The softfood, in my opinion, should never be mixed with water but given in a dry greasy state, as this makes the particles adhere to the livefood, minced greenfood and fruit and in no time the young birds will be taking it quite freely. When seen to be doing this the food can be given in separate vessels; this diet must then be kept up at all seasons.

Do not attempt to ration the livefood until the birds are through the first moult, then and only then can the amount of livefood be at all rationed. My birds eat plenty of softfood but none-the-less have livefood before them at all times, they must be given the choice. It is not unusual to find that one day the softfood is all eaten while another it is barely touched, and the same goes for greenfood and fruit; the birds should have it before them all the same, as the need for a particular food at certain times is apparent to the birds themselves to regulate their needs, even if it is not to you. The greatest variety of foods that your birds will eat should always be the aim, as I am sure that constant variety gives good results in moulting, showing, breeding or just keeping the birds for their song and looks.

Never waste milk that has turned sour, let it curdle and then pour it in a muslin bag or silk stocking and you have good soft cheese liked by all softbills. I also give an occasional drink of fresh milk and a bit of beef dripping mixed with honey in the softfood. Watch the feet and eyes of your bird, any sign of soreness in either means that the diet is lacking in something. If this should be noticed, treat the feet first with a good antiseptic ointment and also bathe the eyes with *Optrex* or boracic acid solution; then improve the bird's diet. This can be helped along with a multi-vitamin liquid called *Abidec* which will fill the vitamin deficiency gap in the food. The first dose can be one drip direct into the gape, thereafter two to three drops in as much water as goes into a 'top hat' drinker, two or three days in the week. It is a good plan, I find, to put this in all the birds' water once a week throughout the year.

149

In some areas tap water is more heavily chlorinated than in others, for this reason water drawn from a stream or fresh water lake is preferable. Rain water from the butt is very good for the bath water, but for all-purpose use it is necessarily short of the minerals which are picked up by water running through the earth, as in streams, lakes or pits. Callow young birds need mineral-rich water most, and a heavily chlorinated tap water is harmful to such tender young things, possibly accounting for early losses in breeding. Avoiding tap water is an extra safeguard; chlorination kills bacteria in the water and may well kill young birds. In addition it is this very bacteria which helps in the breaking down of the food in the intestines. D.D.T. is also a danger; while it kills lice and red mite it also kills young nestlings, as I have found to my cost.

Figure 11.5 Jars with pierced tops containing live Mealworms (left) and Gentles
Courtesy: Arthur Hissey

PART 5 — OBTAINING LIVE FOOD

Mealworms

Mealworms have always been considered as a standby with softbill fans. They are very useful and suitable for all large softbills, having the advantage of being with us all the year round; however, they are indigestible insects for small birds and all small species, such as tits, wrens, treecreepers, goldcrests, chiff-chaff, are susceptible to obesity if fed with mealworms too liberally. Obesity will cause high blood pressure and so losses will occur by fits. The best advice is to cut up just one or two daily, if other livefood is scarce.

Many fanciers breed mealworms successfully, using a strong box with a well fitting lid. The lid should be provided with a ventilation hole covered with very fine gauze to prevent the worms and beetles from crawling out. Cover the bottom of the box with bran then fold some damp sacking over it, add another layer of bran and sacking and place the mealworms on top. Put the box in a fairly warm position. Mealworms do require a fair amount of water so the box should be inspected every week or two and the sacking dampened as necessary. It is very helpful to put in a cabbage leaf or sliced carrot to help maintain the moisture level.

Mealworms have a rather long life-cycle and it will be some weeks before supplies will be available for feeding to the birds. The mealworms which you put into the box will firstly change into pupae and then into black beetles. The beetles lay the eggs which, in turn, hatch into minute mealworms. These shed their skins as they grow and complete another cycle. By leaving some mealworms to pupate a continuous supply can be obtained after the first life-cycle has been completed. Mealworms do best if they are kept in a constant warm temperature all the year round.

Gentles

While mealworms are very clean to handle, gentles when first bred are, perhaps repulsive, as they are bred from offal and must be cleaned in sand before being offered to softbills. One method of breeding gentles is to use fish heads. Prop open the mouth with a piece of matchstick, place in an open tin and leave in the sun; when the fly has deposited its eggs, wrap up the fish head in paper and put it back in the open tin. Store this in a dry place and, when the gentles are large enough, they will emerge through the paper. Examine the fish head occasionally; when gentles are of good size place wrapped head in a wire frame and lay it on top of an open tin containing clean sand. As the gentles grow they will push through the paper and so drop into the sand; examine these after two days and feed to your birds those that have lost the dark line through the body, this denotes that the food from the offal has passed from the gentles and that they are now a clean and useful food.

Wasp-grubs

A valuable addition to livefood are wasp-grubs, however, until experience is gained in wasp destroying it can be an uncomfortable business. The wasps may well have two entrances to their home and if you have only poisoned one and not noticed the other it will be found when you attempt to dig out the nest the next day that many wasps are still very much alive. A good nest can contain eight tiers of cone, being full of grubs and weighing as much as six pounds. Cook these cones in a hot oven for several minutes and then lay them out to cool. Store in a cool dry place in a cardboard tray and use the grubs, as wanted, from the cone. This type of livefood is relished by all insectivorous birds and is obtainable from May to September. Feed the white grubs to small birds and the partly and fully formed ones to the larger species.

Ant Eggs

These are not eggs of the common or garden ant but of the large, black ant found in pine woods. Ant eggs or cocoons are a valuable food for softbills and can be gathered in large quantities, as the wood ant builds a high nest of pine needles, usually 2-3 feet (0.6-1 m) high, containing thousands of eggs from May to July. The method of collecting these eggs is to don a pair of gloves and cycle clips around the bottom of trousers then, armed with a trowel and large tin, having a tightly-fitting lid, proceed to open the nest by removing the top layer of pine needles with the trowel. As soon as eggs are visible transfer these to your tin; close the lid when full and bring to the open sheet. This sheet should be spread out in the sun with each corner tied to pegs driven in to the ground and formed like a biscuit tin lid, that is with turned-up sides. Place bracken or evergreens around the inside and tip the ant eggs all over the sheet. Ants which have been collected with the eggs and pine needles will immediately carry the eggs to the sides and under the bracken out of the sun.

After a time you can lay the bracken aside and pick up clean ant eggs with a spoon; these can be used alive, but for future use cook them in a hot oven for five minutes. This kills the germ, otherwise they would hatch out. Do not over-cook and store in open cardboard trays, the same as for wasp grubs, and the eggs will not go mouldy. Ant eggs, if cooked correctly, will keep provided they are kept open in shallow trays in a cool, dry place and shake occasionally to allow access to fresh air.

Wasp grubs should be left in their cones and laid out in the same way, just one tier high; after being cooked I have successfully kept ant eggs the whole year round, but wasp grub for only a few months. Gentles quickly turn into chrysalises and then hatch in to flies; to prevent this place them in a tin of clean sand fitted with an ordinary lid and sink this into the garden covering it with a foot of soil. In this way gentles will keep for several weeks.

Earwigs

These are useful for most insectivorous birds, either given alive or killed. Earwigs are present when dahlias are growing and a good way to secure a regular supply of this livefood is to fit a small flower pot, inverted with a little hay inside, over the dahlia stake. Use a glass jam jar to hold the earwigs; a few can be given alive, which the birds will soon pounce on. To store, tip a jar full of earwigs into a bowl of boiling water, strain off onto a clean cloth and when dry lay on cardboard trays to keep for use.

Caterpillars

Smooth caterpillars are the only ones which should be used for softbills — never hairy ones. Caterpillars can be gathered from cabbages at the time white butterflies are on the wing; many can be found hanging from trees and, if found on fruit bushes, can be gathered by holding an open umbrella close to the bush and giving the latter a sharp tap; the caterpillars will then fall into the umbrella.

Woodlice

Woodlice can be found all the year round and should be offered alive to all large birds; small softbills are not keen on them. Place some old sacking against a fence or wall at an odd corner of the rubbish heap and you will breed a good supply. A piece of rotted wood is also useful as a breeding place.

Earthworms

Ordinary garden worms are useful only for the thrush and blackbird families; the former will also relish a snail daily but the most useful worms are the small red ones found in decayed rubbish heaps. If cleanings from cage and aviary are put in a corner of the garden this will attract many small worms, if the rubbish is turned over occasionally. Many of the small softbills will benefit if given one or two worms a day as a change.

Whiteworms

White worms are appreciated by some birds. They can be bred in a box of damp peat or compost by adding a white worm culture to it. The worms require regular feeding with a little porridge and bread and milk, which should be placed on top of the culture. Put a piece of glass over this and cover with a sack. The worms will be attracted to the glass and they may then be scraped off and fed to the birds.

Spiders

These act as a medicine should an insectivorous bird be ailing — just one or two spiders will attract the bird and will, almost invariably, put new life into it. Never overfeed spiders, however, as too many at a time are apt to stick in the bird's throat and so choke it.

Greenfly and Garden Pests

Such delicate feeders as wrens, flycatchers, goldcrests, chiff-chaff and treecreepers will benefit if given a sprig from a rose infested with greenfly. This garden blight is with us at about the time that small softbills are breeding and so are very handy as a rearing food for these handsome little sprites. Various kinds of garden blight will be found useful for all small species and picking a sprig from a fruit tree or bush and such–like containing blight provides the birds with good exercise. Many useful insects to offer to softbills can be found when digging or weeding the flower or kitchen garden: one such is a white grub with a brown head about an inch in length, enjoyed by all species of softbills. Centipedes, wireworms and all kinds of grubs are useful.

At various seasons of the year slug eggs are found just under the surface of the soil, often in clusters looking like a bunch of pearls. The slug itself is certainly not accepted by any self respecting softbill, but large birds enjoy the eggs.

Fruit flies

Fruit flies (*Drosophila*) may be cultured by placing rotten fruit, especially bananas, in jars or bowls. In warm conditions the jar will soon be swarming with small flies; this can be placed in the cage and removed when most of the flies have been eaten. Be careful to place a lid on the jar with a few very small holes in it — this will enable the flies to escape but prevent the occupant of the cage from becoming wedged in the neck of the jar.

Figure 11.6   Chickweed — a useful wild plant

PART 6 — BASIC DIETS

For quick reference basic diets for the various species are listed on the following pages for the help and guidance of new fanciers and breeders, or those who take up a new species for the first time. Birds can be kept in good condition on these diets, but we do not claim that they are necessarily complete nor that they are the only foods on which the birds can be maintained. Indeed, many birds have individual preferences and it is as well to study these carefully to find the foods which suit them best.

Birds in aviaries need a richer diet than those kept in cages, where care has to be taken with some species that they do not become too fat. Breeding birds also require extra foods, especially when rearing young.

All **seedeating birds** must have a continuous supply of mineral grit, clean water for drinking, regular baths, a constant supply of a good quality British Finch Mixture and all the wild seeding plants which can be gathered as they come into season. It is best to purchase the British Finch Mixture without hemp so that this can be fed in regulated amounts according to the species. All finches can have a continuous supply of maw seed, as this helps to prevent illness.

Useful wild plants include: chickweed, dandelion, annual grasses, knot grass, groundsel, shepherds purse, plantain, sow thistle, knapweed, nettles, persicaria, dock, charlock, ragwort, fat hen, hawksbeard, meadow sweet. Many seaseaters are also fond of privet berries, blackberries, blackcurrants and will often take sweet apples, pears and boiled or raw carrots. Brassicas which have gone to seed and similar greenfoods are useful. Some birds will also take blowfly chrysalises or, more frequently, the smaller common house fly chrysalis.

Care should be taken not to supply foods in a frosted condition.

Softbills live almost exclusively on an insectivorous and fruit diet. They must have clean water for drinking and constant baths. Grated cuttlefish bone should be mixed with insectivorous foods and, periodically, chopped green food is a useful addition. A little minced meat or mutton and beef suet is often enjoyed and larger softbills appreciate elderberries, hawthornberries, hips, haws, mountain ash and the like.

Please refer to the following tables for details of feeding the different species.

SPECIES	STOCK FOODS	STOCK FOODS (to be supplied in small quantities)	EXTRAS WHEN BREEDING
Bullfinch	finch seeds, wild foods, berries	hemp, sunflower seed	fruit flies, green flies etc., egg food
Brambling (Bramble Finch) Chaffinch	finch seed, wild foods, blowflies, houseflies, spiders, mealworms	hemp, maw seed, sunflower	all insects, caterpillars etc., egg food, maggots
Crossbill	finch seed, plenty of sunflower, fir cones	hemp, maw seed	any live food they will take
Goldfinch	finch seed, hemp, maw seed, teazle, wild foods, thistles	extra niger	fruit flies, greenflies, etc., egg food, groundsel, annual grasses
Greenfinch	finch seed, wild foods, sprouted seed, grass seed	sunflower, maw seed	fruit flies, greenflies etc., egg food especially, annual grasses
Hawfinch	finch seed, sunflower, fruit stones, berries, garden peas, mealworms	hemp	all insects, caterpillars, etc.
Brown Linnet	finch seed, wild foods	hemp, maw seed	fruit flies, greenflies etc., egg food, small moths & beetles, larvae
Lesser and Mealy Redpoll	finch seed, wild foods	hemp, maw seed	fruit flies, greenflies, etc. egg food
Siskin	finch seed, wild foods, seeding grasses	hemp, maw seed	fruit flies, greenflies, etc., egg food
Twite	finch seed, wild foods	hemp, maw seed	fruit flies, greenflies etc., egg food, small moths & beetles, larvae
Cirl Bunting Corn Bunting Reed Bunting Snow Bunting Yellow Bunting (Yellowhammer)	plain canary seed, maggots, mealworms, grain, grass seeds, berries	any other seeds that they will eat	any live food, egg food slugs, spiders, millipedes, small earthworms
Meadow Pipit Rock Pipit Tree Pipit	fine insectivorous food, maggots	mealworms, small insects, ripe fruit, wasp grubs	continuous supply of live food, caterpillars, ant eggs etc.
Redstart Black Redstart	fine insectivorous food, maggots	mealworms, small insects, ripe fruit, wasp grubs	continuous supply of live food, smooth caterpillars, ant eggs

SPECIES	STOCK FOODS	STOCK FOODS (to be supplied in small quantities)	EXTRAS WHEN BREEDING
Longtailed Tit	fine insectivorous food, maggots	mealworms, small insects, ripe fruit, wasp grubs, peanuts	continuous supply of live food, smooth caterpillars, ant eggs
Blue Tit **Great Tit**	fine insectivorous food, maggots, weed seeds and berries	mealworms, blue-bottles, fruit flies, small insects, ripe fruit, wasp grubs, peanuts	continuous supply of live food, smooth caterpillars ant eggs
Starling	coarse insectivorous food, maggots	mealworms, small insects, ripe fruit	continuous supply of live food of all kinds
Blackbird **Song Thrush** **Mistle Thrush**	coarse insectivorous food, maggots, boiled vegetables, (Thrushes — snails), berries	mealworms, small insects, ripe fruit, earthworms, slugs	continuous supply of live food of all kinds
Waxwing	coarse insectivorous food, ripe fruit, soaked currants	berries, maggots mealworms crumbled fruit cake	continuous supply of any live food the birds will take
Grey Wagtail **Pied Wagtail** **Yellow Wagtail**	fine insectivorous food, maggots	mealworms, small insects, ripe fruit	continuous supply of live food, smooth caterpillars
Blackcap **Nightingale** **Whitethroat**	fine insectivorous food, maggots	mealworms, blue-bottles, fruit flies, small insects, ripe fruit	continuous supply of live food, smooth caterpillars
Pied Flycatcher **Spotted Flycatcher**	fine insectivorous food, maggots	mealworms, blue-bottles, fruit flies, small insects, ripe fruit	continuous supply of live food
Stonechat **Whinchat**	fine insectivorous food, maggots	mealworms, small insects, ripe fruit	continuous supply of live food, smooth caterpillars
Tree creeper	fine insectivorous food, maggots	mealworms, small insects, ripe fruit	continuous supply of live food
Wheatear	fine insectivorous food, maggots	mealworms, small insects, ripe fruit	continuous supply of live food, raw meat, liver etc.
Magpie **Jay** **Jackdaw**	coarse insectivorous food, maggots, woodlice, acorns, beetles.	raw egg, cod liver oil mealworms, raw meat, young mice	

CHAPTER 12

Exhibition

THE PREPARATION AND EXHIBITION OF SEEDEATERS AND THEIR HYBRIDS
by Walter Lewis

Bathing

There is one most important role for the keeping of birds for exhibition — they must have access to water for bathing regularly and it is really the most essential matter if you are to be successful on the show bench.

Some birds are reluctant to bathe, but usually when they see or hear other birds bathing they follow suit. If they do not they should be sprayed, even if it is an unnatural method — there being no alternative. I know a lot of successful exhibitors who always spray their birds but I like a bird to bathe naturally and the majority will, if given the opportunity. When a bird bathes it relaxes and allows the water to penetrate the feather; if sprayed it behaves as if it is trying to avoid the water and 'tightens' up.

Without any doubt rain water is the best to use — this is the water wild birds use and, as everyone knows, the wild bird always carries a 'sheen' or gloss on the feather which, undoubtedly, is obtained by bathing frequently.

Show Cages

It is desirable that a bird gets used to its show cage before it is exhibited. Some birds take to a show cage 'like a duck to water' as the saying goes, but others do not like to be confined. These birds should be run into a show cage for very short periods and eventually they get accustomed to it. Occasionally one does meet a problem bird but it is surprising how it will eventually accept a show cage. Very often a bird, when shown at a small show for a few hours, gains confidence and, once acquired, it is never lost.

Some birds — just a few — have the nasty habit of facing the back of the cage. Birds like this, *seldom* overcome this bad habit. The ideal exhibition bird always faces the front of the cage.

Although experience over the years teaches us — or should — the handling or management of birds it is, after all, only common sense.

The staging or presentation of British seedeaters, mules and hybrids is very important if the exhibitor is to be successful. Many years ago fanciers had various ideas about the types of show cages and interior colours which suited a particular species or variety. Consequently we saw all types of cages — 'bow' fronts of different types and also different interior colours. For some years now, the specialist societies have decided that green is a natural colour

158

and undoubtedly the best, suiting all species and varieties. There is a slight difference in the sizes of show cages advocated by the Scottish British Bird and Mule Club, but we are all agreed that green is the acceptable colour for interiors and black for exteriors.

It is very important that exhibits are staged in the sizes we advocate for the particular species or varieties, but there can be exceptions. Occasionally a hybrid of outstanding size requires a size larger cage than we have recommended: it is always permissible to use the larger size but *never* a smaller size. Please remember that the sizes recommended and adopted are the minimum sizes and, in the main, are the most suitable. It must be remembered also that it is possible that a new hybrid may appear, such as a hawfinch hybrid, which would require a show cage of a size which would have to be determined by the exhibitor. It is most important that show cages are made by a skilled cage maker who specialises in this particular job.

It is very important that decoration of the show cage is of the highest standard both internally and externally. Sometimes we see show cages which are poorly constructed and poorly decorated: a good bird deserves a good cage — it certainly enhances a bird's chances on the show bench providing the exhibit is of a high quality.

To maintain a cage in good condition it is important that you always clean your show cages after a show; wash them thoroughly, particularly the perches and place them in your carrying case ready for your next show. They will also need repainting periodically — the brand of green enamel which we consider to be best and that which the National British Bird and Mule Club have adopted, is Brolac Georgian Green; British Standard 14E 53 is almost identical.

Many fanciers have show cages in perfect order, decorated with Aspinell's Jade Green or a similar colour. When the cages require repainting we ask exhibitors to decorate them with the recommended brand. In addition all drinkers used must be painted green inside and out. A list of sizes is given later.

For those who are just commencing exhibiting birds it must be pointed out that birds are only allowed to be in show cages for seventy-two hours and while being transported to and from the shows. At other times, apart from training sessions, the birds must be kept in the recommended stock cages.

Colour Feeding

The colour feeding of British seedeaters is a controversial subject nevertheless I am quite sure some species are improved by its use. Nowadays *Carophil* Red* is available and its use in the drinking water is quite simple and effective. My method is to dissolve a small teaspoonful in a container by pouring boiling water on to it. Leave it for about fifteen minutes to thoroughly dissolve. This will make a three and a half-pint bottle of solution, pour the solution into the bottle and top-up with water. Put a good splash into the drinking water; do not be too fussy about the amount. *Change* every other day. Put a dish of clean water into the cage or aviary in the morning, removing it when the birds have bathed and replace it with the *Carophil* Red* solution.

*Registered trade name

Bullfinches, bramblings, redpolls, buntings, chaffinches and linnets are undoubtedly improved by its use. Greenfinches and siskins are far better and more attractive when they are fed naturally and are not colour fed.

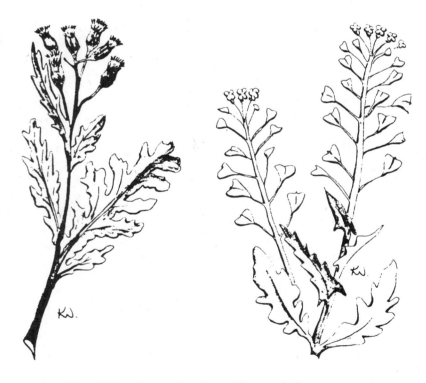

Figure 12.1   Groundsel (left) and Shepherds Purse

STAGING SOFTBILLS
by Colin H. Clark

The following notes may be of interest and help to anyone considering taking up the exhibition of softbills. There are four factors to take into account: cages and materials and of course large and small softbills. Softbills are much more active than hardbills and require more space to show themselves off and to be seen to their best advantage. Suitable cage sizes are listed later.

It is worthy of mention that some species are best suited to the conventional box type cage and others are enhanced by the desk pattern, the latter now being widely used by fanciers. In general large softbill exhibitors do not employ cage decoration although it is used by some with thrushes, jays, magpies and such and on several outings have done very well. My view is that they look far better without any. I would draw the border line at, say, waxwing and starling body size but I must point out, however, that it is left to the exhibitor and the choice is left to both fancier and judge as to whether they like it or not — there are no rules to say one cannot use it.

With large softbills a clean cage is of the utmost importance and when the *standard* asks for a white interior it means white and not cream or off-yellow. The size of large softbill cages and the obvious inconvenience to promoting show societies in staging them often leads to a cage front having the paint chipped off or being misshaped — nothing looks worse than two tones of paint colour. Bear in mind that there are ten points allocated within the *standard* for staging — the same as for the small softbill section, where cages normally are decorated.

Usually enthusiasts who want to decorate their cages can find something suitable within their own back garden or at least close by. The type of material which is best used can be allocated according to the normal show classification: for example, the class including wrens, titmice, goldcrests can have small sprays of ivy (the wall climbing variety) cotoneaster, silver fir or similar, tastefully placed so as not to drown the birds. Perches for this type of bird should be of a springy nature and I find the tops from dead elderberry bushes, scrubbed elm twigs and grapevine very suitable.

The class of wheatears, 'chats and 'starts can be presented on small stumps and rocks; a little heather, broom and bracken can be arranged to give a heathland effect and make the cage very eye-catching. Old hedgerow stumps wearing a weather beaten look are attractive and are readily accepted by the exhibit which, when properly cage trained, soon shows its gait and stance to perfection.

The majority of leaf warblers, including nightingales and blackcaps, are constantly on the move and are often hidden from the eye of the officiating judge by having too much 'backing'. Small clusters of plants like rhododendrons, laurel and copper beech sprays have the desired effect: try to arrange them either side of the perches, fanned to or from the cage centre. Various types of mosses can be used to give contour and elevation as well as floor covering.

Reedlings and marsh-living birds require to be shown as the name suggests. Several types of ornamental grasses and reeds can be employed with success as well as reeds and rushes which can be gathered from the local pond or from a weekend outing. The rushes can be stood in water. Fixing can sometimes constitute a problem: I find a piece of wood pressed tightly at the base of whatever is used is helpful and can be hidden by the floor covering of moss. Alternatively, use a potato or piece of swede with the cut, flat side down on the cage bottom. Holes can be made in the potato with a thin gauge piece of wire, pencil or such. The suction holds the material firmly and the moisture keeps the arrangement fresh and upright. Small pot plants of a ferny nature can be used (sometimes they need to be trimmed a little) and can look very effective. The use of synthetic materials is not recommended and if natural materials cannot be obtained it is better not to decorate the cage at all.

In conclusion, the essential and basic rules of showing softbill birds to perfection is to have everything clean — including all food and water vessels. Get your birds used to the idea of decorated cages before showing them — do not make hiding places for them within the cage.

BRITISH BIRD COUNCIL RECOMMENDED EXHIBITION RULES

1.	**Entries:**	The completion of an entry form implies an express understanding that the exhibitor accepts these rules as binding and final, and any breach of the rules will render the exhibitor liable to be disqualified and to forfeit all entrance fees.
2.	**Law:**	All exhibitors and exhibits must comply with the Wildlife and Countryside Act 1981.
3.	**Cages:**	All exhibits shall be staged in the correct standard show cages for the species as specified by the B.B.C.
4.	**Food:**	All exhibits must be provided with all necessary utensils fitted to enable the stewards to clean and replenish, and an adequate supply of food for the duration of the show.
5.	**Bone Fide:**	All exhibits must be the *bone-fide* property of the exhibitor.
6.	**Rings**	All birds exhibited must be ringed with either a split ring or a closed ring or both.
7.	**Entry Fees:**	Must be sent with the entry form, which must be signed in the appropriate places. Entry fees will be forfeited if any exhibit does not arrive at the exhibition hall before the final time for staging.
8.	**Loss:**	The show promoters will not be responsible under any circumstances for any loss or damage sustained by exhibits or exhibitors and their property nor any consequential expenses from any cause whatsoever whether these be sustained either on the way to, at or during, or returning from the exhibition.

9. **Wrong Class:** The judge, whose decision is final, shall decide if any bird is wrongly classed, or if a bird is ineligible due to the nationality of the species. He shall mark the cage label accordingly, and any such exhibit is automatically disqualified from all competition.

10. **Dishonest:** The judge, whose decision is final, shall decide if any bird has drawn, stained or trimmed plumage, or is in any way dishonestly shown. He shall mark the cage label accordingly. Any such exhibit is automatically disqualified and will be removed from the exhibition hall forthwith.

11. **Untrained:** The judge, whose decision is final, shall decide if any bird is insufficiently trained. He shall mark the cage label accordingly. Any such exhibit is automatically disqualified and will be removed from the exhibition hall forthwith.

12. **Sale:** British birds will not be sold at or during the exhibition under any circumstances. Mules and hybrids, however, may be sold subject to the show promoter's rules.

13. **Breeders' Classes:** Are confined to birds being exhibited by the actual breeder, and must be wearing his or her own closed recorded ring of the correct size for the species and issued by the British Bird Council. Any bird wearing any other ring will be disqualified. (See Protests Rule No. 20).

14. **Resident Status:** Where two exhibitors reside at the same address and both exhibit British birds, they must both exhibit in the highest status of either one. This rule also includes juveniles.

15. **Partnerships:** Any two names on an entry form will constitute a partnership.

16. **Novice:** A Novice can exhibit in Novice Classes for three calender years and will then automatically become a Champion.

17. **Juvenile:** A Juvenile is an exhibitor between the ages of 6 and 16 who has not competed in any other section in an open show. Junior awards and specials will only be given to birds exhibited in Junior Classes.
A Juvenile may, if he wishes, exhibit in a higher status, but will not then be eligible for any Junior award or special. Once having done so, he cannot revert to Junior status.

18. **Status:** An exhibitor can only exhibit in one status. This rule also applies to Juveniles.

19. **Visitors:** The committee have the right to eject any person from the exhibition hall without assigning any reason if they consider it necessary or desirable. Dogs will not be allowed in the exhibition hall under any circumstances.

20. **Protests:** Any exhibitor wishing to make a protest must make it in writing to the show secretary, *during the show*, and pay £5 deposit. The protests will then be considered by the Committee, whose decision will be final and binding. If the protest is sustained the £5 deposit will be refunded.

21. **Committee:** The exhibition promoter's committee will deal with all matters arising out of the exhibition, whether provided for in the foregoing or not, and their decision is final and absolute.

22. **Judges:** Judges are not allowed to exhibit at any show where they are judging.

STANDARD SHOW CAGE SIZES

British Hardbills, Mules and Hybrids

The recommended colours are black outside top, bottom, back and sides with a bright medium gloss green inside and on the outside of the wires and on both top and bottom rails.

All drinkers should be painted green to match.

Floor covering: seed only.

Size 2: for goldfinch, lesser and mealy redpoll, siskin, linnet and twite. All mules and other British bird hybrids whose size does not exceed the hardbills in this category including redpoll × bullfinch.

Length 11 inches (28 cm); height $9\frac{1}{2}$ inches (24.2 cm); width $4\frac{1}{2}$ inches (11.5 cm); No. 14 gauge wires set at $\frac{5}{8}$ inch (1.5 cm) centres; drinking hole $\frac{7}{8}$ inch (2.85 cm) diameter; bottom rail $1\frac{1}{2}$ inch (3.75 cm) high; top rail (shaped) 1 inch (2.5 cm) at the outside sloping to $\frac{1}{2}$ inch (1.25 cm) at the centre.

Size 3: for bullfinch, greenfinch, chaffinch, brambling, yellow, reed and cirl buntings, bullfinch hybrids, goldfinch, linnet, twite and greenfinch mules, and other British bird hybrids whose size is similar to the hardbills in this category.

Length 12 inches (30.5 cm); height 10 inches (25.5 cm); width 5 inches (12.75 cm); No. 14 gauge wires set at $\frac{3}{4}$ inch (2 cm) centres; drinking hole $1\frac{1}{8}$ inch (3 cm) diameter; bottom rail $1\frac{1}{2}$ inches (3.75 cm) high; top rail (shaped) 1 inch (2.5 cm) at the outside sloping to $\frac{1}{2}$ inch (1.25 cm) at the centre.

Size 4: for hawfinch, crossbill, corn bunting, snow bunting and Lapland bunting and all mules and other British bird hybrids whose size is similar to the hardbills in this category.

Length 14 inches (35.5 cm); height 12 inches (30.5 cm); width $6\frac{1}{2}$ inches (16.5 cm); No. 14 gauge wires set at 1 inch (2.5 cm) centres; drinking hole $1\frac{1}{4}$ inch (3.25 cm) diameter; bottom rail 2 inches (5 cm) high; top rail (shaped) $1\frac{1}{2}$ inches (3.75 cm) at the outside sloping to $\frac{3}{4}$ inch (2 cm) at the centre.

British Softbills and Their Hybrids

The recommended colours are black outside including wire fronts with white interior. Food and water vessels should be inside the cage. Floor covering is optional, but blotting paper, damp peat or moss for small softbills and very coarse sawdust for large softbills is recommended. Softbills, being so much more active than hardbills should always be shown in as large a cage as possible. The following minimum sizes are suggested:

Size 5: for small softbills up to the size of a waxwing

Length 16 inches (40.5 cm); height 13 inches (33 cm); width 8 inches (20.25 cm).

Size 6: for thrush family except mistle thrush.

Length 18 inches (45.5 cm); height 15 inches (38 cm); width 12 inches (30.5 cm).

Size 7: for mistle thrush and other large softbills.

Length 24 inches (61 cm); height 20 inches (50.75 cm); width 14 inches (35.5 cm).

Size 8: for magpie, jay and similar.

Length 30 inches (76 cm); height 20 inches (50.75 cm); width 14 inches (35.5 cm).

NOTE

Under the new Wildlife and Countryside Act 1981 most show cages will have to be changed within a few years (probably five). The new requirements have not been clarified at the time of going to print and are under discussion with the Department of the Environment.

As soon as the exact requirements are known the British Bird Council will issue leaflets giving full details which will be available from the Secretary.

Figure 12.2   Show Cage for a small Seedeater

STANDARD OF POINTS AWARDED FOR EXCELLENCE
OF SHOW QUALITIES

Points

LIGHT MULES

Size	To be of good size compatible with that of the parents	15
Shape	To be of stout cone shape, with broad bold head, and close–fitting wings and tail	15
Colour	To be deep and rich in colour naturally and when colour fed to be considerably intensified	10
Markings	To be distinctly characteristic of both parents, and the clearer the plumage the better	20
Quality	The plumage to exhibit the highest possible smooth glossy surface throughout	15
Condition	To be sound in condition in every part	10
Steadiness	The bolder and firmer the stand on the perch the better	10
Staging	To be shown in clean condition and a clean cage	5
		100

DARK MULES AND BRITISH BIRD HYBRIDS

Size	The larger the better, compatible with that of the parents	15
Shape	To be of stout cone shape with broad bold head	10
Markings	To show distinctly and nicely blended the chief characteristics, markings and colour of both parents	15
Colour	To be rich, deep and distinct	20
Quality	The plumage to possess the highest possible smooth glossy surface	15
Condition	To be sound in condition in every part	10
Steadiness	To be bold, firm and steady and fearless on the perch	10
Staging	To be shown in clean condition and a clean cage	5
		100

BULLFINCH

Size	As large as possible	10
Shape	Cobby, with roundness everywhere (long bodied birds undesirable)	15
Head and neck	Broad, expansive black cap well back over head; razor like clean cut around its edge, on a nicely rounded head (flat heads with narrowing caps deemed faults) with clean cut black bib under lower mandible (not necessarily large). Neck to be distinctive from the shoulders; a fault reveals itself where the head, neck and shoulders are concertinered into one	20
Wings and Tail	Compact and short	5

Points

Body	Light slate–blue colour back; well defined bar in wings;	
Colour	bright crimson even colour throughout, starting from	
	throat, down chest and belly, underneath and between	
	the legs and on flanks; fading of colour anywhere	
	considered a fault	20
Steadiness		5
Quality and		
Condition		15
Staging		10
		__100__

As in all species yellows and buffs are evident, more noticeable in the hens. The yellow hens have a chocolate coloured breast whilst that of the buffs is slate colour.

BRAMBLING

Size	As large as possible	15
Shape	As in chaffinch and little more boldness	10
Markings	Well defined spangles or V shape markings on head,	
	neck, back and flanks, over the back they should be in	
	even rows (if possible); jumbled up spangles or V	
	markings on back, or lack of them constitutes a fault to	
	a certain degree. Spangles on older birds' heads (3 to 4	
	years) usually disappear and are replaced with a black	
	hood or mantle	15
Colour	Rich and well defined, even, rusty or reddish brown on	
	chest, forming an apron shape and well down towards the	
	belly if possible. White rings or spectacles around the	
	eyes are a fault, particularly in full adult plumage,	
	young birds usually show some ringing	20
Steadiness		20
Quality and		
Condition		10
Staging		10
		__100__

Hens as above, except not too plentiful in apron and rich coloration. Flank V or spangle markings very important in an exhibition hen.

CHAFFINCH

Size	As large as possible	15
Shape	Thick set with bold front and well across the perch	20
Markings	Wing markings well displayed	5
Colour	Slate blue on head (spring condition), olive-green back,	
	rich victoria plum colour chest, colour carried evenly	
	down the belly and between the legs and on flanks; the	

Points

ideal colour is same shade throughout, without variation
or fading   20
Steadiness   20
Quality and
Condition   10
Staging   10
                                                                            _____
                                                                               100

Hens — points allotted as cocks, with possible exception of size — which
should have increased number of points at the expense of colour.

CROSSBILL

Size	As large as possible	20
Shape, head and neck	Short body, very thick set throughout, broad bold head and neck	20
Colour	There are three distinct phases in the colour cycle: grey green — juvenile; copper — second season cocks; yellow, sometimes with copper streak — older and mature cocks	25
Steadiness		10
Quality and Condition		15
Staging		10

                                                                               100

GOLDFINCH

Size	As large as possible	10
Shape	Well proportioned and bold	10
Head	A large expansive blaze is most desirable extending well down throat and back behind the eye and on skull; the whole with clear razor cut edge; blaze to be rich vermilion red colour — the brighter the better, as free from black in or on the face and around the base of the mandible as is possible, also free from black lines cutting into the blaze at an angle from both sides of the base of the lower mandible; the squarer the blaze the better; black cap should be wide on the top of the head and not broken by light feathering	35
Wings and Tail	Visible golden flights, with well defined pairs of markings known as buttons on wings and tail	5
Body	Well tanned on chest and flanks. All tanning being even	
Colour	and clear cut and well defined with contrast	15
Quality of Feather and Condition		15
Staging and Steadiness		10

                                                                               100

Points

GREENFINCH

Size	As large as possible	**30**
Shape	Well rounded and to be as short as it is thick, as it is long; really thick set (small Norwich with half the tail length)	
Head and Neck	Broad, well rounded head set on a thick well defined neck compatible with body size	**30**
Wings and Tail	Short compact wings with well defined yellow bars, also well defined yellow edging to feathers in tail	**5**
Colour	Clear and as bright a green as possible, devoid of smokiness or too much slate grey over body feathering	**20**
Steadiness, Quality and Condition, Staging		**15**
		100

Yellows and buffs are very evident in this species. When a good sized yellow appears on the show bench of good size and shape it will do a lot of winning. The richly coloured buff bird is also a grand bird to possess especially when it possesses good quality feather.

It is a difficult task for any judge to decide which is the better of the two examples. If the two birds are of similar shape and size naturally the yellow bird will win, but if the buff is of superior size and shape the buff bird should win.

Hens are similar to the above in all respects, except colour, which is not so rich. A brownish hue is superimposed over the body.

HAWFINCH

Size	As large as possible	**15**
Shape, head and neck	Short body, very thick set at shoulders and through the body (avoid Yorkshire type); broad bold head and neck with well defined clean-cut large thumb nail shaped bib, or as near to that shape as possible	**20**
Markings	Well defined, steel blue, glossy wing markings, glossed with purple with edging of white	**10**
Colour	Cap of cinnamon and chestnut brown, dense in centre; shaded off all around with bluish grey; body colour rich brown with nut-brown tannings on chest well into the centre and down flanks	**25**
Steadiness		**10**
Quality and Condition		**10**
Staging		**10**
		100

Hens, same as above, but without rich colouring.

Points

LINNET

Size	As large as possible	15
Shape	As nearly cone shaped as possible	15
Head and Neck	Head well rounded, well lined or ticked on top, neck to have distinctive, well defined lines under lower mandible	5
Markings	Small, fine, evenly broken up tickings, starting well up the the chest, continuing as even and distinct as possible into and towards the centre (narrow) white line of the chest and down the flanks and under flue	20
Wings and Tail	Well defined white edges to primaries and compact tail	5
Steadiness		20
Quality and Condition		10
Staging		10
		100

Hen linnets, as above, except that they should carry heavy, plentiful well defined clear cut lines on chest and flanks (not fine tickings).

LESSER REDPOLL

Size, Shape and Head	As in Greenfinch on a smaller scale	25
Markings	Well defined, plentiful, distinct lines on chest and flanks; lines well towards centre of chest with reasonable amount of bib	25
Colour	Deep rich nutty brown	25
Steadiness		5
Quality and Condition		10
Staging		10
		100

Hens, similar to above; difficult to sex.

MEALY REDPOLL

Size, Shape and Head	As in greenfinch	25
Markings	Well defined, plentiful lines on chest and flanks well into centre of chest, with reasonable amount of bib	25
Colour	According to the variety; mostly rich, nutty brown types are seen; occasionally the light greyish greenland and arctic types are seen and accepted, but they are not adorned with plentiful lines on chest and flanks	25
Steadiness		5

		Points
Quality and Condition		10
Staging		10
		100

Hens, similar to above. Difficult to sex.

SISKIN

Size, Shape and Head	Size as in redpoll; head to have good broad black cap with even lacings and clean cut bib	20
Markings	Well laced flanks and distinct pencilling on back	25
Colour	Clear and bright with good yellow base colour devoid of smokiness	30
Steadiness		5
Quality and Condition		10
Staging		10
		100

As in the greenfinch the yellows and buffs are very evident in the species. Colour and markings are a very important point in the exhibition siskin cock.

Hens as above, without black cap, but possibly another five points for markings — markings 30, colour 15, and size shape and head 30.

Markings to be well defined and plentiful well broken up over breast and well laced flanks.

TWITE

Size	As large as possible	10
Shape	Cobby, with neat round head — well lined on head	15
Markings	Clear and well defined lines on chest, well into the centre, and down the flanks, defined white bar in wing	20
Colour	Rich, nutty brown throughout	20
Steadiness		15
Quality and Condition		10
Staging		10
		100

Hens, similar to above, slimmer in head and neck. Cocks can be distinguished from hens by the plum colour feathering at the top base of flue. In some birds the plum colour turns to creamy yellow.

Points

CIRL BUNTING

Size, Shape and Head	As in yellow bunting; yellow and olive-green on head sides; black streak through eye	20
Markings	As in yellow bunting	20
Colour	Rich chestnut as above, streaked with black, breast rich nutty colour; abdomen and base feather pale colour yellow; chin and throat black	20
Steadiness		20
Quality and Condition		10
Staging		10
		100

Hens, as above, except not the rich profusion of yellow base colour.

CORN BUNTING

Size, Shape and Head	Large as possible; thick, defined neck with bold head	15
Markings	Bold; well defined, with rich, deep nutty brown profusion	15
Colour	Sound throughout, but brown above, sandy buff underbody	15
Steadiness		35
Quality and Condition		10
Staging		10
		100

Hens, similar to above, but slimmer. Oftimes hens are best coloured and marked. Difficult to sex.

REED BUNTING

Size and Head	As large as possible; head well rounded	10
Shape	Cone shape or near cone	10
Markings	Jet black head and throat with black, even-cut, well defined black apron extending well down the chest; well defined clear cut lines on flanks	20
Body Colour	Rufus brown streaked with black	20
Steadiness		20
Quality and Condition		10
Staging		10
		100

Hens similar to above, just two black streaks down throat with slight, sometimes invisible streaks of black. No black mask on head. Body colour more brown. Hens are usually steadier than cocks. Points for size could be reduced and added to size and markings. Full plumage is not usually assumed until near breeding season.

Points

SNOW BUNTING

Size	As large as possible	**10**
Shape	Similar to hawfinch — thicker at back end	**10**
Markings	Well defined	**10**
Colour	Good sound pure white base colour; the more white the better, with deep nutty brown markings at side of head and shoulders, fading to buffish grey down the wings	**30**
Steadiness		**20**
Quality and Condition		**10**
Staging		**10**
		100

Hens very similar to above except they are more grey, lacking the profusion of white and nutty brown.

YELLOW BUNTING

Size and Shape	As large as possible. Good length of body. Thick set	**25**
Colours and Markings	Well defined, light chestnut brown on outer body feather, somewhat darker on sides of head and neck; base feather colour rich, deep yellow, as distinct a V shaped marking on head as is possible (NB. no yellow bunting is without some fine ticks in centre of V markings) and distinct cheek marking	**30**
Steadiness		**25**
Quality and Condition		**10**
Staging		**10**
		100

Hens similar to above, with far less yellow on head and devoid of V markings, and not so rich base yellow colour and carry heavy body markings.

MEADOW PIPIT

Size	Well developed	**15**
Shape	Full chest tapering to vent	**20**
Colour and Markings	Olive brown striped with black Eye cere sandy buff	**30**
Quality of Feather and Condition		**15**
Staging and Steadiness		**20**
		100

Points

ROCK PIPIT
Size	Well developed	10
Shape	Full chest tapering to vent	15
Colour and Markings	Olive brown covered with slaty blue hue, mottled markings	30
Quality of Feather and Condition		20
Steadiness and Staging		25
		100

TREE PIPIT
Size	Well developed	15
Shape	Full chest tapering away to vent	15
Colour and Markings	Upper parts brown streaked blackish; creamy-buff below	30
Quality of Feather and Condition		20
Steadiness and Staging		20
		100

REDSTART
Size	Well developed	10
Shape	Chubby	10
Colour and Markings	Eye markings and head shield well frosted; rich russet brown breast well frosted	40
Quality of Feather and Condition		20
Steadiness and Staging		20
		100

BLACK REDSTART
Size	Well developed	15
Shape	Chubby	15
Colour and Markings	Pure metallic colour well frosted and defined	30
Quality of Feather and Condition		20
Steadiness and Staging		20
		100

LONGTAILED TIT
Size	Well developed	15
Shape	Somewhat slim	10
Colour and Markings	Black and rose, well defined	35
Quality of Feather and Condition	Tight as possible	20
Steadiness and Staging		20
		100

Points

STARLING

Size	Looking strong	15
Shape	Cone shape	15
Colour	Black and reflections of green, purple and violet	20
Markings	Evenly and profusely spangled	30
Quality of Feather and Condition		10
Steadiness and Staging		10
		100

BLACKBIRD

Size	Well developed	15
Shape	Bold	20
Beak and Eye Cere	Rich crocus colour	10
Colour	Rich glossy black	20
Quality of Feather and Condition		20
Steadiness and Staging		15
		100

SONG THRUSH

Size	Well developed	15
Shape	Bold	15
Colour and Markings	Above olive brown, breast and lower body bright golden buff, with even dark spots	35
Quality of Feather and Condition		20
Steadiness and Staging		15
		100

MISTLE THRUSH

Size	Large	15
Shape	Stout build	15
Colour and Markings	Above rich ashy brown, breast buffish white tinged with gold, profuse dark spots	35
Quality of Feather and Condition		20
Steadiness and Staging		15
		100

WAXWING

Size	Must be neat and compact	15
Shape	Large thumb nail shaped bib	15
Colour and Markings	Dark cinnamon brown with slate blue flush, chestnut brown cap, waxings in wings and tail sharply defined	40

Points

Quality of Feather and Condition		15
Steadiness and Staging		15
		__100__

GREY WAGTAIL

Size	Well developed	10
Shape	Clean cut, cone shape	15
Colour and	Blue grey back, lemon yellow breast	
Markings	shading	35
Quality of Feather and Condition		20
Steadiness and Staging		20
		__100__

PIED WAGTAIL

Size	Well developed	10
Shape	Clean cut, cone shape	15
Colour and		
Markings	Slate black and white, colour well defined	35
Quality of Feather and Condition		20
Steadiness and Staging		20
		__100__

YELLOW WAGTAIL

Size	Well developed	10
Shape	Clean cut, cone shape	15
Colour and	Olive yellow back, pure yellow breast shading	
Markings	off to light yellow	35
Quality of Feather and Condition		20
Steadiness and Staging		20
		__100__

TREE CREEPER

Size	Well developed	15
Shape	Neatly proportioned	15
Colour and	Brown tinged with golden buff, striped with	
Markings	ashy grey	30
Quality of Feather and Condition		20
Steadiness and Staging		20
		__100__

Points

BLACKCAP

Size	Well developed	15
Shape	Chubby	15
Colour	Body good slate grey with olive flush; broad well cut cap	30
Quality of Feather and Condition		20
Steadiness and Staging		20
		100

NIGHTINGALE

Size	Well developed	15
Shape	Nice and round with a good belly line	15
Colour and Markings	Upper parts a warm rich brown with whitish, brown front and a brownish chestnut tail	30
Quality of Feather and Condition		20
Steadiness and Staging		20
		100

WHITETHROAT

Size	Neatly proportioned	10
Shape	Perky and full	15
Colour and Markings	Underparts very pale pinkish–buff with brownish grey extending to the nape and down the back with a pure white throat	35
Quality of Feather and Condition		20
Steadiness and Staging		20
		100

WREN

Size	Tiny and neat	10
Shape	Nice and plump and round	15
Colour and Markings	Closely barred brown, rich in colour with a short cocked tail	35
Quality of Feather and Condition		20
Steadiness and Staging		20
		100

WHINCHAT

Size	Well developed	10
Shape	Stocky, short-tailed appearance with a cottage loaf shaped head	30

Points

Colour and Markings	A good prominent eye stripe with streaked brown cheek crown and upper parts and warm buff throat and breast	25
Quality of Feather and Condition		20
Steadiness and Staging		15
		100

WHEATEAR

Size	As bold as possible	15
Shape	Nice and full with an upright stance	10
Colour and Markings	Varying shades of buff with a nice light grey back with blackish ear patches, wing edges and tail tips with a bright white rump	35
Quality of Feather and Condition		20
Steadiness and Staging		20
		100

JAY

Size	Well developed	10
Shape	Stout	15
Colour and Markings	Pinkish brown body with streaked black and white erect crown feathers, white patch on wings with blue and black barred wing coverts, also a good bright pale blue eye	35
Quality of Feather and Condition		20
Steadiness and Staging		20
		100

MAGPIE

Size	Well developed	10
Shape	Bold and fearless	15
Colour and Markings	White flanks and belly with white bars on wings; remainder black glossed blue, green and purple	35
Quality of Feather and Condition		20
Steadiness and Staging		20
		100

RING OUZEL

Size	Well developed	15
Shape	Bold	15
Colour and	Dull black plumage with lightish feather edges	

Points

Markings	and a white gorget or crescent	30
Quality of Feather and Condition		20
Steadiness and Staging		20
		100

FIELDFARE

Size	Large and strong	10
Shape	Bold	15
Colour and Markings	Pale grey head and rump with a chestnut back, throat and breast rusty yellow streaked with black, mottled flanks	35
Quality of Feather and Condition		20
Steadiness and Staging		20
		100

CHOUGH

Size	Well developed	15
Shape	Good broad width of head, nicely curved and uncrossed beak	15
Colour and Markings	Glossy blue black plumage; long curved red bill (not crossed) and red legs	30
Quality of Feather and Condition		20
Steadiness and Staging		20
		100

JACKDAW

Size	Well developed	15
Shape	Thick and sturdy, but compact	15
Colour and Markings	Black with grey nape and ear coverts, underparts dark grey with a good pale grey eye	30
Quality of Feather and Condition		20
Steadiness and Staging		20
		100

NUTHATCH

Size	Bold	10
Shape	Stubby and neat	10
Colour and Markings	RAF blue crown and back, carrying well down to the tail with buffish underparts, chestnut flanks and a nice bold black streak through eye	40
Quality of Feather and Condition		20
Steadiness and Staging		20
		100

Points

DUNNOCK
Size	Nice body size	10
Shape	Chubby	15
Colour and Markings	Rich brown and dark grey upper parts streaked with black, head and neck slate grey, underparts slate grey with dark streaked flanks	35
Quality of Feather and Condition		20
Steadiness and Staging		20
		100

REDWING
Size	Slightly smaller than song thrush	10
Shape	Bold and neat	15
Colour and Markings	Rich olive brown above with a broad buff eye stripe paler underparts with streaked breast and chestnut flanks and under the wings	35
Quality of Feather and Condition		20
Steadiness and Staging		20
		100

STONECHAT
Size	Well developed	10
Shape	Plump with a good upright pose	15
Colour and Markings	To have a distinctive black head and throat, with a broad white half collar, underparts rich chestnut shading to a warm buff	35
Quality of Feather and Condition		20
Steadiness and Staging		20
		100

SPOTTED FLYCATCHER
Size	Nicely proportioned	15
Shape	To be of an upright watchful pose	15
Colour and Markings	Ashy brown plumage with spotted crown and lightly streaked whitish breast	30
Quality of Feather and Condition		20
Steadiness and Staging		20
		100

Points

LESSER WHITETHROAT

Size	Small and neat	10
Shape	Compact with short tails	15
Colour and	Grey upper parts with dark ear coverts	
Markings	giving a masked appearance	35
Quality of Feather and Condition		20
Steadiness and Staging		20
		100

Figure 12.3   An interesting group of Hybrids
1. Ticked Siskin-Canary. 2. Unevenly marked Goldfinch-Canary. 3. Redpoll-Goldfinch.
4. Bullfinch-Canary.

CHAPTER 13

Recognition of Birds

There are many books on the market which give detailed descriptions of birds on the British list and every British bird enthusiast should have one. Most have coloured plates but it is not always easy to relate these to birds seen in the wild or even in one's garden. Few explain how to recognise a bird and it is hoped that these notes will assist those who are just starting to study the birds around us. Those taking up the breeding of British birds should also study their selected species in the wild and follow nature as far as possible.

One should first study and learn the topography of a bird, so that descriptions naming these parts can be understood. It is not, however, necessary to be able to recognise all the British species before being able to enjoy watching birds. For some the collection of lists of birds seen, like train spotting, is reward enough for the time and energy expended. The British bird keeper, however, will want to know much more. What is the bird doing, what is it feeding on, where is it nesting, why is it in this particular location, and indeed how does it live its life?

Most people will only ever see about three quarters of the birds on the British list and it is not necessary to be able to recognise all of these before starting to watch birds. A start can be made on the birds around the garden and those which are attracted to the bird table in bad weather. It is a great help to make a sketch of the bird at the time it is seen, noting the main colours and any markings noticed so that this can be compared with illustrations and a process of elimination used to arrive at the correct identification.

Some of the things to look for when attempting to identify birds are:

Size — compare the size of the strange bird with that of a well known bird such as a sparrow, blackbird or rook.

Shape — is it plump and round like a robin, or slender like a wagtail? Is the beak short and conical like a sparrow, pointed like a wren, longer and stronger like a starling or flat like a duck; or perhaps long and curved like some of the waders? Does it have a crest like the crested tit, skylark or lapwing?

Behaviour — if the bird is on the ground notice how it moves. Does it walk like a blackbird, run spasmodically like a wagtail or shuffle along like the hedge-sparrow (dunnock)? Does it use its tail in a characteristic way like a wagtail, wagging it up and down, quivering it like a redstart, or cocking it up like a wren? If it climbs trees, does it move in short jerks like a woodpecker, run up and down like a nuthatch or climb upwards in spirals like a tree-creeper? If the bird is on water, does it swim high in the water like a moorhen or low with the body almost submerged like the grebe, and does it dive? Does it stand in the shallows for long periods like the heron or run along

182

TOPOGRAPHY

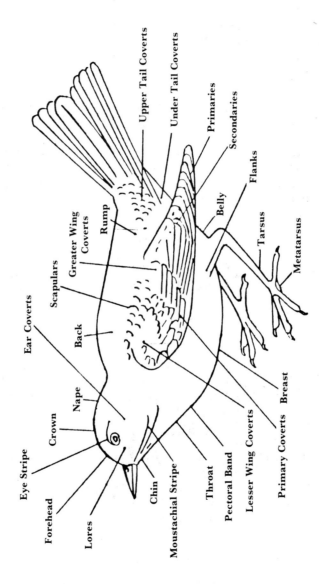

Eye Stripe

Forehead

Lores

Crown

Nape

Ear Coverts

Scapulars

Back

Greater Wing
Coverts

Rump

Upper Tail Coverts

Under Tail Coverts

Primaries

Secondaries

Flanks

Belly

Tarsus

Metatarsus

Chin

Moustachial Stripe

Throat

Pectoral Band

Lesser Wing Coverts

Primary Coverts

Breast

Figure 13.1   Principal Parts of a Bird

the margins like a sandpiper? If it is in the air how does it fly? Does it fly straight like the starling or zig zag like a snipe? Does it beat its wings slowly like the heron or rapidly like a mallard; or maybe with alternate wing beating and stooping like the fieldfare?

Plumage and field marks — some birds can be recognised by colour and size alone, but it is usually necessary to look for field marks. First note the general colour or colours and whether these are on top of the bird or underneath, then look for the field marks, streaks and spots and eyestripes, for example, the spots on the underside of a song thrush. Wing bars are a very important feature in the identification of some birds.

Habitat and season — by noting the type of habitat and time of year in which the bird is seen it is possible to establish the species. For example a water bird is unlikely to be found in a wood, and a summer visitor is unlikely to be seen in the winter, as is a winter visitor unlikely to be seen in the summer.

Song and call notes — are the best identification of all, but generally speaking the most difficult to learn. Records of bird songs can be obtained and played over and over again until the different songs become familiar, but it takes a lot of practice.

SCIENTIFIC SYSTEM OF NAMING

Many people have difficulty in understanding the scientific naming of birds and it is hoped that the following explanation will be helpful:

1. Birds are first divided into orders or groups which clearly have some relationship to each other, such as *Arderiformes*, geese and ducks, *Strigiformes* owls, *Passeriformes*, perching and singing birds, *Ciconiiformes*, herons and storks, *Falconiformes*, birds of prey, *Charadriiformes*, waders and gulls. All these names end in *iformes*.

2. Each order is split into families which names end in *idae* for example *Corvidae* (crow family).

3. Each family is split into genus which indicates the type of bird in the family. It is a single word.

4. Each genus is sub-divided into species which are the individual birds. The species name is two words; the first word is the generic name and the second the specific name, that is the genus and the species.

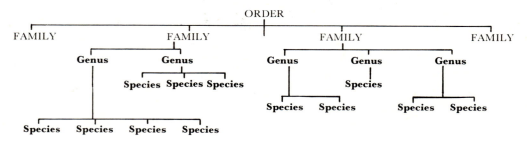

The species is the fundamental unit of classification and the name consists of two words usually derived from Greek or Latin. For example the common gull is *Larus canus*. The first word indicates the genus and the second word an adjective describing the first. The two words together constitute the scientific name of the species.

5. Sub–species (or race): species are sometimes divided into sub–species to denote birds which are slightly different from the main population usually due to geographical isolation.

APPENDIX

1. **When to Look and Listen for Migrants**
2. **Interesting Natural History Organisations**
3. **British Bird Council Constitution**
4. **Bibliography**
5. **Wildlife and Countryside Act**

1. WHEN TO LOOK AND LISTEN FOR MIGRANTS

The British Isles are particularly well situated for migrants, both with regard to position and climate. These can be divided into three main groups:
1. Species that visit Britain to breed. (Spring and Summer visitors).
2. Species that come here for the winter (Autumn and Winter visitors).
3. Species that pass through twice a year to their breeding areas in the North, and on return to their wintering grounds in the South.

Below is a list of the more common migrants and the periods when they are most likely to be first seen in England and their departure times. The arrival dates for summer migrants will be later in northern England and Scotland and variations according to weather conditions can be expected.

Species	Usual Arrival Time	Usual Departure Period
Chiffchaff	3rd week March	October
Wheatear	3rd week March	October
Sand Martin	4th week March	October
Willow Warbler	4th week March	September
Sandwich Tern	4th week March	September
Ring Ouzel	1st week April	October
Swallow	1st week April	October
Blackcap	1st week April	September
Yellow Wagtail	1st week April	September
Redstart	1st week April	September
Common Tern	1st week April	September
Common Sandpiper	2nd week April	September
Tree Pipit	2nd week April	September
House Martin	2nd week April	October
Cuckoo	2nd week April	September
Sedge Warbler	2nd week April	September
Nightingale	2nd week April	September
Whitethroat	3rd week April	September
Grasshopper Warbler	3rd week April	September
Garden Warbler	3rd week April	September
Whinchat	3rd week April	October
Pied Flycatcher	4th week April	September
Swift	4th week April	August
Turtle Dove	4th week April	October
Reed Warbler	4th week April	September
Spotted Flycatcher	1st week May	September
Nightjar	2nd week May	September
Snow Bunting	September	April
Redwing	September	May
Hooded Crow	September	April
Brambling	September	March
Woodcock	September	April
Teal	September	April

Pink-footed goose	September	April
Wood Pigeon	September	April
Curlew	September	April
Starling	October	March
Waxwing	October	March
Fieldfare	October	May
Kestrel	October	March

2.   INTERESTING NATURAL HISTORY ORGANISATIONS

Government Departments

1. *Nature Conservancy* Natural Environment Research Council, 19 Belgrave Square, London SW1
Performs scientific work on the conservation of the flora and fauna of Great Britain. Also establishes, maintains and manages statutory nature reserves.
2. *The Countryside Commission*   1 Cambridge Gate, Regents Park, London NW1
Manages the ten National Parks and twenty–four areas of outstanding natural beauty in England and Wales. It is also concerned with the preservation of the countryside and its use for outdoor recreation.

Voluntary Organisations

1. *British Ornithologists' Union*   c/o Bird Room, British Museum (Natural History), Cromwell Road, London SW7
The senior ornithological society in Great Britain instituted for the advancement of the science of ornithology. Publishes the quarterly journal *Ibis*.
2. *British Trust for Ornithology*   Beech Grove, Tring, Hertfordshire
Formed for the advancement of knowledge of British Birds by field studies. Organises enquiries into particular species of birds.
3. *International Council for Bird Preservation*   (British Section), c/o British Museum (Natural History), Cromwell Road, London, SW7.
Investigates matters dealing with international law and protection. I.C.B.P. headquarters are in Switzerland.
4. *Royal Society for the Protection of Birds*   The Lodge, Sandy, Bedfordshire.
Establishes non–statutory reserves, carries out research and educational projects. Publishes bi–monthly magazine *Birds*.
5. *Scottish Ornithologists' Club*   17 Regent Terrace, Edinburgh 7
Has branches in major centres in Scotland holding meetings and outings.
6. *Society for the Promotion of Nature Reserves*   c/o British Museum (Natural History), Cromwell Road, London SW7
Details of Trusts in your own county can be obtained from this society.
7. *Wildfowl Trust*   Slimbridge, Gloucestershire
A unique collection of wildfowl from all over the world. Well worth a visit. Also a research organisation concerned with ducks, geese and swans. The Trust also owns a number of other centres.
8. *County Bird Watching Societies*   Natural History Societies and County Conservation Trusts.
Most counties have their own societies which usually have programmes of indoor lectures and films and outdoor field meetings, and sometimes arrange ornithological enquiries. Details can usually be obtained through the local museum, public library or information bureau.

3. BRITISH BIRD COUNCIL (AFFILIATED TO THE N.C.A.)
THE CONSTITUTION

1. **Name:** *The British Bird Council.*
2. **Constitution:** The Council shall be constituted of two delegated members from each of the member specialist societies who shall serve for a period of three years, and shall be eligible for re-election immediately. The Council shall have power to co-opt on to the Council any individual or delegates from other societies if they, the Council, by a simple majority think fit.
3. **Objects:** To promote and further the hobby of keeping, breeding and exhibiting British birds in all its aspects.
4. **Mandate:**
    To enquire into the keeping, breeding and exhibiting of British birds.
    To collate information on breeding results and to make such information available to the fancy.
    To investigate, report on and recommend the size of cages suitable for the exhibition of British birds and to issue directives thereon to the specialist societies.
    To determine the size of close rings suitable for each species and to direct the specialist societies as to their use.
    To act as a Council or by an authorised representative, who need not be a Council Member, as representing the British bird fancy.
    To seek representation on the Home Office Advisory Committee dealing with the protection of birds.
    To further the goodwill and co-operate with all bodies who have as their objects the protection of British birds.
    To seek such assurances as necessary that the legitimate exercise of the freedom to enjoy the hobby shall not be restricted by further legislation without full consultation and consideration of any representations made by the Council.
    To affiliate with the National Council of Aviculture.
5. **Chairman:** The Members so appointed shall appoint a Chairman, whose term of office shall be for a period of three years, and shall be eligible for re-election immediately.
6. **Vice Chairman:** The Members so appointed shall appoint a Vice Chairman whose term of office shall be for a period of three years, and shall be eligible for re-election immediately.
    The Vice Chairman's duties shall be to assist the Chairman in every way and to take over the Chairman's duties if and when the Chairman, for any reason is unable to perform them himself.
7. **Secretary and Treasurer:**
    The Members so appointed shall appoint a Secretary and a Treasurer, whose terms of office shall be for a period of three years, and shall be eligible for re-election immediately.
    His duties shall be to convene and organise, to keep the minutes and deal with correspondence. The Secretary shall not make any decisions on behalf of the Council, and shall not be responsible for the decisions the Council take.
    It will be the treasurer's duty to receive all monies on behalf of the

Council, to pay all bills and expenses and keep a proper account thereof.

8. **Ring Registrar and Breeding Records Officer:**

   The Members so appointed shall appoint a Ring Registrar and Breeding Records Officer whose term of office shall be for a period of three years, and shall be eligible for re-election immediately.

   His duties shall be to issue council rings in whatever way may be decided by the Council, and keep proper records thereof, and to receive and keep full records of all Breeding Achievements of British Birds.

9. **Council Meetings:**

   Seven members of the Council, which may include the Chairman, Secretary or Ring Registrar, shall form a quorum and no business shall be transacted unless such a quorum is present.

   The Meetings shall be held at such place and at such time as the Members shall agree, or failing agreement, as determined by the Chairman and Secretary who shall have regard to the convenience of the Members of the Council.

10. At all meetings the Chairman shall have a casting vote in addition to his vote as a Member of the Council.

    All matters before the Council shall be decided by a simple majority of the Members present.

    A Member of the Council shall lose his seat thereon if he does not attend a meeting for one year.

    In the event of the resignation or death of any Council Member, the Secretary shall call upon the specialist society whose delegate he is, to appoint another delegate without delay.

11. The Council's year shall be from January 1st to December 31st.

Individual Membership of the British Bird Council

For some time the Council has been giving consideration to according membership to those British Bird Fanciers who wish to identify themselves more closely with the work of the Council.

The Council has now agreed to accept individual fanciers into membership and has drawn up the **Standing Orders** listed below. Whilst these Orders do not entirely describe the full benefits of membership, it will be apparent that belonging to the Council, whose contacts with the various Government Departments, MPs and other bodies, is able to accord protection of rights in many directions, will be worthwhile, and you will be providing an insurance for your hobby in the future.

1. The fee will be £5 per annum (subject to revision at an Annual General Meeting) January to December each year, except fees paid after November 14th in any one year shall be applicable for the whole of the following year.

2. An official receipt must be given as soon as possible after receipt of the fee.

3. Date of operation will be from 1978.

4. The Council reserve the right to refuse membership to any individual without explanation.

5. If a protest is received in connection with item 4, a sub-committee comprising Chairman, Secretary, Treasurer, Publicity Officer and one Council member shall be appointed to consider the case. This can be

dealt with in correspondence if necessary, Secretary in the initiative.

6. Subscriptions may be made by Banker's Order on an appropriate form provided by the Council.

7. The fact of accepting individual membership of the BBC does not affect the present Constitution of the Council and such individual members will have no voting rights at meetings of the Council. An Annual General Meeting will be called to which all members may attend to discuss Council policy. Any suggestions such members care to put forward in regard to improvements, etc., to the working of the Council, or any ideas, would be welcomed and receive consideration, by invitation of the presiding Chairman.

8. Individual members shall be sent as much information of the business of the Council as is deemed reasonable, shall receive all benefits of the services of the Council and shall have the right to have any questions they raise answered to the best ability of the Officers.

9. Individual membership shall be open to anyone interested in the keeping and breeding of British birds in cages and aviaries or to anyone else interested in the work of the council.

10. If in the fullness of time the fanciers themselves decide that they require one organisation to represent the British Bird Fancy, or a Specialist Society through its AGM or EGM decides to transfer its organisation and membership to the BBC and thus relinquishes its individuality, then these Standing Orders will require to be altered/amended etc. to make provision for such changes.

4. BIBLIOGRAPHY

Woodland Birds   Eric Simms. Collins, 1971

Man and Birds   R. K. Murton. Collins

Finches   Ian Newton. Collins, 1972

The Bird Table Book in Colour   Tony Soper. David & Charles, 1977

Watching Birds   James Fisher & Jim Flegg. Poyser, 1974

Pine Crossbills   Desmond Nethersole–Thompson. Poyser, 1975

Bird Spotting   John Holland. Blandford Press, 1959

Birds in Colour   Bruce Campbell. Blandford Press, 1974

British Thrushes   Eric Simms. Collins, 1978

British Tits   Christopher Perrins. Collins, 1979

The Oxford Book of Birds   Bruce Campbell & Donald Watson. OUP, 1964

Finding Nests   B. Campbell. Collins

Bird Migration   A. Landsborough Thomson. Published by H. F. & G. Witherby, 1943

Migration of Birds   F. Lincoln

Studies of Bird Migration   G. Rudebeck

Owls   J. Sparks & T. Soper. Published by David & Charles, 1970

The Life of the Robin   David Lack. H. F. & G. Witherby, 1965

Bird Watching for Beginners   Dr. Bruce Campbell & R. A. Richardson

The Atlas of Breeding Birds in Britain and Ireland   J. T. R. Sharrock. Published by the British Trust for Ornithology, 1976

The Hamlyn Guide to Birds of Britain & Europe   B. Bruun & A. Singer. Published 1970

Bird Observatories in Britain and Ireland   edited by Roger Durman. Published by Poyser 1976

How to feed and attract the Wild Birds   H. M. Batten. (B.T.O. Field Guide)

The Popular Handbook of British Birds   P. A. D. Hollom. H. F. & G. Witherby, 1978

Birds of Britain and Europe in Colour   Avon and Tilford. Blandford Press, 1975

Reader's Digest Book of British Birds   J. E. Cooper. David & Charles, 1979

Nesting Birds, Eggs and Fledglings   Winwood Reade & Eric Hosking. Blandford Press, 1975

First Aid and Care of Wild Birds   J. E. Cooper. David & Charles, 1979

Every Garden a Bird Sanctuary   E. L. Turner. H. F. & G. Witherby, 1936

Collins Guide to Bird Watching   R. S. R. Fitter. Published by Collins

Nest Boxes   Edwin Cohen and Dr. Bruce Campbell (B.T.O. Field Guide No. 3)

Reference Books generally obtainable at libraries

The Handbook of British Birds   H. F. Witherby

The Hawfinch   Guy Mountfort

5. The Wildlife and Countryside Act 1981
which replaces the previous Protection of Birds' Acts

The following explanation of the *Wildlife and Countryside Act* insofar as it affects aviculture, particularly British species, is given for the help and guidance of bird keepers and lovers, but the Council accept no responsibility for its legal accuracy. It is an attempt to explain the intention of the *Act* in layman's terms and has been agreed by the Department of the Environment (who sponsored the Bill) at the time of going to print, but is subject of course to any subsequent amending order or Act of Parliament.

The **British Bird Council** urges all fanciers to make themselves familiar with the provisions of the *Act* and to ensure that they keep within the law at all times. If any fanciers are not clear on any point the Secretary of the Council will be pleased to obtain an explanation for them if they will contact him.

Further, the Council will, whenever necessary, produce leaflets listing any amendments, which may be made from time to time which will be available to anyone from the Secretary for a small charge which will be fixed, to enable the Council to recover the cost of printing and postage.

Protection

All wild birds, their eggs and nests are protected

It is an offence to kill, injure, take, damage or destroy or attempt to do any of these things. All birds on the British list are included. That means not only resident species but also those which are regular or passage migrants which visit these shores, including quite a number which are rare. (Foreign bird keepers must also check whether any species which they wish to keep is on the British list). The total is over 400.

It is not unlawful to kill a bird if a person can prove to a court that it was necessary to prevent serious damage to crops etc. or to take a bird in order to tend and release it, or to kill a disabled bird, other than one disabled by his own act, provided that the bird is so badly injured that it is unlikely to recover.

Injured Birds

If an injured bird is taken solely for the purpose of tending it and then releasing it when it is no longer disabled, no offence is committed. This does not allow the bird to be kept permanently and anyone keeping such a bird might have to satisfy the court both that he intended to release the bird as soon as he could humanely do so and that the bird had not been disabled by his own act. Birds which are permanently disabled, and thus cannot be released back to the wild, may be kept without licence.

Possession

It is an offence to have in one's possession or control any wild bird on the British list unless obtained under licence. Wild bird means any bird which has not been bred in cage or aviary and proof by ringing or registration or both may be required.

Ringing and Registration

The method of ringing and registration is to be in accordance with regulations made by the Secretary of State and he may make different provision for different birds or birds in different sections.

Imported Birds

All birds on the British list are protected, whether they originate from this country or not, and birds imported from the continent or elsewhere are protected in the same way. (Foreign bird keepers must check the British list to ensure that the birds they wish to keep are not included). While the scientific name of each bird is given in the various schedules there could well be difficulties with some sub-species which are very similar to the main race.

Nests and Eggs

It is illegal to take, damage or destroy the nest of any wild bird while that nest is in use or being built, and it is illegal to take or destroy or damage an egg of any wild bird in any way so that it will not hatch.

Marking

A licence is required to ring or mark any wild bird.

Wild Bird

The term *wild bird* within the *Act* means any bird of a kind which is ordinarily resident in or is a visitor to Great Britain in a wild state. It does not include any bird which is shown to have been bred in captivity, providing that its parents were lawfully in captivity when the egg was laid.

Traps

The killing and taking of any birds by the use of gin traps, hooks and lines, bird lime, poisonous baits, gas, maimed live decoys etc. is strictly prohibited and constitutes a separate offence to taking the bird itself.

Aviculture

This means the breeding and rearing of birds in captivity. A bird shall not be treated as bred in captivity unless its parents were lawfully in captivity when the egg was laid.

Sale

It is illegal to sell or offer for sale or to advertise birds for sale other than those in Part I of Schedule 3 and these birds must be bred in cages or aviaries and ringed. It is also illegal to sell or advertise birds' eggs, dead birds or their skins. Sale includes hire, barter and exchange.

Registerable Birds

It is an offence to have in one's possession or control any bird included in Schedule 4 which has not been registered and ringed or marked in accordance with regulations made by the Secretary of State.

Exhibition

Only birds listed in Part I of Schedule 3 can be exhibited and they must be ringed. It is an offence to show or permit to be shown any live wild bird other than captive bred and ringed birds in Part I of Schedule 3 for the purpose of any competition or in premises in which a competition is being held or any live bird one of whose parents was such a wild bird.

This means that hybrids can only be shown if both parents appear in Part I of Schedule 3 and Mules can only be shown if the parent, other than the canary, appears in Part I of Schedule 3.

Show Committees

As the club running a show is a corporate body it is an offence if they allow any bird which should not be exhibited to be shown and in such cases the club, the club officials and show committees are deemed to be as guilty as the exhibitor himself and they are liable for the same penalties.

Cage Sizes

It is an offence to keep or confine any bird whatsoever in any cage or other receptacle which is not sufficient in height, length or breadth to permit the bird to stretch its wings freely. These conditions do not apply:-
(a) while the bird is in the course of conveyance or
(b) while it is undergoing treatment by a veterinary surgeon or practitioner or
(c) while the bird is being shown for the purpose of public exhibition or competition for not more than 72 hours.

Schedules

In each Schedule the common name or names is given first for guidance only. In the event of any dispute or proceedings only the scientific name is to be taken into account.

Power to vary Schedules

The Secretary of State may by order either add any bird to, or remove any bird from any of the Schedules 1 to 4 or any part of those Schedules.

Schedule 1: Part I

Birds which are protected by special penalities at all times.

Common name	Scientific name
Avocet	*Recurvirostra avosetta*
Bee-eater	*Metrops apiaster*

Bittern	*Botaurus stellaris*
Bittern Little	*Ixobrychus minutus*
Bluethroat	*Luscinia svecica*
Brambling	*Fringilla montifringilla*
Bunting, Cirl	*Emberiza cirlus*
Bunting, Lapland	*Calcarius lapponicus*
Bunting, Snow	*Plectrophenax nivalis*
Buzzard, Honey	*Pernis apivorus*
Chough	*Pyrrhocorax pyrrhocorax*
Corncrake	*Crex crex*
Crake, Spotted	*Porzana porzana*
Crossbills (All species)	*Loxia*
Curlew, Stone	*Burhinus oedicnemus*
Divers (All species)	*Gavia*
Dotterel	*Charadrius morinellus*
Duck, Long-tailed	*Clangula hyemalis*
Eagle, Golden	*Aquila chrysaetos*
Eagle, White-tailed	*Haliaetus albicilla*
Falcon, Gyr	*Falco rusticolus*
Fieldfare	*Turdus pilaris*
Firecrest	*Regulus ignicapillus*
Garganey	*Anas querquedula*
Godwit, Black-tailed	*Limosa limosa*
Goshawk	*Accipiter gentilis*
Grebe, Black-necked	*Podiceps nigricollis*
Grebe, Slavonian	*Podiceps auritus*
Greenshank	*Tringa nebularia*
Gull, Little	*Larus minutus*
Gull, Mediterranean	*Larus melanocephalus*
Harriers (All species)	*Circus*
Heron, Purple	*Ardea purpurea*
Hobby	*Falco subbuteo*
Hoopoe	*Upupa epops*
Kingfisher	*Alcedo atthis*
Kite, Red	*Milvus milvus*
Merlin	*Falco columbarius*
Oriole, Golden	*Oriolus oriolus*
Osprey	*Pandion haliaetus*
Owl, Barn	*Tyto alba*
Owl, Snowy	*Nyctea scandiaca*
Peregrine	*Falco peregrinus*
Petrel, Leach's	*Oceanodroma leucorhoa*
Phalarope, Red-necked	*Phalaropus lobatus*
Plover, Kentish	*Charadrius alexandrinus*
Plover, Little ringed	*Charadrius dubius*
Quail, Common	*Coturnix coturnix*
Redstart, Black	*Phoenicurus ochruros*
Redwing	*Turdus iliacus*
Rosefinch, Scarlet	*Carpodacus erythrinus*
Ruff	*Philomachus pugnax*
Sandpiper, Green	*Tringa ochropus*
Sandpiper, Purple	*Calidris maritima*
Sandpiper, Wood	*Tringa glareola*
Scaup	*Aythya marila*
Scoter, Common	*Melanitta nigra*
Scoter, Velvet	*Melanitta fusca*
Serin	*Serinus serinus*
Shorelark	*Eremophila alpestris*
Shrike, Red-backed	*Lanius collurio*
Spoonbill	*Platalea leucorodia*
Stilt, Black-Winged	*Himantopus himantopus*
Stint, Temminck's	*Calidris temminckii*
Swan, Bewick's	*Cygnus bewickii*
Swan, Whooper	*Cygnus cygnus*
Tern, Black	*Chlidonias niger*
Tern, Little	*Sterna albifrons*
Tern, Roseate	*Sterna dougallii*

196

Tit, Bearded	*Panurus biarmicus*
Tit, Crested	*Parus cristatus*
Treecreeper, Short-Toed	*Certhia brachydactyla*
Warbler, Cetti's	*Cettia cetti*
Warbler, Dartford	*Sylvia undata*
Warbler, Marsh	*Acrocephalus palustris*
Warbler, Savi's	*Locustella luscinioides*
Whimbrel	*Numenius phaeopus*
Woodlark	*Lullula arborea*
Wryneck	*Jynx torquilla*

Schedule 1: Part II

Birds which are protected by special penalities during the close season which in general is the 1st February to the 31st August.

Common Name	Scientific Name
Golden-eye	*Bucephala clangula*
Goose, Greylag	*Anser anser*
(In Outer Hebrides, Caithness, Sutherland and Wester Ross only)	
Pintail	*Anas acuta*

Offences in connection with birds on this Schedule incur a fine of up to £1000 in respect of each bird, nest or egg.

In addition the court shall order the forfeiture of any bird, nest or egg in respect of which the offence was committed and may order the forfeiture of any vehicle, animal, weapon or other thing which was used to commit the offence.

Schedule 2: Part I

Birds which may be taken or killed by authorised persons outside the close season which in general is the 1st February to the 31st August.

Common Name	Scientific Name
Capercaillie	*Tetrao urogallus*
Coot	*Fulica atra*
Duck, Tufted	*Aythya fuligula*
Gadwall	*Anas strepera*
Golden-eye	*Bucephala clangula*
Goose, Canada	*Branta canadensis*
Goose, Greylag	*Anser anser*
Goose, Pink-footed	*Anser brachyrhynchus*
Goose, White-fronted	*Anser albifrons*
(in England and Wales only)	
Mallard	*Anas platyrhynchos*
Moorhen	*Gallinula chloropus*
Pintail	*Anus acuta*
Plover, Golden	*Pluvialis apricaria*
Pochard	*Aythya ferina*
Shoveler	*Anas clypeata*
Snipe, Common	*Gallinago gallinago*
Teal	*Anas crecca*
Wigeon	*Anas penelope*
Woodcock	*Scolopax rusticola*

Schedule 2: Part II

Birds which may be taken or killed by authorised persons at all times.

Common Name	Scientific Name
Crow	*Corvus corone*
Dove, Collared	*Streptopelia decaocto*
Gull, Great Black-Backed	*Larus marinus*
Gull, Lesser Black-Backed	*Larus fuscus*
Gull, Herring	*Larus argentatus*
Jackdaw	*Corvus monedula*

Jay	*Garrulus glandarius*
Magpie	*Pica pica*
Pigeon, Feral	*Columba livia*
Rook	*Corvus frugilegus*
Sparrow, House	*Passer domesticus*
Starling	*Sturnus vulgaris*
Woodpigeon	*Columba palumbus*

Authorised Person   This means:

(a) The owner or occupier, or any person authorised by the owner or occupier, of the land on which the action authorised is taken.

(b) Any person authorised in writing by the local authority for the area within which the action authorised is taken.

(c) In connection with wild birds, any person authorised in writing by the Nature Conservancy Council; a water authority; statutory water undertakers or a local fisheries committee, but these authorisations do not confer any right of entry upon any land.

Offences in connection with birds on this Schedule incur a fine of up to £200 in respect of each bird, nest or egg.

In addition the court shall order the forfeiture of any bird, nest or egg in respect of which the offence was committed and may order the forfeiture of any vehicle, animal, weapon or other thing which was used to commit the offence.

Schedule 3: Part I

Birds which may be sold alive at all times provided that they are bred in captivity and ringed. They can also be exhibited if ringed, and it is only birds in this Schedule which can be sold alive or exhibited.

Common Name	**Scientific Name**
Blackbird	*Turdus merula*
Brambling	*Fringilla montifringilla*
Bullfinch	*Pyrrhula pyrrhula*
Bunting, Reed	*Erberiza schoeniclus*
Chaffinch	*Fringilla coelebs*
Dunnock	*Prunella modularis*
Goldfinch	*Carduelis carduelis*
Greenfinch	*Chloris chloris*
Jackdaw	*Corvus monedula*
Jay	*Garrulus glandarius*
Linnet	*Carduelis cannabina*
Magpie	*Pica pica*
Owl, Barn	*Tyto alba*
Redpoll	*Carduelis flammea*
Siskin	*Carduelis spinus*
Starling	*Sturnus vulgaris*
Thrush, Song	*Turdus philomelos*
Twite	*Carduelis flavirostris*
Yellowhammer	*Emberiza citrinella*

Exhibition

It is an offence to show or permit to be shown any live wild bird other than those in this Schedule for the purpose of any competition or any live bird one of whose parents was such a wild bird.

It is an offence if either parent of a hybrid is not on this Schedule and it is an offence if a mule is shown if the parent other than the canary is not on this Schedule.

Show Committees

If any offence is committed the club officials and show committee are deemed to be as guilty as the exhibitor and are each liable for the same penalties.

Offences in connection with birds on this Schedule incur a fine of up to £200 in respect of each bird, nest or egg.

In addition the court shall order the forfeiture of any bird, nest or egg in respect of which the offence was committed and may order the forfeiture of any vehicle, animal, weapon or other thing which was used to commit the offence.

Schedule 3: Part II

Birds which may be sold dead at all times.

Common Name	Scientific Name
Pigeon, Feral	*Columba livia*
Woodpigeon	*Columba palumbus*

Schedule 3: Part III

Birds which may be sold dead from the 1st September to the 28th February.

Common Name	Scientific Name
Capercaillie	*Tetrao urogallus*
Coot	*Fulica atra*
Duck, Tufted	*Aythya fuligula*
Mallard	*Anas platyrhynchos*
Pintail	*Anas acuta*
Plover, Golden	*Pluvialis apricaria*
Pochard	*Aythya ferina*
Shoveler	*Anas clypeata*
Snipe, Common	*Gallinago gallinago*
Teal	*Anas crecca*
Wigeon	*Anas penelope*
Woodcock	*Scolopax rusticola*

Offences in connection with birds on these Schedules incur a fine of up to £200 in respect of each bird.

In addition the court shall order the forfeiture of any bird in respect of which the offence was committed and may order the forfeiture of any vehicle, animal, weapon or other thing which was used to commit the offence.

Schedule 4

Birds which must be registered and ringed or marked in accordance with regulations made by the Secretary of State if kept in captivity.

Common Name	Scientific Name
Avocet	*Recurvirostra avosetta*
Bee-eater	*Merops apiaster*
Bittern	*Botaurus stellaris*
Bittern, Little	*Ixobrychus minutus*
Bluethroat	*Luscinia svecica*
Bunting, Cirl	*Emberiza cirlus*
Bunting, Lapland	*Calcarius lapponicus*
Bunting, Snow	*Plectrophenax nivalis*
Chough	*Pyrrhocorax pyrrhocorax*
Corncrake	*Crex crex*
Crake, Spotted	*Porzana porzana*
Crossbills (All species)	*Loxia*
Curlew, Stone	*Burhinus oedicnemus*
Divers (All species)	*Gavia*
Dotterel	*Charadrius morinellus*
Duck, Long-tailed	*Clangula hyemalis*
Falcons (All species)	*Falconidae*
Falcon, Gyr	*Falco rusticolus*
Fieldfare	*Turdus pilaris*
Firecrest	*Regulus ignicapillus*
Godwit, Black-tailed	*Limosa limosa*
Grebe, Black-necked	*Podiceps nigrocollis*
Grebe, Salvonian	*Podiceps auritus*
Greenshank	*Tringa nebularia*
Hawks (True)	*Accipitridae*
(Except Old World Vultures) i.e. Buzzards, Eagles, Harriers, Hawks and Kites. (All species in each case)	(Except the Genera *Aegypius, Gypaetus, Gypohierax, Gyps, Neophron, Sarcogyps* and *Trigonoceps*)
Hoopoe	*Upupa epops*
Kingfisher	*Alcedo atthis*
Oriole, Golden	*Oriolus oriolus*
Osprey	*Pandion haliaetus*

199

Petrel, Leach's	*Oceanodroma leucorhoa*
Phalarope, Red-Necked	*Phalaropus lobatus*
Plover, Kentish	*Charadrius alexandrinus*
Plover, Little Ringed	*Charadrius dubius*
Quail, Common	*Coturnix coturnix*
Redstart, Black	*Phoenicurus ochruros*
Redwing	*Turdus iliacus*
Rosefinch, Scarlet	*Carpodacus erythrinus*
Ruff	*Philomachus pugnax*
Sandpiper, Green	*Tringa ochropus*
Sandpiper, Purple	*Calidris maritima*
Sandpiper, Wood	*Tringa glareola*
Scoter, Common	*Melanitta nigra*
Scoter, Velvet	*Melannita fusca*
Serin	*Serinus serinus*
Shorelark	*Eremophila alpestris*
Shrike, Red-backed	*Lanius collurio*
Spoonbill	*Platalea leucorodia*
Stilt, Black-winged	*Himantopus himantopus*
Stint, Temminck's	*Calidris temminckii*
Tern, Black	*Chlidonias niger*
Tern, Little	*Sterna albifrons*
Tern, Roseate	*Sterna dougallii*
Tit, Bearded	*Panurus biarmicus*
Tit, Crested	*Parus cristatus*
Treecreeper, Short-toed	*Certhia brachydactyla*
Warbler, Cetti's	*Cettia cetti*
Warbler, Dartford	*Sylvia undata*
Warbler, Marsh	*Acrocephalus palustris*
Warbler, Savi's	*Locustella luscinioides*
Whimbrel	*Numenius phaeopus*
Woodlark	*Lullula arborea*
Wryneck	*Jynx torquilla*

Registration

It is an offence to have in one's possession or control any bird included in this Schedule which has not been registered and ringed or marked in accordance with regulations made by the Secretary of State and such an offence incurs a special penalty of a fine of up to £1000 in respect of each bird concerned.

False Statements

If any person makes a statement or representation or furnishes a document or information which is false or which he knows to be false in a material particular for the purpose of obtaining either for himself or another, a registration in accordance with the regulations or the grant of a licence, he is guilty of an offence. Such an offence incurs a fine of up to £500. In addition the court shall order the forfeiture of any bird in respect of which the offence was committed.

Exhibitions

Birds in Schedule 4 are not allowed to be exhibited for competition and it is an offence for any of these birds to be on show in any premises in which a competition is being held. The show-promoting society will be equally responsible. Offences in this connection incur a fine of up to £200 in respect of each bird and the court shall order the forfeiture of the bird or birds. Birds which can be exhibited are shown in Schedule 3 Part I.

Sale

Birds in Schedule 4 cannot be sold under any circumstances and again offences will incur a fine of up to £200 for each bird and the forfeiture of the bird. However, for those birds in Schedule 4 which are specially protected species and are therefore also shown in Schedule 1 (and most of them are) a fine of up to £1000 can be incurred.

Inspection

Any person authorised in writing by the Secretary of State may, at any reasonable time, and upon producing evidence that he is authorised, enter and inspect any premises where any birds included in Schedule 4 are kept, for the purpose of ascertaining whether an offence under this section is being or has been committed on these premises. Any person who intentionally obstructs him in this inspection is guilty of an offence which again will incur a fine of up to £200.

Anyone having been convicted of any offence covered in this Act other than birds on Schedule 4, or any offence involving the ill-treatment of birds will be prohibited from keeping any bird listed in Schedule 4 for a period of up to three years from the date of that conviction.

Anyone having been convicted of any offence in connection with any bird listed on Schedule 4 will be prohibited from keeping any bird listed in Schedule 4 for a period of up to five years from the date of that conviction.

Any person who disposes of or offers to dispose of any bird listed in Schedule 4 to any person who has been convicted, within those periods is also guilty of an offence which can incur a fine of up to £200 in respect of each bird.

General

Licences

The Secretary of State after consultation with whichever one of the advisory bodies he considers is best able to advise him as to whether the licence should be granted, or the Nature Conservancy Council has power to grant licences for:

(a) Scientific or educational purposes.
(b) The purpose of ringing or marking or examining any ring or mark on wild birds.
(c) The purpose of conserving wild birds.
(d) The purpose of protecting any collection of wild birds.
(e) The purpose of falconry or aviculture.
(f) The purpose of any public exhibition or competition.
(g) The purpose of taxidermy.
(h) The purpose of photography.
(i) The purpose of preserving public health or public or air safety.
(j) The purpose of preventing the spread of disease.
(k) The purpose of preventing serious damage to livestock, foodstuffs for livestock, crops, vegetables, fruit, growing timber or fisheries.

If any person makes a statement or representation or furnishes a document or information which is false or which he knows to be false in a material particular for the purpose of obtaining either for himself or another the grant of a licence he is guilty of an offence which will incur a fine of up to £500 in respect of each bird.

Advisory Bodies

The Secretary of State may establish any body or bodies consisting of such members as he may from time to time appoint and assign their duties.

It shall be the duty of an advisory body to advise the Secretary of State on any question which he may refer to it or on which it considers that it should offer its advice in connection with the *Wildlife and Countryside Act 1981* or the administration of this part of the *Act*.

The advisory body may publish reports relating to the performance of its duties.

The Secretary of State may contribute towards the expenses of an advisory body provided that this is approved by the Treasury.

The Secretary of State shall consult such persons or bodies as he thinks fit before appointing a person to be a member of the advisory body.

British List

This is the list of British Birds published by the British Trust for Ornithology, Beech Grove, Tring, Hertfordshire.

Enforcement

If a constable suspects with reasonable cause that any person is committing or has committed an offence under the *Act* the constable may without a warrant:

(a) Stop and search that person if he has reasonable cause to suspect that evidence of the commission of the offence is to be found on that person.
(b) Search or examine anything which that person may be using or have in his possession.
(c) Arrest that person if he fails to give his name and address to the constable's satisfaction.
(d) Seize and detain for the purpose of proceedings anything which may be evidence of the commission of the offence or may be liable to be forfeited.
(e) A constable who suspects with reasonable cause that any person is committing an offence under the Act may enter any land other than a dwelling house.

Warrant

If a Justice of the Peace is satisfied by information on oath that there are reasonable grounds for suspecting that an offence has been committed and that the evidence of the offence may be found on any premises, he may grant a warrant to any constable (with or without other persons) to enter upon and search those premises for the purpose of obtaining that evidence.

Individual Rights

Even if there is reason to believe that the law is being broken no one, other than a policeman, has any right to enter private land or premises unless the owner expressly gives his permission. They can make enquiries and can offer advice. They can call a police constable and ask him to search the garden if the constable is satisfied that there are reasonable grounds for doing so, but no one else can accompany the constable on to private land without the owner's express permission. The owner can, if he wishes, make them wait outside. The constable can, if he believes it necessary, obtain a warrant to search a house, but only the person or persons named on the warrant have any right to enter the house, and the owner can, if he wishes, make anyone else wait outside.

Any access to private property gained without permission or other lawful authority amounts to a trespass which is actionable at law.

The representatives of the R.S.P.C.A., R.S.P.B., or any other protection society have no right to handle any bird or birds whatsoever. The owner can if he wants, give his express permission to allow them to handle the birds. A police constable however does have authority and must be allowed to handle the birds if he wishes to do so.

In the same way an official of a protection society does not have any authority to confiscate birds or equipment and should be refused. A police constable on the other hand does have authority to confiscate birds or equipment if he thinks they will be needed as evidence in court proceedings.

The onus for the safe keeping of any birds confiscated by the constable falls directly on to the police authority concerned. The owner can advise on their feeding etc. since otherwise they may be allowed to die through ignorance of their requirements.

When birds are confiscated with the intention of being examined by experts the owner should insist that he has an expert to examine the birds at the same time on his behalf, and if this expert disagrees with those appointed by the authority he should say so in no uncertain terms.

If the birds are ringed when confiscated the owner should state in writing that he believes the rings to be correct. Furthermore the owner should insist that there should be no attempt to remove the rings unless the owner is present and preferably in the presence of an independent expert.

The owner should obtain from the constable a detailed receipt for all birds and equipment which are confiscated at the time that they are taken.

Proceedings

Proceedings for an offence may be brought within a period of six months from the date on which evidence came to the knowledge of the prosecutor.

Commencement dates

So far as the protection of birds is concerned, the Secretary of State may appoint the day when this Act shall come into force and he may appoint different days for different provisions, different purposes and different areas. Meantime the existing Bird Protection laws will be operative until any appropriate section is superseded.

Birds not on Schedules

It is perfectly legal to keep and breed birds which do not appear in the Schedules in the Act, providing that the stock was legally obtained, but they cannot be sold or exhibited. Fanciers who are breeding these birds at the present time are strongly recommended to register them with the **British Bird Council** immediately as this will help to prove that the birds and their progeny are legally in captivity later on.

This has nothing to do with the compulsory registration of birds on Schedule 4 with the Department of the Environment. It is only for the fanciers' own protection.

The *Wildlife and Countryside Act 1981* covers many things to do with the countryside, wild plants and wild animals. In the above summary we have only attempted to explain the part which affects aviculture.

INDEX

Numbers in **bold** refer to main entries
Numbers in *italics* refer to illustrations